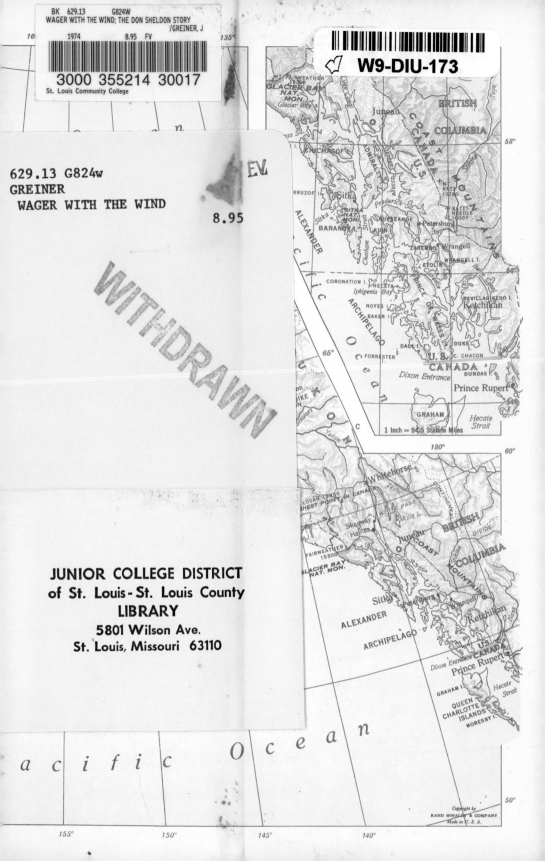

Wager with the Wind

Wager with the Wind

with the

THE DON SHELDON STORY

by James Greiner
foreword by Bradford Washburn

illustrated with photographs

Rand McNally & Company   Chicago / New York / San Francisco

For Mickey, who taught me how to fly just well enough to solo; Ed, who then summoned up the raw courage to let me try; and most of all for Hal, who did both when check-ride time rolled around. Finally, for my dear mother, who, though not quite understanding, gave her blessings as I struck out for Alaska years ago, and my wife, who, like a true Alaskan, poured the coffee as this was written.

Frontispiece: Don Sheldon and his Super Cub
on the vast surface of Ruth Glacier. The
rugged Moose's Tooth is in the background.
Photo by Bradford Washburn.

Library of Congress Cataloging in Publication Data
Greiner, James.
  Wager with the wind.

  Bibliography: p.
  SUMMARY: A biography of the Alaskan bush pilot
emphasizing his thirty-three year flying career and his
contribution to the development of bush aviation.
  1. Sheldon, Donald Edward, 1921–   2. Aeronautics
—Alaska—History.   3. Alaska—History. [1. Sheldon,
Donald Edward, 1921–   2. Aeronautics—Alaska—History.
3. Alaska—History] I. Title.
TL540.S455G73   629.13′092′4 [B] [92]   74-16323
ISBN 0-528-81856-2

First printing, October, 1974
Second printing, November, 1974

Contents

Foreword   7

Acknowledgments   9

Introduction   15

A Step And A Half   19

Talkeetna   29

From the River to the Air   37

Back to the Territory   54

"Eight G Lake"   62

The Man from Boston   71

The Bait   80

A Hell of a Good Pilot   96

A Red Fox and a Black Leather Bag   109

Layer Cake and Lemon Drops
and a 300-Pound Lady   120

Devil's Canyon   128

"The Famous Last Ride of 55 Xray"   135

Senator Boecher's White Bear   142

Mount McKinley's "Highest Airport"   157

The Intrepid Italians   176

"Both Sides of the Fence"   183

Emergency on 3411   193

Death on the Mountain   209

The Mountains Strike Back   221

"Five Little Flowers"   234

Postscript   246

Bibliography   251

Index   253

Foreword

Don Sheldon is a legend that is still very much alive! While all of us who have flown with him and know him well have heard perhaps a third of the formidable array of Alaskan history, delightful yarns, and anecdotes that fill these pages, nobody before Jim Greiner has ever had the inspiration and the patience to set them down.

We are deeply indebted to him for wringing them out of this modest hero—not only for the record but for all to marvel at and to enjoy.

Don is a rare combination of warmth and efficiency, mirth and seriousness, conservativeness and just sheer guts. Few professional pilots are blessed with his refreshingly youthful joy at drinking in the wonders of the country over which they ply their daily trade— and few pilots anywhere on earth have such a superb spot in which to ply it.

Don is many things to many people. To mountaineers, he has been the catalyst which made possible their great pioneer ascents on the forbidding virgin walls of McKinley, Huntington, Deborah, Hunter, and Logan. To the hunter, fisherman, climber, and airman in distress, he has been a rescuing angel for nearly 30 years. To his family and friends in Talkeetna, he has been a warm, thoughtful, ever-generous father, neighbor, and friend.

Those of us who know Don really well and have shared many of these experiences firsthand with him sense that this has been a rare privilege. It has been exciting to watch him grow in wisdom and competence over this quarter-century. And to have been able to contribute ever so slightly to his achievements has made my own friendship with Don ever more rewarding.

It is my sincere hope that this book will bring back thrilling memories to a select few—and kindle in thousands of others a keen desire to meet Don, to fly with him, and to see his country at first hand. It is North America's most magnificent wilderness.

BRADFORD WASHBURN
Cambridge, Massachusetts
February 18, 1974

Acknowledgments

It is always a truly difficult task to thank individually all of the friends and strangers who give freely of their help in a major project, such as that of writing a factual book. It is therefore my most sincere hope that those who are not specifically included herein will know that I am deeply grateful.

I shall begin then by naming my very close personal friend Chuck Keim, professor in the University of Alaska's Department of Journalism and former dean of the College of Arts and Letters. It was the result of his subtle prodding and encouragement that I took a deep breath and plunged ahead in this project, my first book. Through the past months, he has given incalculable advice on the many facets of proper technique and the legalities of book writing as well as complimentary encouragement that was perhaps not always deserved. Our relationship was made easier because, having guided for big game with this man through the years, I have learned that though he sets a brutal pace in the mountains, his word and opinions are as solid as Klondike gold.

Also, my deepest gratitude to Dr. Bradford Washburn, director of the Boston Museum of Science, who found time in his busy schedule, and while conducting the mapping project of the Grand Canyon, to tell his side of the Don Sheldon story. He also provided several hours of tape taken directly from his extensive diaries. He is indeed the world's foremost expert on Mount McKinley and the rest of Alaska's high places, a fact that was proven to me repeatedly while I researched this book. Special thanks must also go to Dr.

Washburn for his comments on the manuscript and the use of his excellent pictures of Mount McKinley.

Others who have helped are Bob Reeve, Don's father-in-law, who offered very early and very gruff encouragement and advice regarding the book; Ray Genet and Marlene Titus, who told me of their part in the Sheldon story over "brownswiger" in Ray's cabin by the Susitna River, a cabin that Ray made available to me during my many trips to Talkeetna; my friend Bud Helmericks, bush pilot and contemporary of Don Sheldon; and lastly, Pete Haggland, my close hunting pal and Super Cub driver extraordinaire, who gave me advice and encouragement.

During the course of researching the book and tracking down all of the photographic illustrations, I was impressed both by the generosity of the climbers of the world's mountains and by their devotion to the man who flew them to their various destinations. Steve Hackett of the Department of Geology, University of Alaska, a guy who never seemed to tire of answering my questions and providing advice during the technical research for the book; Bucky Wilson of the university's Geophysical Institute, for the same; Bob Goodwin of the Alyeska Pipeline Corporation, for his superb photos and facts dealing with the Cassin and Raithel Expeditions that are described herein; Paul Crews and Dr. Rodman Wilson of Anchorage, for their advice on the Day-Bading incident; George Hall, retired superintendent of Mount McKinley National Park, for his personal in-depth description of the Wilcox Expedition; Gary Brown, chief ranger at McKinley Park, for his help with the Micheko Sekita story; Les Viereck of the University of Alaska's Forestry Lab and participant in the Thayer Expedition on McKinley, for his pictures and advice; and all of the others who came to the fore with information relative to little-known aspects of other incidents that I have included in the Sheldon story.

Special thanks must go to Barry McWayne, excellent photographer at the University Museum, University of Alaska, for the many hours he spent copying expedition photos, taking his own, and offering valuable advice on the illustrations of the book, and to all of the other people who gave freely of their personal photo collections in the interest of telling the picture story of Alaska's bush pilot among bush pilots—he is their friend as well as mine.

Finally, all biographies have a singular aspect and ingredient—the personal interaction of those individuals who share in the subject's everyday life. Roberta Sheldon, Don's wife, has been the catalyst without which this story could never have come to print. She has been the unruffled go-between in many situations that, in retrospect, would have been insoluble without her firm but gentle feminine touch. Her talents as a diplomat have never been quite so obvious as they were during the past two years.

Speaking of wives, I would be sadly remiss were I not to mention my own, for she provided not only hot coffee and an ear that never tired but the final typing of the manuscript that was offered for publication. In time there may be other books, but there will certainly never be another Ida.

Finally, I must thank Don's sister, Berniece of Arlington, Virginia, whose early encouragement and help were invaluable.

In conclusion, and before this truly enjoyable task of expressing my gratitude is at an end, there is one last person I am compelled to mention—Don Sheldon. He has for many years been a highly admired and close personal friend, who convinced me early on of his lack of enthusiasm for what had been written about him in the past. It seemed to Sheldon that these writers allowed exaggerations of fact to take precedence over his personal motivations and true life-style. As a result, my constant efforts throughout the writing of his story have been to represent him as he truly is—a man of very deep personal integrity, unparalleled ability, and practical modesty.

JIM GREINER

Wager with the Wind

Introduction

The story of Alaskan bush aviation is not an old one. It began on July 4, 1913, when the tiny log-cabin settlement of Fairbanks saw the first airplane to fly in Alaska take to the sky. Billed as The Aerial Circus, James Martin was hired to travel north from Seattle, and when the wheels of his tractor biplane rose above the dust of the ballpark, the townsfolk cheered from nearby sod rooftops. Ten years later, a quiet North Dakota schoolteacher named Carl Ben Eielson, who had arrived in the frontier town in 1922, took off from the same ballpark Martin had used, to begin a flying career that would take him "where the airplane had no reason to be."

During the late twenties, there were no roads in the Territory of Alaska, and the Alcan Highway would not be built until the war years of the forties. Alaska was a distant place believed to be populated by igloo-dwelling sourdoughs who spent each passing season of the year in the dark clutches of a never-ending snowstorm. Even in the light of Eielson's considerable efforts, the resident population of the continental United States, a place that Alaskans would someday refer to as "the South 48," stood firm in the belief that Alaska would remain a place best described as a refrigerated wasteland, and yes, the folly of a man named William Seward.

With Eielson breaking trail across the boundless skies of a land that had never heard the drone of an aircraft engine, others followed. Noel Wien, Joe Crosson, Fred Moller, Harold Gillam, and Bob Reeve—men who shared the quiet schoolteacher's boundless optimism in the future of Alaska—would become legends in their own time.

There have been countless thousands of words written about these early "bush pilots," and almost without exception, these stories have created a universal image of reckless derring-do in an untamed land. It is true that the "challenge" of Alaska had motivated these early airmen. However, what made them tick was their simple faith that their flimsy wire-strung machines represented the key to the Pandora's box called the Territory of Alaska. Proof of this faith is easily found in the fact that those hearty individuals who survived bush aviation's infant years went on, almost to a man, to concentrate their efforts on the formal development of aviation in the Far North.

Eielson spent the last years of his young life in pursuit of a dream that called for a network of airlines through Alaska to Asia and Europe. Noel Wien and his brothers would later found the prestigious Wien Airlines (now Wien Air Alaska, Inc.), a firm that is still one of Alaska's largest carriers, while Gillam, using his uncanny ability to understand and cope with the Territory's fickle weather, opened the way for the development of early navigational aids. And finally, there was the dynamic Bob Reeve who founded Reeve Aleutian Airways, still a highly successful carrier in both Alaska and Canada.

When Eielson, Crosson, and the others came to Alaska, Don Sheldon was a stringy youngster with his own personal dream. Like Eielson, the Wien brothers, Crosson, and Reeve, he grew up during the predepression years in an environment of self-sufficiency that seemed to breed Alaska's early fliers. Like them also, he was reared in the north-central states. Sheldon, however, came to the Territory searching not for a place to fly an airplane, because he did not yet know how to fly, but simply for a place in which he would be free to choose his own way.

He watched the arrivals and departures of these early aviators during his first season in the north, and because "going by airplane was better than beating yourself to death on a pair of snowshoes," he quickly learned to fly. To those hearty souls who have traveled on foot in the endless snow of a winter in the interior of Alaska, the logic in this succinct statement is not only obvious but sufficient, and those who understand the wide spectrum of reasons that make men fly airplanes can easily read between the lines.

Unlike most of the original "drivers" of bush aircraft, Sheldon learned his basic trade in Alaska, and like many others before him, he has gone on to become a highly specialized bush pilot. During his colorful flying career, he has seen vast changes in the Territory. Where at one time the sight of a single airplane made everyone's day, air service now is available to the most remote village. This development occurred at a phenomenal rate. In order to indulge in what he now refers to as his "specialty," Sheldon was early forced into the role of shrewd competitor in the ever-marginal business of general-charter aviation. And while many other pilots failed, he not only survived but excelled. Talkeetna Air Service has long been one of the most successful ventures of its kind. The reason it has flourished is that Sheldon, now 53 years old, is one of only a handful of the world's pilots who make high-risk mountain flying a full-time, everyday vocation.

The events which have occurred in the 36 years since he came to Alaska and which have contributed to Sheldon's undisputed rank among airmen the world over are far too numerous to be contained between the covers of any single book. This fact has necessitated limiting the selection of incidents to highlights that best describe this man—what he has done and what he continues to do. It is my most sincere hope that Don Sheldon, my close friend and a highly unique individual, will become familiar to all who read his fascinating story. It is the story not only of Sheldon the aviator but of flying in Alaska's great mountains, especially Mount McKinley, North America's highest peak and a place that he calls his own.

A Step And A Half

The mountain, 60 miles northwest of where he stood on his dirt airstrip in Talkeetna, always gave him a clue to the approaching weather. On this Christmas day of 1958, he could see from the cloud layers building up around the mountain that a storm was brewing. More than any other man alive, Donald Edward Sheldon knows Mount McKinley—its soul-inspiring beauty and its basic savagery. He understands the lure of the mountain, called "Denali" by the Athabascan Indians, and respects the almost unparalleled mental and physical stamina needed to meet the challenge of this forbidding giant. Sheldon's love affair with this monolith of a forgotten Ice Age began with his first sight of North America's tallest mountain, rising 20,320 feet above Alaska's spruce-cloaked interior. She has been his mistress ever since.

The brisk wind tugged at his clothes and banged the sliding hangar doors. Snow blown off the roof swirled around him. Sheldon was glad he had hangared four of his planes before the blizzard could begin. As he stepped inside to check his schedule for the day, he heard the jangling of the phone barely rising above the noise of the wind. It was a dispatcher from Tenth Rescue Division at Elmendorf Air Force Base in Anchorage.

The news the dispatcher gave Sheldon was anything but good. A huge military C-54 transport was overdue. It had left Anchorage the day before en route for Shemya, in the Aleutian Islands, but it never got there. Radio contact had been lost after the big plane —carrying passengers, Christmas packages, and the payroll for the troops at Shemya Air Force Base—called a position report 100 miles southwest of Anchorage. At the time of the last report, the plane had been flying in heavily overcast weather.

The Alaska Peninsula spawns a system of foul weather that has affected the entire history of Alaskan aviation. In the early forties, during the Second World War, both the Japanese and American war machines were hard pressed to cope with it, and Dutch Harbor became a word that most GIs and military tacticians would like to forget—permanently. The long string of tiny treeless islands, with names like Attu, Umnak, Atka, and the Rats, are strung out from the peninsula into the vastness of the North Pacific, where they are steeped continually in the heavy fog, wind, and zero-zero overcast for which such maritime environments are notorious. The weather does not get much better is it approaches the base of the peninsula near Port Moller and Cold Bay.

"Tenth Rescue didn't initiate a search because of the weather, and the guy asked me if I'd be interested, to which I said, 'You bet!' After I hung up, I looked at the weather south of town, and I knew that this wouldn't be any lark, 'cause she was stacked up like sour biscuit dough as far as I could see, which wasn't very far."

Into the Super Cub's boot, Sheldon loaded cans containing four extra hours of gasoline, a pair of snowshoes, and his survival gear, which as always was packed into a big red nylon bag that closely resembles a fat sausage. He had decided to begin his search somewhere in the north quadrant of Mount Iliamna, a 10,016-foot active (smoking) volcano, 180 miles south of Talkeetna. The peak is on a direct airway to Shemya and 1,200 miles to the northeast.

After topping off his wing tanks and slipping into his parka and felt-lined overshoes, he took off to the south and set a course that would take him over the braided and frozen Susitna River to Cook Inlet. Once there, he planned to follow the coastal flats to the vicinity of Tyonek and Trading Bay. This course would place him just a short hop from Iliamna.

"Tenth Rescue had told me that they had layered clouds in the vicinity of Iliamna, and man they weren't kiddin'. It looked like a milk shake, and the trip down had been like the old roller coaster. I had just recently installed a powerful HF radio in the airplane, and I figured that I could call New York City on 3411 if I had to. Right now, I was busy just lookin' for a place to start lookin'."

The tiny Super Cub, 7163 Delta, jumped like a scalded cat as

Sheldon closed with the base of Iliamna. Looking for a break in the low ceiling, he flew south to the vicinity of Iniskin Bay.

"I noticed right off when I got to Iniskin that the wind, which was blasting out of the south, was thinning the cloud deck on that side of the mountain, but the north side was a swirling mass of snow, pushed by a wind that I estimated to be blowing at about 30 to 40 knots."

Sheldon now had to play what cards he had or get out of the game. Once on the north side of Iliamna, there would be no room for even a carelessly drawn breath, because low-level flight along the slopes of any mountain is risky when there is high wind and little visibility.

"I got as low as I could after I ducked into the clouds, and like I figured, couldn't see a thing except occasional snow and rocks. I could smell the stinking sulfur fumes from the volcano rifts as I got downwind of 'em through the cracks in the Cub's door, and it was a bad scene. Each time I punched a hole in the low clouds, I hoped they weren't stuffed with rocks.

"In a deal like this one, all you can do is follow your hunches, and you'll last longer—unless, of course, they turn out to be wrong. The hunch I had told me first that they were on the north side of the mountain, and then it said to look higher. I had the growing feeling that if I could only get to 8,500 or 9,000 feet, I'd find something. At this point, the wind is rippin' and tearin', and I'd been in the overcast for about half an hour. I started to look for a hole to go up through."

During his entire career, Sheldon has been a firm believer in what he casually calls "good hunches," and he was willing to play his hunches here on the jagged slopes of a mountain that was, for the most part, unfamiliar to him. On McKinley, he has come to know the mountain so intimately that he can get but a momentary glimpse of rock and ice and know exactly where he is and in which direction he is traveling, but not here.

"I was headed north and climbing, and in the process of making a turn to the left. I had just about made up my mind for the 8th time that I'd never get to nine grand [9,000 feet] when out of the corner of my eye, I spotted something that made my old ticker stand still. There she lay, and would you believe—the transport was scattered for half a mile."

Sheldon swung the Super Cub in a dangerously steep bank to

negate the chance of losing the site of the crash. On his first return pass, he thought he could see numbers, but he needed to get closer.

"The damned scud and sulfur fumes, which smelled like rotten eggs, were streaming across my line of vision, and the Cub was bouncing up and down in the turbulence. The numbers of the plane were on the tail fin, and because of their size, I ended up readin' 'em on my 7th pass at 50 feet of altitude."

Sheldon hastily jotted the registry of the plane on a scrap of brown paper as he climbed away from the grizzly scene. During the course of the seven on-the-deck sweeps he had made over the broken plane, death had been but a single moderate downdraft away.

"I pulled out over the ocean on the south side and gave Elmendorf a holler on 3411, and they came in like the guy was sittin' next to me."

"Ah, Roger 63 Delta, go ahead," said a calm military voice.

"I say, 'Hey, are these numbers correct?' and then I read 'em off."

The military voice verified the plane's registry. Sheldon "hauled anchor" and landed on the beach in a wind-sheltered cove near Trading Bay only long enough to dump the red 80-octane gas he carried through the chamois-skin strainer and stretch his cramped legs. Then it was back to Talkeetna for a Christmas turkey and a game of poker at the Bucket of Blood Bar.

Sheldon received a special citation from the U.S. Air Force for his efforts in finding the lost plane.

An interesting incident closely related to his location of the C-54 would occur six years later. He was asked by an amateur treasure hunter from the Talkeetna area to take him to Mount Iliamna to look for "base metals."

"I hauled this guy, along with 2,000 pounds of gear, down there in the ski plane, and when I finally got him landed, I suddenly realized we were at 8,250 feet, just 2 miles west of the snow-buried site of the 1958 disaster. The military had, of course, put the place off limits and listed it as an unrecoverable disaster. This was six years later, and the off limits designation wouldn't be removed till the following year. My flesh crawled when it suddenly dawned on me what this dude had in mind. I walked up to the guy and said, 'If you plan to salvage the valuables from that C-54, mister, you're going to do it over my dead body, and you got just 20 more seconds to get your butt into this here Cub, or I'm headed for Elmendorf.' "

Sheldon knew that in addition to the personal effects that lay beneath the snow, the payroll for the military installation at Shemya was still there too.

"We almost had a knockdown battle right there on the side of old Iliamna before the guy thought better of it and hopped into the Cub. He sulked as I took him back to Talkeetna, and after backhauling all that gear, I figured here was one trip I'd never collect for, but I was wrong. He paid off later, but since that day to this, I'm definitely not on his list of favorite speaking acquaintances."

From the flickering shadow of a tiny airplane on the rugged granite face of a remote mountain to the momentary darkness of spring clouds racing over an endless sea of bunchgrass prairie is an effortless shift in time for one who remembers well.

Donald Edward Sheldon was born in Mt. Morrison, Colorado, on November 21, 1921. In 1923, the family moved to Wyoming.

Sheldon's world then consisted of a small ranch—a few hundred acres owned by his father—and the surrounding federal lands that were leased to the ranchers to provide grass for their cattle. The grazing lands always seemed to renew themselves as if by magic, or so it seemed to young Sheldon. A sudden rainstorm would drench the red earth and renew the bunchgrass that had shriveled during a hot, dry summer. Water, dammed and held in reservoirs much as it is today, was readily available. A comfortable but unstable self-sufficiency prevailed.

"This place was near the great Red Desert in the sovereign state of Wyoming," Sheldon explains, "and the nearby settlement of Lander straddled the still-evident ruts of the old Oregon Trail that wound through South Pass. School was five long miles on horseback for me and my older sister."

Sheldon recalls his early life in a series of sharp, though often detached, impressions that almost exactly mirror his unique personality as a man—the undulating prairie grass; the musk of newly turned sod; the weathered ranch buildings content in their declining years to shelter a rancher, his wife, and their two children; and above all, the exciting plethora of wildlife. Smiling in his disarming fashion, Sheldon recalls the flash of white antelope rumps and the heavy prairie chickens that were a delight to behold both on the wing and on the black iron wood stove as they cooked to tender goodness. Sheldon's consummate interest in the big-game animals of Alaska—the moose, caribou, and the giant shuffling grizzly bear —is the perfect counterpart of his childhood fascination with elk, bison, and bighorn sheep. His interest, now as then, transcends the ordinary and zeroes in on the habits of the animals—how they survive, where they spend their lives, and how they can be approached. On the plains and in the mountains of Wyoming, he was training in the best, and perhaps least expensive, school of all to become a self-made naturalist, and at the same time, was cultivating a deep and abiding respect for the basic forces that shape our environment. Even during these early years, the lad was always influenced by the relentless natural force of the weather, which would regulate and almost define his adulthood—the driving snowstorms of winter and early spring; the hot, dry, grass-scorching summers; and the violent winds that would become his constant companion and adversary in his final chosen vocation. To Sheldon the bush pilot, the marrow-chilling cold on the high mountains of Alaska would be little different from the cold he remembers as a boy when he and his older sister, Berniece, became trapped in a gale-force blizzard en route to the small country schoolhouse five miles from their ranch.

Like other boys of similar places and times, Sheldon learned to ride, and he vividly remembers the throbbing scrapes and bruises left by unyielding rocks after a fall from the back of a skittish horse that had been panicked by the flashing rump patches of a jumping band of pronghorns. The horse was the only available means of transportation for young Sheldon, and riding required confidence and considerable personal skill. Perhaps one might speculate that his almost total reliance upon the airplanes he flies today found early root here.

Ranch work was hard and bone wearying for the boy. The gathering and storing of the neck-prickling hay that would forestall hunger for the livestock during the winter and the harvesting of three complete crops of alfalfa during the summer and early autumn made for a never-ending cycle of labor. Blisters of spring turned to calluses of summer, and young stringy muscles became wiry and hard during school vacations spent learning to earn a living from the land.

In autumn, the same hard work continued. Corn and wheat were harvested instead of hay and alfalfa. Inevitably, the shocking of wheat for the threshing machines and the harvesting of the corn were accompanied by a sudden succession of stubble-frosted mornings and clear, cool days. Scurling like clean slate haze beneath mile-high blue skies, the pungent scent of wood smoke, always present but never so meaningful, ushered in the undeniable winter. Year-round, the youngster's life became a closely regulated succession of effort, always disciplined by the weather. He learned to accept the satisfaction of doing hard work in order to survive. Today Sheldon's life has not changed a whit from these very early beginnings. It probably never will.

When he was eight years old, his father died, and young Sheldon's hard-earned and yet unidentified sense of rising above at least a few of the early frustrations of growing up was shattered. Sheldon and his sister were taken to Lander, Wyoming, by their mother. Here Mrs. Sheldon would operate a successful rooming house and follow her rancher husband in death during Don's 12th year.

After their mother's death, Berniece went to live with relatives in Denver, and Sheldon moved in with LaVerne and Pat Norman, his aunt and uncle, on their ranch near Lander. After several years spent in the relative confinement of town, he had been elated to return to the work he knew best on the ranch at the north fork of the Popo Agie River.

When he was 13 years old, he became a summer-vacation wage earner. At his uncle's urging, he took a job with the long-established Wyoming Tie and Timber Company. This concern harvested timber, which was then hand-hewn for the manufacture of railroad ties. The logs were flumed to the mighty Wind River and then floated down to Riverton, Wyoming, and a pickling plant there.

Young Sheldon had been mildly reluctant to take the job with the tie company, but after he had been with a timber-cutting crew awhile, he found that he liked the work.

These cutting crews were constantly on the move, much like the cowboys of this country during earlier years. With good luck, the tie drivers could travel 10 to 15 miles each day. Sheldon's job was to help move the tie camps ahead of the tie drivers and to assist the cook in the outdoor kitchens at each new location. He remembers the mouth-watering aromas of succulent roasts, thick crumbly blueberry cobblers, bread, and other delicacies cooked in a Dutch oven by filling the lipped top with hot coals from the campfire. The chief cook in Sheldon's first camp was an old Norwegian, Adolf Solum, who was "a true master of the Dutch ovens. He could, with uncanny accuracy, estimate the exact time required to bake bread and other delights to a state of utter perfection."

The drives terminated at the pickling plant in Riverton. All hands were then given jobs on the plant conveyer, recovering and processing the tie logs from the waters of the Wind River.

Sheldon worked for the tie company during each school vacation through the summer of 1938. By then, with high-school graduation a thing of the past, his thoughts had begun to center more and more on a place far to the north, a place he had never seen—the Territory of Alaska. He had heard and read much about the raw land where gold was still a warm attraction and game was said to be plentiful beyond belief. By now, his imagination, nourished by a quiet, thoughtful manner, had provided an impetus that could no longer be ignored. Like so many others before him, and even more since, young Sheldon could not really explain this attraction. Alaska promised adventure to be sure and the heady exhilaration of strange new sights and sounds, but most of all, it carried the gilt-edged promise of being a worthy place for Sheldon to fulfill his burgeoning desire to be truly self-sufficient. He was 17 years old.

When operations at the tie plant ended for the summer, Sheldon and two friends, Charlie Shatto—called "Yarlie" by his pals—and Roy Graham, purchased a well-used Model-A Ford and departed Riverton for Seattle. On their epic journey across the states of Idaho and Oregon, they "rebuilt the 'A' three or four times." Finally, the trio reached the port city of Seattle just in time to watch the steamship *Yukon* depart Pier Number One for Alaska. Following a period of serious deliberation and a few words of farewell, Shatto and Graham headed for the peach orchards of Oregon, while Sheldon vowed to wait for the next boat. He spent a long week at the Seattle YMCA before he could board the next northbound steamer.

As the journey progressed, Sheldon became increasingly inspired by the magnificent Inside Passage, with its fjords, rugged foothills and mountains, the spruce forests rising to timberline, and the cold, gray-green waters of the North Pacific. The steamship docked at Seward after an eight-hour layover in Juneau, and here, at its southern terminus, Sheldon boarded the Alaska Railroad for the final leg of his journey.

Upon alighting from the train in Anchorage, Sheldon's nostrils were assailed by the cool, moist air of the sea, and he heard the incessant gulls, sounding like a chorus of rusty gates in a steady wind. The mist-softened outlines of the Chugach Mountains to the east somehow tempered the stark newness of this place. Sheldon felt the electric surge of confidence that has inspired all newcomers who are destined to a lifetime infatuation with Alaska. This feeling was soon moderated by the practical realization that because of his unplanned week in Seattle, his pockets had become alarmingly light.

After the expensive trip north, Sheldon was forced to meet reality eye to eye. He soon discovered that even in a big city of 2,500 souls, one still needs money, which Sheldon even then was referring to as "resource." In 1938, Anchorage was yet to feel the ultimate effect of the expansion that occurred after the Second World War. Her streets were mostly unpaved, and her residents transients. Gold miners from the outlying districts spent their money in Anchorage, and the commercial fishing industry was growing to supply the increasing needs of the areas to the south. At first glance, the town seemed impressive but closer inspection soon revealed its true nature, a facade of rather fragile and definitely temporary design. Anchorage in 1938 could perhaps be likened to the young Don Sheldons of the time—everchanging, restless, yet saturated with an optimism that has somehow endured. With a tenacity that was the godchild of need, the city clung for its very life to the edge of the mud flats of Cook Inlet.

Only after a considerable investment of what shoe leather he still possessed did Sheldon find employment in the job-hungry city with a firm called the Step And A Half Dairy. Though its unlikely name did not conjure up visions of grandeur, it did seem to promise something even more important to young Sheldon—a means to solvency. The means was a 16-hour work shift, 7 days each week, for which he was paid an even $40 per month. His duties consisted of working in the bottling plant and driving the delivery trucks on their appointed rounds during all but the earliest morning hours, when he slept.

Six interminable weeks passed. Unknown to Sheldon he had established a record of dubious value. Due to the unheard-of long hours and submarginal pay—even in that day—a stay of longer than a week or two at the Step And A Half Dairy was defined as no mean accomplishment.

On a brisk autumn morning—the air, with its faint odor of fish

27

and the sea, cooler yet somehow more demanding of one's attention than usual—Sheldon drove his delivery truck down Fourth Avenue and almost ran over a fellow who looked familiar. He quickly recognized Jim Cook, a sailor he had met in Juneau on the trip north. After a brief reunion, the pair decided to pool their wealth, most of which would prove to be Sheldon's, and travel as far north on the venerable Alaska Railroad as the sum would allow. Sheldon needed no excuse to leave the dairy, and Cook also had itchy feet. Later that same afternoon, Sheldon would find that their $12 had "just barely" purchased two one-way tickets punched for Talkeetna, Alaska. The month was October, and the year 1938.

Talkeetna

Its name—meaning "where the rivers meet" in the Indian tongue—still rings of old-time Alaska. Located where the Susitna, Talkeetna, and Chulitna Rivers come together, the town is as slow moving today as it was in the autumn of 1938 when two young cheechakos debarked from the train, whose engine still wheezed from the exertion of pulling the gradual 112-mile grade of the Susitna River drainage. Then as now, Talkeetna consists of one dirt street three blocks in length, beginning at the yellow-frame Alaska Railroad depot and ending abruptly at the north bank of the muddy Susitna. In the dun October overcast, puffy snowflakes settled lazily to earth, dogs barked and yapped, and a host of miners and other transients yarned idly in front of log buildings. The still, damp air was laden with the heady perfume of wood smoke, fish, moose jerky, and the ubiquitous booze fumes that seeped from the doors of the Fairview Inn, Talkeetna's most prominent bar, and from home-brew vats in the local cabins.

Here at last was the Alaska that young Sheldon had visualized as he passed the endless days at the Step And A Half Dairy in Anchorage. It was all here—the teams of walleyed sled dogs picketed in the grassless, dung-littered spaces between squat log buildings, an Indian settlement along the nearby Talkeetna River, and best of all, the congenial way of life that the lanky Sheldon had been reared to appreciate but had seen little of in the city of Anchorage.

Sheldon would soon learn a basic fact of life, which at first seemed to contradict the complacency that Talkeetna exuded. The town was the first in what Sheldon describes as "a series of sand traps that stretched from the front steps of the Fairview to the South 48."

"There were about 50 mines in the nearby Cache Creek area, and the Talkeetna social season began when the miners arrived in town from the hills to the north and west. They were pretty well heeled, and the first challenge that faced them was to make a clean break away from Talkeetna. Most of 'em couldn't hack it."

Many of the miners talked excitedly of returning to their homes in Norway, Ireland, Sweden, and Germany; but by the time the snow began to speckle the ground, they had been in the hills for "a whole lot of months," had fought mosquitoes, and had sweated the clock around in the 24-hour daylight of the Alaskan summer. After they rolled into town, it became increasingly difficult for them to break away, and more often than not, the grubstake that was to have taken them across the sea disappeared into the top of a barmaid's dress, the dust's passage from view somehow made acceptable by the booze it had bought.

"Those few who got on the train with their pokes intact then had the Anchorage social whirl to contend with, and it was a dandy. The occasional miner who made the steamship south was a rare bird, and even he usually ended up dead broke in the city of Seattle, writing home to some buddy in Talkeetna for enough of a stake to get back home on." With a sigh and a grin, Sheldon summarizes the whole process: "All somebody had to do was get their hands on some resource. The shock was too great for their systems, and they went ape when they got to the bright lights."

Though their spirits were high as they stepped from the wheezing train at Talkeetna, Sheldon and Jim Cook realized that their survival would be short-lived if they couldn't find a job. They soon struck up an acquaintance with one Benjamin Mayfield, the portly town commissioner. Sheldon's reminiscences of his early days in Talkeetna are punctuated regularly by recollections of this man.

"We had to find some gainful employment with which to better our cupboard, and I mentioned this fact to the commissioner. I had heard around town that there were jobs to be had cutting wood, and Cook and I were game. Mayfield pointed us in the right direction, and we were soon swinging an ax and running a two-man Swede saw. By the time December rolled around, we had quite a pile of birch and spruce stacked, and in the process, had earned enough to keep from starving."

Another of Sheldon's early acquaintances in the village by the Susitna during those early days was Belle McDonald, the proprietress of the Talkeetna General Store.

"Belle was a fine lady, and she'd made a small fortune in Alaska but had given it all away in grubstakes to the miners, who were very seldom able to pay back the favor in money or time. She'd made mention of the fact that she would dearly like to get hold of some moose meat."

For some reason, moose had been scarce that winter, and Sheldon resolved to shoot one of the huge mule-eared critters if the chance came his way. The way it worked out, he didn't have long to wait.

"The legal territorial moose season had long passed, and Cook and I were living at the edge of town in a cabin owned by an old homesteader named Perkins. Early one morning—it was still dark outside—I woke up to the sound of muffled footsteps just beyond the cabin wall. I crept to the door, opened it a crack, and there stood the biggest bull moose that I had ever seen."

In his brief time at Talkeetna, Sheldon had seen only a few of the ponderous animals, and then usually at a distance and during the day. The moose he looked at now, a bull with sweeping antlers and a weight of about 900 pounds on the hoof, was magnified to even greater stature by the soft moonglow of the mid-December morning.

"I reached stealthily back behind the door for my small-caliber .250 Savage rifle. With great reservations, I took one shot at the moose, and he fell like he'd come out of a coal chute."

The shot, considering the poor light and Sheldon's pounding pulse and shaking hands, was a lucky one. It centered the moose's broad forehead directly between its big hazel-colored eyes. Later, in the dawn light, he rapidly converted the moose to a form conducive to a swap for some of Mrs. McDonald's groceries. For two quarters of moose, Sheldon got a bag each of sugar and flour.

"I learned very soon thereafter that the commissioner had heard I'd shot a moose. I was soon stewing about what he would think of my shooting an illegal one and then trading it for groceries, so I took him part of the liver. To my surprise, he was grateful to get it and didn't say a word. I found out later he didn't really need the meat, and he was working hard to help a couple of green kids."

Other than moose, the only outside source of meat was beef, called "boat meat." It was of decent quality but prohibitive in price and "never really did measure up to a good cut of moose."

About the time of that first trade with the gracious McDonald woman, Cook lit out for warmer climes and a post with the Merchant Marines.

After a while Sheldon tired of living in the cabin alone. When a fire claimed the home of a miner named Thompson, Sheldon grabbed the opportunity to invite the old man to spend the rest of the cold winter with him at what he now called his "stump ranch." Thompson was a trapper during the winter months, and in the long aurora-filled nights that followed, he regaled Sheldon with the lore of setting beaver traps, his specialty, and skinning the spade-tailed animals.

"Beaver were worth 25 bucks apiece, and I bought several traps. By the time the beaver season rolled around, I was ready to try my hand at it. The day after I set my traps, I caught by first beaver, and it took me two days to skin it."

With the coming of spring and a warm May sun, breakup became a reality. In the most significant of all seasonal changes in Alaska, the rotten ice came surging down the rivers on the crest of the swelling waters below. The booming shear of the moving river ice as it slid and tumbled between banks where pussy willows had grown through the slushy remnants of winter snow was a sight and sound that no Alaskan—the sourdough or the greenhorn cheechako —could ignore.

Bets on "the day the ice goes" seemed as old as gambling itself, and the event almost overnight set the stage for the long-awaited and fireweed-filled summer. Muskrat hunting became the topic of the day among the Indian faction, and the miners assembled the gear and supplies they would take with them to the Cache Creek and Fairview Mines, a 50-mile walk from Talkeetna.

Sheldon had met most of these miners during the long winter. One of them, an old, flint-eyed gold gopher named Jenkins, offered him a job at his mine near Cottonwood Creek.

"The job would pay five bucks a day for ten hours of work, without a break for Sunday," but Sheldon, long fascinated by the thought of mining for gold, hired on gladly.

Old man Jenkins had first gone to Nome, where he had already spent a good number of his years scratching in the black sands of the beaches for his rightful share of the warm yellow stuff. After coming to Talkeetna, he had discovered a rich placer deposit in the Cache Creek area, and so on a warm sunshiny May morning, Jenkins—along with his wife, two lads named Ira Dease and Joey Burtel, and Sheldon—eagerly headed back through the thawing snowdrifts to his Cottonwood Creek holdings.

"The standard practice those days was to get a head start on the mining season, which begins in June, by moving freight and spare parts to the mines before they were really workable. For the cross-country haul of 50 to 55 miles, Caterpillar tractors, horse-drawn wagons, dogsleds, and packboards were used, and the caravans made noisy and colorful progress as they left town for Cache Creek and the Fairview."

Jenkins was a dyed-in-the-wool early bird, and they arrived at the diggings on May 1, 1939, to begin the summer of backbreaking labor that Sheldon will never forget. The endless succession of days was filled with the various tasks involved in mining for gold— sluicing, shoveling, repairing equipment, and watching the boxes that tailed the riffle boards from which the harvests of gold, or "cleanups," came. The first of these cleanups came in late June, and Sheldon clearly recalls the drama of the event.

"The gold was really a shock to me. It was bright yellow and very pure, and it often occurred in a kind of blue clay, which really set it off."

There were seven cleanups that summer, and as the last one was completed, Sheldon was struck with an itch to move on. He had been corresponding with his friend Dease, who had injured his back working in the mine and had gone to Anchorage. They decided to spend the approaching winter trapping, and they hatched a plan to build some line cabins at a place called Kroto Creek. Sheldon promised to meet Dease on the trail back to Talkeetna.

On August 30, at 6:00 P.M., he shouldered a 70-pound pack and departed the Jenkins Mine in a heavy downpour of late summer. It took two round trips, some ten miles over the soggy, rough trail through the spruces, to get all of his belongings to the rendezvous point, a place called the Elwell Location. At two in the morning, shortly after Sheldon's last trip, Dease materialized out of the darkness. The pair spent a sleepless night in a rundown cabin near the trail laying plans and listening to the steady drum and drip of rain on the mossy cabin roof. At nine the next morning, the once-a-month Cat train they awaited hove into sight through the hazy warm sunshine, and they rode the rest of the way to Talkeetna in high style.

After their arrival in town, Dease and Sheldon found the Civil Aeronautic Authority (CAA) busily engaged in the construction of one of its many new airstrips, this one for Talkeetna. An offer of an-unheard-of $2.50 per hour convinced the pair that to pass up a job with the government agency to go trapping would be folly. Besides, they could always do the latter after the airfield was finished later in the winter.

By early October, the season's first snow began to dust the hills near the town, and the Canada and white-fronted geese were moving from the Yukon River and the swamplands of Minto Flats far to the north. Sheldon savored the new smells of frost-dampened leaves and paused at increasing intervals in his brush cutting to gaze at Bald Mountain with its new mantle of stingy snow. His fascination with the changing season was second only to his interest in the work of the surveyors on the strip, and with each passing day, his resolve to somehow learn their craft became stronger. Unknown to Sheldon, old man Jenkins, along with his wife and Joey Burtel, were past the making of plans for an optimistic future, for they had been bludgeoned to death at the mine near Cottonwood Creek.

A miner named Clark had discovered the bodies early one morning, and after a long fast hike to Talkeetna, told the gruesome story to Commissioner Mayfield. Clark, a French Canadian, had more bad news. Earlier that same morning, on a claim near the Jenkins holdings, he had discovered the mortal remains of another miner, a man named Dick Francis, who had been shot twice through the right temple. At first glance it had appeared that Francis had bushwhacked the Jenkins crew and then committed suicide, but since no man can shoot himself in the head twice with a single-action revolver, the theory was quickly ruled out.

"There had been considerable friction between Francis and old man Jenkins, and they'd been in and out of court many times over the years trying to settle boundary disputes. To this day, the murders go unsolved, but the indications are quite strong that the French Canadian Clark was implicated. They formed a posse consisting of several FBI agents and some deputies, headed rather unexpectedly by Clark, which immediately departed for the mine."

After a two-week investigation, which according to Sheldon was fraught with classic examples of how not to find clues, the posse returned to Talkeetna. Before leaving the Jenkins holdings, Clark appointed one of the posse members as custodian of the place. He was to stay there through the following winter and assure that vandalism to the mine did not occur.

"When the posse left, the caretaker took over. By the 15th of November, the old man grew tired of feeding the wood stove and watching the snow fall. It was also very spooky there, what with the wind howling through the rafters of the old mine cabin."

The caretaker grew edgier as time passed, and finally, down to his last spoonful of coffee and with his wood supply nearly exhausted, he resolved to take his leave of the Jenkins Mine. This would mean a hike of about 65 miles to Talkeetna over 5-foot snowdrifts, but so be it.

"By this time, Dease and I had established one of several cabins in the Kroto Creek area, and right on the trail to the Cache Creek mines. Late one miserable, stormy night, there was a knock on our door, and we opened it to find the old caretaker, who we didn't know at the time, standing there on his snowshoes. We invited him in for some warmed-up, leftover stew."

The old man was exhausted and said little about either his reason for traveling or the origin of his journey. He did mention that he was en route to Talkeetna, and with that, he turned in on the pole-floored loft of the cabin. Before Sheldon and Dease blew out the lamp for the night, they were convinced of two things. The old man carried an unusually heavy pack, and he was noticeably close-mouthed about his comings and goings.

"About two in the morning, I heard a few small sounds overhead but paid them little attention and went back to sleep. At seven, it had gotten light enough for me to see that the old man had left during the night, and all he left behind was a fading set of snow-shoe tracks that disappeared in the direction of Talkeetna."

Two days later, Sheldon was summoned to Talkeetna. When he arrived, he discovered that the old man who had stayed with them was the caretaker of the Jenkins Mine and that he was being detained in Talkeetna under very unusual circumstances.

"I learned that as soon as the old guy hit town that night after he left us, he took up residence in the Bucket of Blood Bar, another of Talkeetna's landmark drinking places. He had missed the south-bound train to Anchorage. As the evening wore on, and the booze began to take effect, he became quite loose tongued about his activities at the mine. He admitted that if he had made his train, he would at that moment be safely in Anchorage with the gold from the Jenkins Mine, which had never been recovered. He'd found the gold, a considerable amount, under the last few sticks of firewood just before he left the mine, and had decided to make a run with it."

Sheldon was needed to identify the seven pokes of gold, for he was the only man alive who could do it. Then he returned to the Kroto Creek cabin and his pal Dease.

As the winter began to fade into the longer days of early spring, their pile of lynx, marten, and beaver pelts had grown to consider-able size. With breakup once more in the offing, Sheldon's interest in surveying had culminated in a decision to go to the University of Alaska at Fairbanks, where he would enroll in the school's highly touted engineering curriculum. As the days became lighter, he could see the odd bush airplane passing overhead, an event that never failed to stir his imagination. He was awestruck by the in-trepid airmen of the day, who traveled in this world of rime frost and haze.

"They looked to me like they came from Mars, and all I could ever think was how much better that kind of travel in this area of no roads was than beating yourself to death on a pair of snowshoes."

From the River to the Air

Sheldon enrolled at the farthest north university in September 1940. In December, shortly after final exam week, he had visitors—Charlie Shatto and Lawrence Anderson. Shatto and Anderson were very capable men. Yarlie was a professional carpenter, and Anderson a skilled heavy-equipment operator. Shatto and Sheldon had exchanged letters earlier that fall, and the subject of trapping had been thoroughly discussed. Sheldon had described the "roomful of fur" that he and Dease had taken in the Kroto Creek country, and Shatto was in Alaska to see if he might do the same. After an evening of talk, the three laid plans for a trapping spree during late winter and spring. Sheldon had already invested his last year's fur receipts in tuition and barely enough was left for the second semester. Besides, he wanted to lay in a stake for a venture that at that moment still had to be called long-range planning; he wanted to learn to drive an airplane. For the moment, however, another crack at the fur-rich Kroto, to be followed by a trip down the Tanana River in the spring, was more than enough to sway Sheldon.

"Those two ex-tie hacks from Wyoming set a fire under my second term at school, and with the promise of two Gs apiece, we were on our way."

During his time in Fairbanks, Sheldon had experienced the minus 50- and 60-degree cold on days when the only tangible proof that a sun still existed was the 3 to 4 hours of weak half light, often shrouded in an ice fog thick with frozen particles of moisture hanging suspended in the cold air. Talkeetna, separated from the weather extremes of the Tanana Valley by the wall of the Alaska Range, was nine long hours away as Sheldon boarded the south-bound train at the Fairbanks station that day in January. The village by the Susitna was his home, a fact that he seldom recognized during those early days, but as the train topped the mountains near the outpost of Cantwell and began the slow descent to Talkeetna, he found his thoughts hurrying ahead in anticipation of the renewal of old acquaintances and the warm familiarity of the place.

Shatto and Anderson met Sheldon in Talkeetna, where they purchased supplies for their late-winter stay in the Kroto Creek country. The trapping expedition came off without a hitch, though the receipts did not quite measure up to earlier expectations. With the new spring, Sheldon and his two pals began to lay plans for the Tanana River trip. They would start their journey at the town of Nenana, at the base of the West Tanana Hills.

Breakup occurred on May 4 that year, and while it was still in progress, they launched a boat that had been purchased and quickly rebuilt for the occasion. For Sheldon, the trip would provide an early opportunity to explore and would lay the groundwork for a knowledge of Alaskan geography that is without peer among the bush pilots of today. It also promised a second chance at fur and a shot in the arm for his stake in the flying game.

"We bought enough supplies to last six weeks and loaded a five-horse outboard, our traps, and a big roll of canvas for building rat canoes. The plan was to follow the breakup downriver to the Yukon and then on to the village of Marshall."

Soon after their departure from Nenana, they were passing the old Indian village of Minto, which squatted benignly on the river's north bank. Almost at its back door, and stretching inland for many miles, lay a swampy flatland bearing the village's name. That the great slough-pocked Minto Flats was the epicenter of the grand-daddy of all muskrat populations is still proven each spring when the entire Athabascan community sallies forth on a rat hunt that knows no equal.

Sheldon and his two chums had tried trapping the multitude of side sloughs along the Tanana without any real success, and since the process slowed them considerably, they soon adopted the

38

Indian method of using a .22 caliber rifle. A carefully placed head shot was mandatory for a salable pelt.

As they harvested the gray-brown pelts, they watched the passage of great wedges of yelping wild geese and thousands of ducks, all moving into their age-old nesting grounds on the flats. They were surrounded by the aroma of coffee-colored swamp water and mud and the exquisite fragrance of new and succulent vegetation fairly leaping to life beneath the warm sun, a sun that even in the Alaskan spring, outlasted the longest midsummer days in the South 48. By the time the tiny settlement of Manley hove into sight, the cargo of muskrat skins had increased to respectable proportions.

Farther along the river, at a point about 15 river miles above the village of Tanana and the anticipated junction with the wide Yukon River, they were treated to a natural spectacle, the memory of which still thrills Sheldon. It occurred at Squaw Crossing.

"We ran onto a tremendous herd of migrating caribou. They were wall to wall and hornless during that time of year, and we just sat there while the current took us and stared."

Like all caribou herds, this one seemed to move in an almost lethargic manner, and it occurred to Sheldon that the rugged gray animals must surely be in great discomfort from the almost-hot spring sun. They still wore their winter coats, though these would soon be shed in great hanging tufts of hollow hair and then be replaced by the flat and glossy chocolate-brown pelage of summer. As the boat drifted silently along, turning slowly with the current boils, Sheldon marveled at the size of the herd that moved slowly in great undulating waves and strings, with a tenacious determination that could not be missed.

With Tanana in sight, Sheldon's eye caught movement along the riverbank, and he pointed to a man waving a blanket. As they crossed over, he wondered if the man needed help, but when they neared the bank, it became obvious that what the man, who spoke with a thick Irish brogue, really wanted was only the chance to pass the time of day and thus garner any news that might be available from upriver. As Sheldon tossed the frayed bowline to the old gent, his nostrils were brutally assailed by a new odor that bore no resemblance to the natural fragrances his nose had come to expect over the past weeks. It was the unmistakable perfume of sour mash seeping from a still that must be nearby.

"Once ashore, we fell into the old guy's good graces. If he said it, his name escapes me, and later he showed us his still, with its copper tubing and gallon jugs. He had it well hidden and had to remove part of the cabin wall to get at it."

Sheldon, a strict nondrinker by preference, remembers that the revelation was far from a surprise.

"We were half swacked from the fumes by the time he gave us the grand tour, so Yarlie and Anderson spent the night drinking white mule with a coffee chaser. That stuff really knocked their eyeballs out of focus!"

The following morning, with Tanana's old garrison buildings disappearing in the river mist off their stern, they continued downriver. By the time Kokrines appeared from behind a bank studded with sweepers—trees lying in the current along riverbanks that had collapsed during high water levels—the cool breeze over the river had helped vanquish the headaches that the white lightning had produced.

At Kokrines, they saw an unnerving sight. Stacked upon the banks of the Yukon were pine coffins, and Sheldon soon learned that they held the bodies of river dwellers who had gone to their reward during the past winter. For some reason, the corpses were brought to this particular village prior to burial, the latter being accomplished during a potlatch held to honor the deceased. He asked a local resident why the bodies were allowed to accumulate and was somewhat taken aback by the simple logic in the answer to his question.

"'Cause ya can't dig a grave when she's 50 below and the ground's froze harder than the hinges of purgatory, that's why."

The trip continued, and the sunny days swept by with increasing speed. Their next stop would be in Ruby, which was abustle with the activities of a major construction project. The CAA was beginning the work on one of several airfields almost identical to the one Sheldon had helped build at Talkeetna.

"We off-loaded our gear, sold the boat, the two canoes that we had made while traveling, and a big stack of muskrat pelts. Then we went looking for a job. Shatto was a heck of a carpenter, and Anderson could peel an orange with a dozer blade. I could run levels and close out within plus or minus a tenth of a foot in the surveying game."

Bradford Washburn

McKinley Survey, 1955: Setting up base camp on the Ruth Glacier, the Moose's Tooth in the background.

Sheldon with Brad Washburn and the pilot's Super Cub, on the strip in Talkeetna prior to the start of the 1955 season.

Bradford Washburn

Photos by Bradford Washburn

Sheldon and his Super Cub at the location
of Dr. Frederick A. Cook's fake peak.

Opposite page (top): Sheldon and Washburn surveying in 1955
near Dr. Cook's fake peak.

Opposite page (bottom): Sheldon seated beside a rock inscribed
by William Dickey, who named Mount McKinley and made the first
estimate of its height. The airplane is Sheldon's Aeronca Sedan,
the one he used in the daring Devil's Canyon rescue.

Mount McKinley towering above the 80-foot-high trees at its base.

Bradford Washburn

Don Sheldon flying by the South Buttress of McKinley.
South Summit (20,320 feet) is at upper left.

Mount McKinley's East Face. A storm with express-train winds
blows across Harper Glacier and Denali Pass. The picture shows both
the North and South Summits of McKinley.

Bradford Washburn

Sheldon in his silver Cessna 180, flying over
the upper Kahiltna Glacier.

Sheldon worked on the Ruby airfield project until summer began to slip away. Then he shipped out for McGrath, where the CAA was constructing an even larger strip. South of Ruby, McGrath, on the Kuskokwim River, was the center for bush-aviation activities in Alaska, and it was here that young Sheldon's interest in flying became chronic.

"There were quite a few bush aircraft at McGrath, and I had a chance to meet some of the luminaries of the flying world—like Oscar Winchell with his favorite Stinson, old 211W, and Jim Dodson, who called McGrath his home base. I also met and talked with a guy named Reeve. He was a rough character and always seemed to be in a heck of a hurry, and he flew an old Boeing with three big radial engines. I knew that he was doing some pretty unorthodox flying down south around Valdez, and some said that he was actually landing airplanes on glaciers, a feat that I found hard to visualize. Later on, he lost the big Boeing in an attempt· to ditch it in the ocean. He was flying priority military cargo to the Aleutians at the time."

Autumn came early to central Alaska that year, and with the McGrath project about to end because of the approaching winter, Sheldon was again ready to move on. In his pockets rested some of the most meaningful resource he would ever make—his flying stake.

"I was heeled, and ready to huckledebuck on down to Anchorage and learn to fly."

When asked how badly he wanted to fly during those early years, Sheldon's reply is quick and to the point.

"Wanted to fly? My God, it isn't tangible. When you bite into a big red apple, ya want to make the thing snap and squirt juice for ten feet. That's what a crack at flying meant to me then and still does."

Sheldon hitched a lift on a plane to the port city, and on his arrival, set a direct course for a place that came highly recommended by the pilots at McGrath—Lars Larson's flight school at Merrill Field. Merrill Field was named in honor of Russell Merrill, who disappeared over Cook Inlet near Anchorage on a flight to Bethel in 1929.

At long last, Sheldon would try his hand at driving an airplane. His mentor would be none other than the well-known Dick Miller, the school's chief flight instructor and a highly competent ex-military pilot. Sheldon, along with 20 other uninitiated students, was soon aloft, feeling the new buoyancy of his unfamiliar surroundings, and in the process, learning to defy gravity. Many years later, Sheldon would reminisce with Ward Gay, one of his fellow students and now owner of the well-known firm of Sea Airmotive, a highly diversified flying service in Anchorage.

"Ward and I have been very close friends through the years, and I pointed out to him one day that of the original 20 guys in that class at Merrill in '41, he and I are the only ones that are still around. Most of 'em have either bought it in airplanes here in Alaska or during the Second World War, and the rest have been scattered to the four winds."

Larson's school had three small fabric-covered airplanes, and Sheldon flew all of them on occasion. One was a tiny J-3 Cub, another a J-5, and the third was a well-worn Aeronca. The J-5 was Sheldon's favorite, and he took it aloft alone after only six short hours of dual instruction with the hard-nosed Miller. Solo flight soon taught him how to handle forced landings, an exercise that modern students merely practice at safe altitudes in high-performance airplanes.

"The J-5 was not equipped with an electrical system and had to be hand-propped to start it. A guy got pretty handy at the job on the ground, but I soon learned that that was the only place you could start it. Shortly after I soloed, the engine quit with carburetor ice, and there was no place to go but down."

As the month of November slipped away, Sheldon was rapidly becoming proficient in making the J-5 do what he wanted it to, and he looked forward eagerly to the day when he would take his long-awaited check ride with a CAA examiner for his private pilot's license. And then came that momentous day in December when the Japanese attacked Pearl Harbor, a place that Sheldon, along with most other Americans, had never heard of.

Unlike multitudes of others, he did not drop everything he was doing to enlist. To understand his reserve, one must understand the man, for Don Sheldon, above all other things, is coolly deliberate and stoically methodical, almost to a fault. Each and every move that the man makes is thought out in advance and then done with a careful slowness that has made others wince with impatience. He applies this attitude to all of his actions, from landing on a murderous glacier to tying the simplest of knots on a box of cargo, and it is this singular virtue that has undoubtedly helped keep him alive during his long years flying Alaska's inhospitable bush country. And so, it was in this manner that he carefully directed his thinking as he reflected upon the advent of the Second World War.

Foremost in his mind was the compulsion to go to his country's aid, and the temptation was almost overpowering. He would have enlisted on the spot, but the thought of going to war in anything but an airplane was totally unacceptable to him. In addition, Sheldon realized that Alaska's geographic location, which would be highly vulnerable in an all-out war with the island empire of Japan, increased the need for airstrips and navigational facilities such as the one at McGrath. Taking everything into consideration, Sheldon promised himself the attainment of three goals: first, to obtain his private flying license; second, to offer his continued help at McGrath; and finally, to someday go to war in a fighter plane.

After realizing the first of these goals when he received his private ticket on a bleak January 4, 1942, Sheldon returned to McGrath, where a new aura of urgency hung like mist over the still-raw landing field. In the months to come, under the direction of his totally dedicated boss, one E. I. Clancy, he worked long shifts under the increasing warmth of the spring sun. Clancy was able to get deferments for most of his men, Sheldon included, because of the priority given to the McGrath project and many others like it.

The exhausting work continued through the summer and autumn of 1942. By the time the Kuskokwim River had frozen over and the hills near McGrath were white with snow, the north-south runway was completed. Sheldon felt he had discharged his second obligation, that of seeing the McGrath project to near completion, and had spoken with Clancy about heading back to Anchorage and joining the Civilian Pilot Training Corps (CPTC) to nail the lid down on the last of the three promises he had made to himself. The Irishman had reluctantly agreed to let him go, and the problem now was centered upon getting out of McGrath in the howling blizzard that signaled the approach of another winter. The dented barrel stove in the partially completed flight-operations building thumped menacingly with each new gust of wind as Sheldon, staring through a small window at the dervishes of grainy snow blowing from the frost-compacted ground, considered his problem. His thoughts were interrupted when his friend Lars Johnson burst into the room.

Johnson was in charge of a small contingent of A-26 bombers that were stationed at the new field. After warming his hands at the barrel stove, he turned and eyed Sheldon.

"Don, I've got a C-47 heading for Anchorage at 2200 hours, and I can get you on it if you still want to go."

"Do I! What about this weather?"

"We'll get there, 'cause I've got two of the best in the business up front to see that we do. Get your gear packed and be ready to go."

That was assurance enough for Sheldon, for Johnson, who would later become head of the Department of Aviation in Anchorage, had an untarnished record and always met his schedules, regardless of the weather.

At the time Sheldon presented himself to the CPTC recruiting officer in Anchorage, he had logged a total of 50-some hours of flying, with 40 of them accumulated while earning his license at Larson's school in Anchorage. The balance of time in his logbook had been flown at McGrath in an old bush plane, a Bellanca that a Fairbanks pilot named Skunahog Schultz flew on his Kuskokwim River run.

After signing the papers enrolling him in the CPTC, Sheldon's next stop was Seattle, where he took skill and aptitude tests along with other young and aspiring airmen. Half of the class passed the tests, but none of them were to enter the coveted flight-training program. The group was told that due to Rommel's incursions in Africa, the Air Force needed gunners rather than fighter pilots. Sheldon's class was assigned to a B-17 bomber-crew school and quickly transported to Kingman Air Force Base in Arizona for a six-month crash course in engineers school. The training was exhaustive, due both to the speed of presentation and to its highly technical orientation. One of the unforeseen results of this particular training curriculum was that upon its completion, Sheldon and the others found themselves qualified not only as gunners but as engine mechanics, who could troubleshoot hydraulic and electrical systems and perform other useful maintenance on the planes in which they would eventually serve.

After the termination of the six-month program, all hands were shuttled to Rapid City, South Dakota, via Amarillo, Texas. From here they left almost immediately for England, and in what Sheldon would later define as the longest, and yet the shortest, trip of his entire life, he was in the war.

He was initially stationed at Snetterton Heath Air Base, and it was from this field that he flew on his first missions, all of them over the vast industrial supply centers of Germany. Sheldon saw action in a total of 26 missions, volunteering for the last because only 25 were required. By the end of August 1944, he had survived two major crash landings in England but was never shot down. After his final mission, Sheldon was placed in charge of a portable skeet range as gunnery instructor until October 1945, when he was discharged. During his tour of duty, the pilot from Talkeetna, Alaska, was awarded the Distinguished Flying Cross and four other Air Medals. While in the service, Sheldon had scrupulously saved the bulk of his pay because he had a new goal—he wanted to purchase two new airplanes.

Back to the Territory

After his arrival in the States, Sheldon immediately headed for Lockhaven, Pennsylvania, and the sales office of Piper Aircraft Corporation, on the banks of the lazy Susquehanna River. After meeting with Jake Miller and seeing the formidable list of back-ordered aircraft, his plans to purchase a PA-12 and a J-3 Cub were smothered. Sheldon accepted a job delivering planes because Miller suggested that to do so might move Sheldon's name closer to the top of the waiting list at a more tolerable rate. With his new job came many long hours in the tiny airplanes, which he flew to many destinations, some as distant as Mexico.

Sheldon's later account of his brief visit to Chihuahua perhaps goes a long way toward explaining why he is so drawn to the land of long winters at the top of the globe. He tells of buxom Mexican women patting tortilla dough on their thighs, then adding chopped coyote meat, or "alley rabbit," and a concoction he describes simply as "beans and torpedo juice."

"The first bite paralyzed your imagination and the second petrified what was left. The Mexican style was definitely not for me."

As a direct result of his short-term encounter with Old Mexico, he would later respond with but an understanding nod when told that Chihuahua is the only place where a local chili-pepper-saturated resident will eat a coyote with no worries whatsoever about the coyote returning the favor.

Sheldon was more than ready to leave, and he caught a bus that would take him back to El Paso, where he would formally leave the land of sombrero hats and jumping beans. The Greyhound was a rolling oven as it swayed through the heat mirage, and he tried to ignore a nagging hunch that he would never really leave this place. Coming to Mexico, he had traveled in style, but returning had all the aesthetic allure of "an Apache torture session complete with ants."

As the bus threaded its way through the outskirts of Amarillo, Sheldon's sluggish thoughts returned to the stop he had made there while en route to England and the war. Though just three short years ago, it seemed like a lifetime. Suddenly, he sat bolt upright in his seat. The bus was passing about a half mile of tied-down aircraft.

As if by predetermined plan, the Greyhound slowed and stopped to pick up more passengers. Sheldon got off, glad to be momentarily free of the vehicle's stifling interior, and learned from a passerby that the dozens of planes across the road were for sale. As soon as Sheldon heard this, he had an inkling that his plane-delivering days were over. After collecting his traveling bag from the bus, he walked across the road and into a civilian office on Amarillo Air Force Base to inquire about the airplanes he had seen.

"Are those birds for sale?"

"Sure are fella. They'll be auctioned off day after tomorrow."

"I'd like to get a little closer look at 'em. They're liaison planes, aren't they?"

"Right, they're L2M Taylorcrafts. Come on, I'll take you over and show you around."

On close examination, he found that two years beneath the white-hot Texas sun had taken their toll. The fabric covering had been weakened, and the engines had swallowed more than their share of windblown dust. They were, however, almost new, and the T-Craft that Sheldon looked at now showed a mere 60 hours of accumulated time on the tachometer.

Two days later, the auction was held, and Sheldon's bid of $1,200 was good enough to secure one of the fragile Taylorcrafts, its registration number a simple 96. He flushed the engine with kerosene to remove the dust and sand. After a few minor adjustments, he was traveling to Pennsylvania in the style he preferred, at an indicated airspeed of 108 miles per hour in his own airplane.

When Sheldon arrived at Lockhaven, he took one last look at Jake Miller's waiting list, which was still as long as Sheldon's arm, and bid Piper Aircraft a fond farewell. Don's sister Berniece Underdahl, then the wife of an Army captain, lived in Moscow, Idaho. She was about to depart for Europe, and Sheldon, who had not seen her for years, decided on a quick visit. The flight west in the T-Craft was uneventful. Then, crossing the Continental Divide near Jackson, Wyoming, he encountered heavy turbulence. As he fought to control the bucking airplane, his mouth went dry as cotton when he heard an ominous ripping sound and felt the T-Craft yaw.

"About 13 feet of the fabric let go at the cap strip on the right wing. The stuff trailed aft and eventually fouled and jammed my right aileron. I had an interesting time getting her down and eventually landed in a hayfield on a dude ranch near the settlement of DuNoir, Wyoming. There was nothing for it but to temporarily recover the wing section that was damaged, so I got some burlap bags, rib-stitched 'em into place, and began to think about more permanent repairs."

In a repair hangar at Riverton, Wyoming, Sheldon replaced the torn burlap bags with new fabric, carefully covered with nitrate dope. By now, he had serious doubts about the rest of the skin on his small plane, but with optimism born of a recent stretch over Europe in far more dire straits, he took off for Moscow, Idaho, and his sister's home.

Sheldon returned to Pennsylvania in the T-Craft and decided he had pushed his luck far enough. He re-covered the entire plane and carefully refurbished it throughout. It was now in mint condition. Then he enrolled at Williamsport Technical Institute in Pennsylvania and graduated with an Airframe and Engineer rating license on February 25, 1947. With the course completed, there was nothing holding him in Pennsylvania, and he longed for the land to the far north.

"It all came back in a rush, and I suddenly wondered if I had froze my brains and they'd just thawed out."

At Williamsport, he had overhauled an aircraft engine, which he loaded in the baggage compartment of his T-Craft. Early one spring morning in April 1948, he took off and pointed the nose of his plane toward Minnesota, where he would cross the Canadian border on his way back home to Alaska.

He spent the night near a border-crossing point north of Minneapolis, and early the next morning, took off into a sunrise the likes of which he had not seen since he left Alaska. The air was cool and dew-fresh, and Sheldon experienced total exhilaration. Noon slipped by, and he began to grow drowsy. He had not slept well the night before, and the drumming of the tiny engine ahead of him began to have a hypnotic effect. He was navigating by charts, so he picked a landmark on the horizon and pointed the nose of the plane in its direction.

After what seemed like seconds, he woke with a start, glanced ahead, and could not recognize the country over which he was flying. He had lost some altitude, but the plane was still flying in a normal manner. His next thought had to do with fuel, and he had a hunch that he had little left. A hurried glance at the gauges was not necessary, for at that instant, the engine coughed and then ran smoothly again. Sheldon knew that he was in a bad spot. He banked gently and began to look for a place to land, but he saw only broken timber and hilly country. Turning the plane in a gradual circle, he finally spotted a small lake, and wonder of wonders, a floatplane was moored along its shore.

"I figured that if I had to stack the plane, I would at least do it near some habitation."

He began to make a slow gliding spiral above the lake, and as his altimeter unwound, he saw something else. At the end of the lake were two cabins and a small clearing. The clearing was a potato patch, and it was being plowed by a man and a team of mules. He had not been able to see the clearing at 6,000 feet, and at 1,000 feet, it still looked like a postage stamp. But it offered the only landing possibility around. To make matters worse, it sloped upward at about 20 degrees. The mule driver, seeing the sputtering aircraft turn into the wind at 800 feet for a landing that was obviously about to occur in his freshly plowed potato patch, promptly led the mules to safety. Sheldon reasoned that he would have to keep power on as he touched down uphill on the soft earth, and his luck held. As he flared for his landing, the engine spit and coughed but kept running until he mushed to a stop at the top of the incline. He had made it on fumes, and the engine died just as the plane settled to a stop in the soft black earth.

The farmer approached cautiously, and as Sheldon jumped down, asked the universal question, "Where ya headed, young man?"

"I'm going to Alaska."

"Jeez, you got a long haul ahead of ya. Think that plane will make it? Sounds like the engine's not runnin' right."

Sheldon told the guy that he had run short on gas.

"But I didn't tell him why," Sheldon said.

After this experience, Sheldon became a firm believer in two things—good navigation and full gas tanks.

Sheldon purchased gas from the logging company that owned the floatplane he had seen on the lake. Then he had to build a runway. It took the combined efforts of Sheldon, the farmer, and an old tractor three days and nights to flatten enough of the potato field to create a runway long enough for Sheldon to take off with the heavy aircraft engine that he carried as cargo. Under full throttle, the tiny T-Craft finally lifted off and became airborne. Sheldon expelled his breath, wagged his wings in inadequate thanks to the farmer, and resumed a northwesterly heading for Alaska.

During later years when he had to fly all-day schedules, Sheldon formed the somewhat unique habit of letting whoever was his right-seat passenger "steer" the plane while he caught ten winks.

The balance of the long trip was uneventful, and after about five days of flying, the muddy Tanana River just south of Fairbanks slid beneath his wings, and he landed at Weeks Field. Since the pioneering days of Carl Ben Eielson, Fairbanks had been aviation oriented, and Weeks Field, a dirt strip at the south edge of town, was the center of bush-aircraft activity in the interior.

Sheldon learned that during April a calamity had occurred. Weeks Field was struck by high winds, and when they finally quit blowing, every airplane that had not been hangared or tied down had sustained moderate to heavy damage. Many of them were beyond repair. While chatting with Sheldon, Fred Seltenrick, who ran an air service at Weeks, began to cast appreciative glances at the mint-condition T-Craft.

"Who did the work on your airplane?"

Sheldon allowed that he had and was prepared to follow up the admission with a bid for a job at Seltenrick's hangar, but the words never left his lips.

"Fred offered me a job on the spot. Because of the windstorm, he had a whole fleet of airplanes that needed repairs."

Sheldon worked for the amiable Seltenrick for several weeks. As the June days slipped by and the hangar on Weeks Field claimed him until long into the daylight nights of summer, Sheldon began to sorely miss his flying. Later, on a chance visit to Talkeetna, Sheldon was beset with air-charter requests, and he realized that a living could be made in bush flying. The mines near Talkeetna represented a good business potential, for there were freight and passengers to be hauled, even though the work would be seasonal. His plane, the T-Craft, was dependable enough but did not offer the extra performance that landings on short rough strips at the mines demanded. With this in mind, he sold the plane that had brought him back to Alaska and invested his money in a new PA-14 Cub. The fate of the T-Craft was sealed, for the two Fairbanksans who purchased it crashed a few short months later, and the plane was a total loss.

By the end of July 1948, Sheldon was back in the village of Talkeetna, and he began making his bid for what, realistically speaking, amounted to rather slim profits in the business of bush aviation. He knew he would eventually have to expand his operation, but for now the PA-14 would have to serve. Sheldon was at the controls as usual that day in July 1948 as he returned two fishermen to Merrill Field in Anchorage. The weather was excellent. Bright sunshine flooded the endless sea of green beneath, and the breeze caused the shadows of the puffy cumulus clouds to move slowly on their inexorable trip to the far horizon.

After landing and unloading two Blazo boxes full of iced trophy-size rainbow trout, Sheldon was checking his fuel tanks for the return trip to Talkeetna when he was approached by a stranger, who was impressed by the size of the fish and was more than interested in where they were caught. After chatting with the man, whose name was Robert Morrison, for several minutes, Sheldon invited the ebullient Irishman to get his fishing gear and accompany him on the return flight. Then as now, the Talkeetna aviator talked a heck of a good fishing trip, and in addition, he preferred to return north with a paying passenger rather than deadheading solo. Morrison returned quickly with his fishing rods, hip boots, and other paraphernalia, and the Cub was soon climbing outbound from sunny Merrill Field.

The fisherman whom Sheldon picked up that day—the man called "Stub" by his friends—would later become his only partner in the bush-aviation business. Morrison proved to be an astute businessman, and besides, he was well heeled. He provided the money for the down payments on several new airplanes, which made an impressive sight on the Talkeetna strip. With the responsibility of repaying the considerable—almost staggering—bank loans came the revolving-door flight schedules that the pilot has learned to accept as part and parcel of the air-charter business, which was named Talkeetna Air Service.

Stub Morrison fell in love with the lake country near Talkeetna on that first fishing trip and later moved to the tiny village with his wife, Lena, a Polynesian by birth. Skilled in the dances of the islands, she soon was operating a dance school for the local citizenry. Lena Morrison had other talents as well, among which shooting pool and consuming large quantities of bourbon were high on the list. Her husband had purchased the Fairview Inn, and it was here that she became a regular at the felt-topped tables.

One night, while engaged in a friendly game of eight ball at the Fairview, Lena removed her jewelry because it was impeding her moves. It was her custom to wear copious quantities of very valuable jewelry, and this night was no exception. She was fetchingly bedecked in a 10-carat emerald-cut diamond necklace, several rings containing a total of 10 or 12 more carats of the shimmering stones, along with several bracelets of native-gold nuggets. History, at this point, does not enlighten us as to whether Lena Morrison was afflicted with acute absentmindedness or had merely imbibed too heartily in the bar whiskey that flowed in its usual good quantity, but it must suffice to say that she placed these valuable jewels in an old cigar box that contained the odds and ends accompanying all pool tables—pieces of chalk, spare cue tips, and a few rubber bands. She became engrossed in the game at hand and later went to bed, completely forgetting where she had left her jewelry. In the morning, after a most thorough search, she decided that she had been the victim of a robbery. Later, Stub would jokingly accuse Sheldon of absconding with the stones and hocking them to make extra payments on his airplanes. Sixteen years after that memorable night at the Fairview, the pool table was sold, and the new owner discovered the bounty in the old cigar box, whereupon they were returned, to Lena's great joy.

Shortly after their arrival in Talkeetna, Stub Morrison was bitten badly by the flying bug, and Sheldon taught him the basics. In Yankton, South Dakota, Stub had been in an unfortunate auto accident, which left him without his left hand and with only partial use of his left arm because the muscles had been badly cut. However, this disability did not really hinder his flying, for Sheldon had welded a special extension to the throttle of the plane he flew. The crippled arm certainly was no distraction in the various other activities that Stub cherished, among them fishing and pitching dice.

One of Stub's most valuable assets was his ability to think and act cool under pressure, a virtue that undoubtedly was honed to a fine edge in the tension of countless high-stake games from Reno to Diamond Head. Morrison was in the habit of backing winners, and in the spring of 1950, he was confident that Sheldon, the air service, and the planes he had financed comprised a young but highly successful venture. One factor that Morrison the gambler seemed to take for granted and accept as his due was luck, whereas Sheldon, through discretion and caution, was learning to make most of his own.

"Eight G Lake"

The moose had dropped their antlers, Uncle Sam had been paid his due, and 1950 looked like it would be even more lucrative than the year just past. Sheldon's contract with the Alaska Road Commission, which had been granted in August of 1949, had been a money-maker, enabling him to pay a substantial amount on the airplane contracts. Working for the commission, he had spent more time in the air between Paxson, Talkeetna, and the west end of Mount McKinley National Park than he had on the ground. He had hauled about 95 percent of the project's transient personnel and support supplies, and emergency equipment consisting of badly needed parts to replace those that broke down or simply wore out as the construction progressed. His landing fields were as varied as the Alaskan weather, and each trip became either a challenge or an ordeal, depending on the circumstances of the day. Where the new roadbed was graded to some semblance of smoothness (the completed Denali "highway" boasts rocks the size of a man's head), he would enjoy the comparative luxury of a reasonably trouble-free and smooth landing. More often, however, he had to find his own landing strips on the tundra and gravel outcroppings near the proposed roadbed.

In a short time, he began to develop what today has often been described as an uncanny ability to see landing spots where none should be. It is perhaps this single factor that separates Sheldon from other bush pilots, regardless of their flying ability.

Landing where no one has ever landed must be "practiced with the utmost of discretion. This holds true for all bush landing areas, such as sandbars and other inhospitable places." Needless to say, these landings, for Sheldon or anyone else brash enough to try them, are fraught with a multiplex of risks both small and large. Under the very best of conditions, they are hard on airplanes, and in a monument to understatement, Sheldon describes them as "abrasive."

Discretion is Sheldon's byword. His judgment, based on a superb understanding of the subtleties of aerodynamics, has been vital to his success. He has become capable of instantly applying his knowledge while standing his aircraft on one wing as he prepares for a landing on, and a subsequent takeoff from, a stump- and rock-littered river bar or a high-altitude glacier.

"Soft sand, obstructions, and the length of the strip are prime considerations. It doesn't do a guy any good to land 200 miles from nowhere and then find out that he doesn't have enough runway to take off on. The tundra is decorated with the remains of planes whose pilots made this mistake."

One of the most changeable and critical of all the factors that relate to Sheldon's work is density altitude, a term used to describe the relative thickness of the atmosphere, or put another way, the number of molecules of air per given volume.

"Density altitude differs with both height above sea level and air temperature, and its value predicts how well any airplane will fly. On a cold day at sea level, planes fly best, while on hot days at high altitudes, such as those often found during the summer on glaciers, performance suffers. In addition, a plane flies better in cool, moisture-free air, and many would-be bush pilots and a surprising number of experienced professionals get caught. They'll land on a short strip one day when the air is cool and dry and take off with no problems. Next day they'll go back, land, and end up stacking the airplane at the end of the runway on takeoff, because today they forgot that the air temperature is 20 or 30 degrees warmer than it was yesterday."

But Sheldon knows that more than discretion and knowledge of aerodynamics is involved. Some lessons have to be learned the hard way. With a realistic outlook, he has the highest regard for simple luck. He was more than lucky in the autumn of 1950. On a tiny green lake in the rugged Talkeetna Mountains, a series of chilling events began which made that year one Sheldon has long tried to forget.

The pilot and an old sourdough friend had just completed dressing two fat moose. Frank Moennikes of Talkeetna and Sheldon had flown to a lake that is 80 miles northeast of Talkeetna and situated at 2,000 feet above sea level, with 800-foot rock ridges jutting upward at its north end. With Moennikes and some of the moose meat aboard, Sheldon taxied the float-equipped Aeronca Sedan to the south end of the small lake for a takeoff into what was now a stiffly turbulent wind blowing from the north.

"I had successfully used this lake for the past three hunting seasons and was wary of the obstructions at the north end. My plan was to fly the perimeter of the lake in a broad circle, first to the right and then to the left. When sufficient altitude had been gained, I would skip over the 800-foot ridges at a 45-degree angle."

With full throttle, the Aeronca shuddered and then rapidly accelerated, blowing a cloud of fine spray in its wake.

"The plane leaped up on the step with the brisk head wind, and using the one-float-roll technique, I was airborne in the first fourth of the lake. Had it not been for faulty turbulence, the takeoff might have been routine. At about 500-foot altitude and on the far perimeter of the lake, I was making a gentle left turn when it became apparent that the plane would not clear the obstructions."

Sheldon's only alternative was to lower the airplane's nose and continue the left turn, while hopefully skirting the edge of the lake as he flew downwind.

"The Aeronca Sedan has a wide fuselage profile, which tends to blanket the airflow of the outside wing in a turn. At slow speeds, or in turbulence, this aircraft must be turned with caution or a stall, or worse yet, a spin will result."

The ridge at the lake's north end filled Sheldon's vision, and he realized that to avoid collision with tons of rock, he would have to steepen his turn to the left.

"I knew that to do this would be to invite the stealthy buffet of a stall. To decrease the bank would guarantee a collision with the rocks, and to point the nose down further would result in a dive into the lake."

Directly downwind and midway into the turn, the Aeronca stalled with authority.

"The right wing dropped sharply, and the plane spun to the right with a vengeance. The impact was in 50 feet of water and straight down."

In the massive concussion and chaos that followed, Sheldon remembers being amazed that he somehow remained conscious, while Moennikes was knocked out cold and jammed under the instrument panel. Indescribable forces tore the windshield from its mountings "by its roots" and jammed the Edo floats tightly against the under-surface of the wings. With impact, dark water gushed in through the windshield opening and quickly filled the cabin. It was at this point that Sheldon spotted Moennikes' foot sticking upward from beneath the panel.

"I reefed on the leg and somehow got to the surface through the windshield opening with Moennikes in tow. It was 50 yards to a small island, and when I got there, I looked back at my $8,000 investment. Only a small part of the rudder was above water. Just then a sleeping bag popped to the surface, and I swam out to recover it. I found that it was surprisingly dry."

Sheldon covered his passenger with the sleeping bag and then piled some moss over him for good measure. It was at this time that Moennikes came to.

"What happened?" Moennikes said.

"We got shortstopped. Can you move everything?"

"Yeh, I'm okay, but I could sure use a drink."

"I'll hike to Gold Creek and get the Tenth Rescue to pick you up."

Sheldon remembers his 50-mile cross-country "stroll" in minute detail.

"I traveled lightly, with a knife, wool shirt, raincoat, and some moose jerky. As dusk approached, a light rain began to fall. I found Portage Creek in high water, bank to bank, and as I swam across the mouth, the current carried me 70 yards down the Susitna River before I got back to the rock wall. Finally, I made a detour up steep rock, which was tundra covered with devil's club and thick alders. Then I smelled bear."

Ahead of him, and almost beneath his feet, a sleeping grizzly exploded from the brush and crashed through the undergrowth. Cursing under his breath about close calls, the pilot continued fighting his way through the brush.

"It was nearly pitch dark as I worked downriver, falling over rotted tree stumps, rocks, and deadfalls. In the far distance, I heard the mournful sound of a freight train, and I poured on the effort to try to catch him at the Gold Creek bridge. I made it to the embankment just as the engine thundered by 30 feet above me."

Sheldon staggered onto the tracks, which still vibrated with the train's passing, and walked uncertainly to the Gold Creek section house near the bridge, where he rapped on the door.

"The early-rising section foreman opened the door, took one quick look, and then slammed it closed. He thought I had survived some kind of gang fight, as my clothes were in rags from the 14-hour stroll. The various collisions had skinned me up from head to toe."

Sheldon was quickly able to get word to Tenth Rescue, and by ten o'clock that same morning, they picked Moennikes up and returned him to Talkeetna.

"Believe it or not, upon their arrival at the lake, they landed in a *no-wind condition.*"

Later, the demolished Aeronca partially surfaced, but though attempts were made, it was unsalvageable. As he flies by, Sheldon never fails to take notice of the tiny lake where the uncontrollable effects of faulty turbulence cost him an airplane. He has dubbed it "Eight G Lake."

Prior to 1951, there were vast areas in the Territory that were still unmapped. A major survey of the Alaska Range was planned, but even with this giant step forward, large yellow regions that were as yet virtually unexplored and unsurveyed would still remain on the map. The rugged Talkeetna Mountains were situated in one of these yellow areas.

"The U.S. Geological Survey was interested in the Talkeetnas and launched a project to map them. To get the surveyors into the area, ten Bell helicopters were staged for the job, nine of them new machines, with the tenth having been built up from scrap parts. After six months' duty in the Talkeetnas, the new machines had been wrecked and scattered all over the country, and you guessed it, the tenth one, the spare-parts orphan, was still going strong."

The USGS and their contracting agent, Alaska Airlines, hired Sheldon to salvage parts from two of the wrecks, one of which was located below Devil's Canyon, on the Susitna River, and the second at Jay Lake, about 30 miles above Devil's Canyon. Sheldon remembers the late September 1950 recovery of the second chopper vividly.

"We had been caught by a storm and darkness as we loaded the last of the salvageable parts aboard my Aeronca Sedan."

Sheldon and the Alaska Airlines mechanic had then tied the plane to some broken rotor blades that had been driven into the soft river sand in the crash. It was a precarious mooring, and at midnight, the two men were rudely awakened by the sounds of driftwood crunching against the floats of the airplane. The flashlight's weak beam revealed that the sandbar was now awash, and whitecaps were tossing the plane like a cork. With sleet rattling on the floatplane's skin, Sheldon decided to taxi downriver to what he hoped would be a more secure tie-up near an old trapper's cabin. It was pitch dark as they cast off.

"The river was running slush ice as we cautiously began to taxi backwards downriver. I had to use half-takeoff power just to hold the plane steady in the heavy current."

The distance downriver to the cabin was about one mile, and in the darkness and sleet, they swept by it. The tiny plane lurched as the current grew heavier, and Sheldon knew that they were being swept into a narrow canyon.

"A takeoff downriver was the last resort. It was now or never."

In the darkness, with the plane's engine howling at full throttle, Sheldon somehow managed to thread his way through the towering rock walls, and after cautiously gaining altitude while negotiating the black maze, climbed the plane to 7,000 feet.

"I decided to try and find Clarence Lake, where we had been stockpiling the helicopter parts, but it was too dark and we couldn't locate it."

There was now only one alternative left—head for Talkeetna, 95 miles to the south. Sheldon lined the plane up on the first leg of a course that would take them there. En route, he checked his fuel gauges with the aid of the flashlight, which now flickered feebly.

"I couldn't believe my eyes. The gauges said empty. I had the equivalent of a barrel of fuel aboard when I took off. Before it had gotten dark, I had topped my wing tanks and loaded one extra five-gallon can in with the helicopter parts. I was still trying to solve the mystery as I adjusted my course ten degrees right to miss Mount Watana."

Minutes later, Sheldon knew beyond the slightest shadow of a doubt that the gauges had not lied.

"Without warning, the engine began to cough and nearly stopped. I pushed on carburetor heat, leaned the mixture fully, reduced throttle, and was able to encourage a few more propeller revolutions."

The complete silence that only an engine failure can produce followed. With the power gone, the plane began to settle rapidly.

"Coming down was like falling out of a coal chute. All I could do was concentrate on nose down and keep the airspeed up. Ahead, in the sleet-spattered murk, something ominous looking loomed, and I turned left. I glanced at the altimeter and saw that we were now sinking through 3,000 feet.

"At the risk of going night blind, I flicked on the landing lights and found myself staring at rocks. More left turn through an opaque fog layer, and then whap. No more whistling float struts and stiff control pressures."

The floatplane bucked and skidded to a stop in the darkness. Sheldon popped his door open for a look.

"We discovered that we were sitting on wet tundra, just off the end of an oversize beaver pond."

Sheldon and the mechanic were delirious with joy and soaked to the skin as they began the task of skinning the green birch poles over which they would skid the plane to the water. A quick examination had shown that the plane was miraculously undamaged in the unscheduled landing, and the last dying beam of the flashlight had solved the mystery of the empty gas tanks.

"One gas cap had been placed in my pocket instead of on the airplane where it belonged, and the flight had lasted just 32 minutes on *full* tanks."

The slipstream and wind rushing over the surface of the wing had quickly vacuumed the gasoline from the tanks, which cross-feed from each other.

"About daylight, with the plane in the water, we unloaded the helicopter parts and other gear, filtered the five gallons of spare gas into the tanks, and blasted off of the beaver pond to idle into Talkeetna on fumes."

Later, that same fall, on a flight from Talkeetna to Anchorage in a Piper PA-14, Sheldon was alone at the controls and considerably more impressed with the total discomfort of a nagging head cold than with any imminent peril that might be in the offing. He was 20 air miles north of Anchorage, where he would pick up a cargo of booze. Cruising at an altitude of about 2,000 feet, he was contemplating the simple act of blowing his nose when suddenly and with no warning whatsoever, he was engulfed in a system of rough air and violent shear turbulence.

"The Cub dropped several hundred feet like a runaway elevator, then snapped upward in the same fashion."

Immediately, he heard a sharp tearing sound at his left and over his head, accompanied by an immediate tendency on the part of the airplane to turn left. He also noticed a change in the position and attitude of the left wing. The ominous sounds of straining metal continued unabated, and the left-turning tendency of the Cub became stronger and much more demanding. As the realization of what was occurring struck home, Sheldon's senses screamed silently. The right wing-spar, the support member that is one of the main beams of the wing, had broken. In each wing of a PA-14, there are two such spars, which parallel each other and extend from wing root to wing tip. Their purpose is to stiffen and support the wing, and since this support was no longer present in the rear portion of the left wing, it was slowly and inexorably folding backward. The wing had already moved about four or five inches in this direction, and all that was holding it now was "force of habit." Suddenly the wing lurched four or five feet aft, and Sheldon was in a vertical attitude as the plane screamed earthward. The ground lay 1,500 feet below.

Early in his flight training, Sheldon had practiced aerobatics in a PT-19 aircraft, and now this training came automatically to his aid. He reached for the flap lever near the floor, his last-ditch chance at lowering the terrible airspeed. Normally, flaps act as air brakes when extended, as they increase the drag on a flying airplane. In this instance, they unexpectedly aggravated the situation, and Sheldon felt his body being jammed down into the seat by the terrible G forces generated by the now-spinning PA-14.

"The G forces were so strong in the spin that my nose blew itself all over the windshield of the airplane."

Somewhere in the third revolution of the spin, Sheldon suddenly realized that he might be able to raise the plane's nose just prior to impact, thereby saving himself. As he looked down, he had a blurred glimpse of a swamp just beyond a grove of 200-foot cottonwood trees.

"The plane spun 1½ more times, and with only 400 feet of altitude left, I pulled back on the controls in an attempt to level it and hopefully make the swamp I had seen moments before. The plane leveled, but I had misjudged the turn and overshot the swamp. Then, everything went ape. As the plane returned to a level attitude, it immediately began a series of snap rolls and became a 1,500-pound projectile with a mind of its own as it collided with the towering cottonwoods beyond the swamp."

Sheldon remembers the sensation as one similar to being fired from a cannon. He recalls the appalling noise, which ceased as abruptly as it had started.

No aviator, regardless of how totally nerveless he may be in an emergency, can repress the consuming panic that postcrash fire creates. Reality smashed at Sheldon, and he reacted instantly. After the impact, during which he once more remained conscious, he hung upside down in his shoulder harness. He released it, tearing all of the fingernails on his right hand. Falling heavily to the roof of the cabin, he lashed out with his feet to kick open the door. Even before the cold air entered, he had become aware that he was being "drowned in gasoline," which poured from the ruptured wing roots. Sheldon jumped and fell 20 feet to the ground.

Once on the ground, the silence was totally unreal. Sheldon's ears still rang horribly from the impact. Drenched in high-octane gasoline, he gazed upward like a man staring at the open lid of his own coffin. Then something else demanded his attention—he realized that the entire engine of the plane was missing. Stumbling around, he found it "in a smoking pile in the snow about 200 feet away. Later, I sold the remnants of the plane for 50 bucks."

What had occurred was one of the imponderables of aviation, and like in-flight fire, a thing that all pilots fear, probably above all others. Structural failure in the air leads to a sequence of events over which there is little or no control. Sheldon, like all competent pilots, clings tenaciously to the unshakable belief that given half a chance, he can either prevent an accident, or at the very least, recover from a bad situation. This faith dissolves with the occurrence of in-flight structural failure and, obviously, when confronted with a midair collision. Both are sudden, unexpected, and almost always fatal; and their eventuality, like a black shadow, rides tucked away in some far corner of every airplane that leaves the ground.

Sheldon continued with his charter and contract flying during the summer of 1950. Stub Morrison flew much of the time, and Talkeetna Air Service held its own despite the loss of two planes. Nevertheless, Sheldon was beginning to realize that he and his partner would somehow have to increase their activities to bring in the extra margin of profit necessary to ensure that the air service could continue to stay out of the red.

The Man from Boston

Don Sheldon met Bradford Washburn on Wednesday, August 1, 1951, and he knew that the scientist was no stranger to Alaska, or for that matter, to the village of Talkeetna. What Sheldon did not know was that this man with the courteous, almost cautious manner would soon bind him irrevocably to a life of high-risk flying in the rugged mountains of Alaska, for Brad Washburn would prove to be an intensely capable, though unlikely, mentor in this unproven art. Sheldon liked the amiable scientist immediately. Washburn, now director of the Boston Museum of Science, was at that time immersed in a long-term study of Mount McKinley and its neighboring peaks, a study that would culminate in the first detailed, large-scale map of the mountain and would require 15 long years of arduous work to complete. On that sunny early-August afternoon, Washburn wanted to fly to the base of the magnificent Ruth Glacier to find a suitable location for a survey station. With Sheldon at the controls of a special four-wheeled Super Cub, they were soon sliding along at a comfortable altitude on their first flight together in the drafty, little plane. There would be many more.

Speaking loudly enough so that the man behind him could hear over the smooth drumming of the Lycoming engine in the Super Cub's nose, Sheldon was soon engaged in what even then was his favorite pastime, pointing down at little-known places of interest with the enthusiasm of a kid on Christmas morning. Washburn, in the rear seat, was carefully appraising the young pilot in the gray knit watch cap. He was impressed with another of Sheldon's trademarks—his cool, almost detached manner, which somehow only magnified the professional smoothness with which he operated the tiny aircraft. Sheldon soon slipped the Super Cub to a landing on a small gravel bar that Washburn had pointed out and rolled to a stop precisely where the scientist wanted to be. This particular plane, with its two pairs of wheels mounted in tandem, was particularly well suited for landings like this.

Later, as the two discussed the wooded moraines and the general lay of the land below the glacier, Sheldon was drawn to the intimacy with which Washburn approached the study of mountains. He found himself seeing them as if for the first time. The pair spent the better part of two hours at the foot of the Ruth, then flew a circuitous route back to Talkeetna.

After their return, each man had reached an unspoken conclusion about the other. Sheldon was convinced that this unassuming man of science was a veritable storehouse of information related to mountain flying. Washburn was well versed in meteorology, airdrop techniques, air-to-ground radio communications, and even the seldom-practiced technique of glacier landings.

Washburn saw a highly versatile and likable pilot, with intense interests other than merely driving an airplane. He felt that Sheldon was a man who, with added experience, would prove an invaluable asset to the McKinley map project. As a result, a close friendship was born—an association that began more than 23 years ago with a shared love for high places and is today earmarked by a deep mutual respect.

Brad Washburn had come to Alaska for the first time in 1930 as a Harvard freshman leading a six-man expedition in an attempt to climb 15,300-foot Mount Fairweather in the St. Elias Mountains. By 1936, he had already made five trips to the Territory, had made the first ascent of Mount Crillon, and had led the first expedition to cross the St. Elias Mountains from Canada to Alaska by dog team in midwinter.

In July 1936, he came to Fairbanks to lead an expedition that was jointly financed by the National Geographic Society and Pan American Airways. The purpose of the project that summer was to take a series of highly accurate and comprehensive photographs of Mount McKinley. At altitudes that often required the use of oxygen, he spent seemingly endless hours squinting through the viewfinder of an aerial camera mounted in the open doorway of a twin-engined

Lockheed Electra. In spite of the discomfort of the cold, thin air, Washburn secured a group of photos that showed the huge mountain in detail never before available. These pictures, published in *National Geographic* magazine, July 1938, would figure prominently in future expeditions and form the inspiration for the complex task of surveying for the first accurate map of McKinley, which Washburn would produce many years later.

By the early thirties, it had become apparent to many scientists, Washburn among them, that this huge mountain—which towers almost four vertical miles above Alaska's interior and is one of the highest mountains in the world, excelled by only two or three of the Himalayan giants—represented an exposed laboratory upon which many barely understood natural phenomena could be closely studied. As yet virtually unmapped, McKinley stood alone, its crown swathed in clouds. At this altitude, 20,320 feet, even the best airplanes of the day were hard pressed to fly for extended periods of time. The mountain, in addition to its awesome height, offered a host of other physical features that were of interest to the scientific world: glaciers; glacial streams; high alpine meadows, which offered countless varieties of flowers and other plant life during the brief Alaskan summer; and at its base, vast moraines, which blended with the unexplored spruce wilderness of the interior.

Between its windswept summit and verdant base were places, many of them as yet unnamed, that were destined to become part of the vocabularies of mountain climbers the world over—places like Kahiltna Pass, the Moose's Tooth, Windy Corner, the West Buttress, and the magnificent Amphitheater and Great Gorge of the Ruth Glacier.

For millions of years, the upper reaches of the mountain have been held in the almost-constant grip of severe coastal storms, which travel inland from the Pacific Ocean and crest along McKinley's South and West Buttresses. These storms consistently produce winds well in excess of 100 miles per hour, with accompanying chill factors that commonly exceed 125 degrees below zero during the summertime. (The warmest night that Washburn would spend in McKinley's Upper Basin during the *summer* of 1942 would be 18 degrees below zero.) When the ubiquitous coastal storms are not pummeling the mountain above 17,000 feet, McKinley, which seems to thrive on malicious perversity, is making its own weather. Due to its tremendous vertical dimension and the accompanying cloud stratification and temperature variation, McKinley is, within itself, a veritable weather factory.

Prior to the year 1930, venturing on foot into this world of freight-train winds and temperatures that make rubber snap like glass was considered pure folly, even by the eternally optimistic Alaskans. In the adolescence of aviation, to fly over the area was known to be highly perilous, and to land upon the flanks of the giant mountain was considered madness. But there were some bush pilots who believed there was a method to flying in the cold, thin air at high altitudes, a method waiting, like the proverbial plum, for the right man.

And Matt Nieminen, a pilot for Alaska Airways, was that man. On August 13, 1930, in a Fairchild Model 71 monoplane, Nieminen, accompanied by his mechanic, Cecil Higgins, made the first flight over the bleak 20,320-foot summit of McKinley. One can only inadequately speculate about the thoughts of Nieminen and Higgins as they gazed at this vast natural spectacle through the frosted windows of the laboring Fairchild that day 44 years ago.

Even when seen from the warm, pressurized cabin of a modern jetliner, the sight of McKinley's summit, usually towering like an icy island above a cloud deck at 16,000 or 17,000 feet, is impressive. At this altitude, the peak seems very small. Then the illusion is shattered when a hole appears in the clouds. The eye is drawn downward, and the awesome height of McKinley is more than obvious.

The second flier to gaze upon the bleak summit of Denali was Joe Crosson, Alaska Airways' chief pilot. With him on that trip in August 1931 was Oscar Darling, a cinematographer with Fox-Movietone News, who took the first pictures ever taken of McKinley from the air.

But Crosson made an even greater mark in aviation history when he accomplished a feat others had only thought and talked about. On April 25, 1932, Joe Crosson, carrying several passengers, became the first pilot to land an airplane in a place others had only ventured to look at from afar. He eased the large homemade, wooden skis of his Fairchild onto the snowpacked Muldrow Glacier on Mount McKinley and unloaded his passengers. With this landing near the 5,700-foot McGonagall Pass on McKinley, a new era of mountain flying was born.

In the years to follow, other pilots would duplicate Crosson's accomplishment. Some would die in the windy, snow-choked vast-ness of the Alaska Range, while a very select few would escape to return on other days. In a tribute to his uncanny "weather sense," Crosson would successfully retrace his first flight to the Muldrow many times during the spring of 1932.

Crosson's passengers were also destined to play an important part in McKinley's history. Allen Carpé, Theodore Koven, Edward P. Beckwith, Nicholas Spadavecchia, and Percy Olten were planning not only the third ascent of McKinley but also a sustained stay on the Muldrow Glacier for the purpose of doing cosmic-ray studies at 11,000 feet. But their expedition would end tragically.

Carpé and Koven were the first on a long list of those who have lost their lives on the mountain in the past four decades. These two men were killed in a skiing accident at the very beginning of their attempt to exist on the Muldrow for an extended period of time. At the time of the 1932 accident, Carpé was without question the number-one climber in North America. It was indeed a senseless tragedy. While an expert *climber*, he was a tyro on skis. Descend-ing from 11,000 feet toward the top of the great Muldrow Icefall, he was unable to turn and skied right into a huge, bottomless cre-vasse. Koven fell in, and was mortally injured, trying to get down to him. The body of Carpé remains deep in the icy heart of the Muldrow Glacier, while Koven's was retrieved later that summer, after being found by the descending Lindley-Liek Expedition, which became the first ever to reach both the North and South Summits on the same expedition.

Other members of Carpé's ill-fated group were also in trouble. Edward P. Beckwith became gravely ill while at the base camp and had to be removed from the mountain by a bush pilot named Jerry Jones, of Fairbanks. Olten, who had stayed at the ailing Beckwith's side until Jones arrived, made his way off the mountain under his own power. Nicholas Spadavecchia was found wandering blindly about in the lowlands. He had been living on porcupines after he got lost attempting to walk out for help. Two McKinley Park rangers, Lee Swisher and John Rumohr, followed his tracks and finally rescued him after a 180-mile trek.

McKinley figured prominently during the Second World War. The U.S. Army put a 17-man expedition onto its slopes for two months during June and July of 1942 to test clothing, food, and equipment. Then, during the fall of 1944, the U.S. Air Force sent a small party to 13,220-foot Mount Silverthrone, just east of Mc-Kinley, to carry out further studies and tests of the effects of extremely low temperatures on the emergency equipment carried in their aircraft flying over cold regions. Brad Washburn was a member of both of these expeditions and led the latter.

From March to May 1945, the U.S. Air Force mounted another research expedition to the frigid slopes of Mount Silverthrone to do further tests of cold-weather food and clothing and to experiment with new methods of air-to-ground supply and communications. In conjunction with the research, Captain Richard Ragle, chief of the USAF Search and Rescue Center at Ladd Air Force Base in Fairbanks, made a number of ski landings on the Brooks Glacier, just above its confluence with the Muldrow, of McKinley. Ragle used an L-1 military monoplane with slotted wings. This feature made it possible to fly the plane very slowly, rendering it ideal for use in glacier landings. The research team was on Silverthrone 40 days, and Ragle flew resupply and other liaison missions for the duration of their stay. He also experimented with free airdrops of supplies at 10,000-foot Silverthrone Pass and perfected the practice to a surprisingly accurate degree. Ragle's methods were carefully logged on the ground for later use by the military, and no one on the scene watched more closely than the man who was coordinating the entire venture. He was, of course, Bradford Washburn.

At the time Washburn met Sheldon in 1951, he was well established as one of the world's foremost experts in mountaineering and in the business of using airplanes and radios in the pursuit of his studies. A small-plane pilot himself, he had flown with the famous Bob Reeve in the coastal mountains of southern Alaska. In 1937, Reeve, flying his ski-equipped Fairchild 51, landed Washburn and Bob Bates at 8,600 feet on the Walsh Glacier of 17,150-foot Mount Lucania. The following year, again with Reeve, Washburn had landed on Mount Marcus Baker.

Reeve, the first Alaskan bush pilot to make glacier landings a successful business, was based at the town of Valdez, on Prince William Sound. He flew the old Fairchilds, a model 71 and 51, and his airplanes were equipped with large wooden skis that could not be retracted to facilitate landings on surfaces other than snow. Reeve solved the problem of taking off at Valdez in the summer by using his skis on the mud flats near town at low tide. The skis that Reeve employed were hand-constructed of hardwood and had their bearing surfaces covered with stainless steel, which provided slickness, strength, and durability.

After the completion of the 1945 cold-weather tests with the Air Force on Mount Silverthrone, Washburn went back to Boston and the Museum of Science, where he was employed, to consolidate plans for his long-term dream of mapping McKinley and the portion of the Alaska Range immediately adjacent to it. In 1947, sponsored by the museum, he returned to Alaska. As always, the bugaboo of finding a capable pilot to provide the vital air support for the expedition had reared its head early in the planning stages. Bob Reeve was flying in the Aleutians, so Washburn selected Haakon ("Chris") Christensen of Anchorage as his pilot. He also chose the Muldrow Glacier as his base position on the mountain, and Christensen, flying a Waco biplane, made many expert and totally successful landings there. While Washburn was on the Muldrow, he also witnessed the landing of a military C-45, flown by two Air Force pilots. This was the first and only landing of a twin-engine aircraft on McKinley. On this 90-day expedition in 1947, Barbara Washburn became the first woman to climb Mount McKinley, and a huge amount of work was accomplished on the map that had been started on Mount Silverthrone in 1945.

In 1951, Washburn decided to carry on his topographic work at the head of the huge Kahiltna Glacier, on the totally unexplored West Approach of McKinley. His close friend Terris Moore, the new president of the University of Alaska in Fairbanks and a highly capable bush pilot who had climbed McKinley with Washburn on the Army trip in 1942, agreed to provide expedition air support with his new 135-horsepower Super Cub. The tiny Super Cub had been born on the drawing boards at Lockhaven and placed in production in the early 1950s. A more successfully designed high-performance bush airplane than the tiny Super Cub will probably never be found. Along with some beefing up of the basic airframe, only the engines in this frail, fabric-covered bird have been changed over the years since its first appearance, and the 150-horsepower Lycoming-equipped version is still considered the ultimate in bush-flying equipment by Sheldon and most other Alaskan pilots.

An innovation that appeared on Moore's Super Cub was the new retractable skis. After leaving a dry-ground airstrip, they could be lowered into position for snow landings by using a hydraulic wobble pump in the airplane's cabin. Moore had helped the Federal Engineering Company of Minnesota design the retractable skis.

Terris Moore landed Washburn's party at the 7,400-foot elevation on Kahiltna Glacier during June 1951 and a month later evacuated the group from a snowy basin at the head of the Kahiltna at an altitude of just over 10,000 feet. As well as doing a large amount of work on the map, Washburn's party had successfully scaled McKinley's West Buttress, a first in the history of climbing on that side of the mountain. The route, pioneered by this group of eight climbers from the Boston Museum of Science and the University of Denver, has become the shortest and safest pathway to Mc-Kinley's now-popular summit. Until that year, the West Buttress had been thought to be unclimbable. Washburn's exploration and confirmation of this way up McKinley was motivated by his desire to find a short route that offered less crevasse danger for use by the Office of Naval Research in subsequent cosmic-ray experiments and other scientific work on the mountain (which actually never took place because the levels of energy produced by man-made accelerators soon made cosmic-ray research of this sort no longer practical or necessary).

During late June and early July, Moore made many landings on McKinley to support Washburn's party, and as testimony to the scientist's thoroughness, Moore once commented, "The strip on the Kahiltna, upon which I made most of my landings, was so well marked by Brad and the ground-to-air radio landing instructions so complete that I considered the task no more difficult than had I been landing at Fairbanks or even Anchorage."

These then were Bradford Washburn's credentials—over 20 years' experience with all phases of mountain flying, air support, mountain climbing, and mountain research. In August 1951, when Washburn met Sheldon, there was one ingredient that was missing in the list that would spell success in the nine-year survey of the mountain which lay ahead, and this ingredient was one that Washburn himself could not supply.

He needed *one* airman who could serve his research project through to its end. None of the pilots who had flown for him in the past—Christensen, Reeve, or Moore—lived near enough to McKinley or would be available for the period of time required by this project. Neither Washburn nor Sheldon realized it when they first met on that lovely summer afternoon in 1951, but Washburn's search for a capable pilot was ended.

78

On the day after his first flight with Don, Washburn went to Anchorage to visit his old friend Bob Reeve. A statement made by the glacier pilot that evening is vividly recalled by Brad Washburn, and it is doubtful that even Reeve realized the accuracy of his prophecy when he said, "I've heard a lot about that kid [Sheldon], and he's either crazy and is going to kill himself, or he'll turn out to be one hell of a good pilot!"

The Bait

Sheldon's unspoken thoughts hit a new low as he stumbled among the moisture-laden tag alders that slapped his face. His shirt, originally dampened by sweat as he unloaded a half-ton of six-inch placer drill casings from his airplane, was now thoroughly soaked. The plane, its engine still warm from the flight in from Talkeetna with an intermediate stop in Anchorage for the casings, rested at the edge of the rough landing strip on a low plateau behind Sheldon. Under happier circumstances, he would now be back home drinking hot tea liberally laced with honey, his favorite libation. Instead, he had spent the better part of two hours trying to follow an almost nonexistent trail to the Fairview Mine in the dark of this October night in 1951. The dense blanket of fog, which now was felt rather than seen, made the darkness absolute. Flying was an impossibility. He was hopelessly grounded, and the only cheerful aspect of the whole situation was that he figured somewhere up ahead was a warm mine shack in which he could spend the night. The vocabularies of pilots everywhere are well supplied with descriptive adjectives that relate to fog, and the most colorful of these belong to the bush pilots of Alaska. There are several kinds of fog listed in the books dealing with meteorology, and the variety that now enveloped Sheldon like a black velvet bag was one of the more common. Called radiation fog, or ground fog, it forms when the ground cools the overlying air to its dew-point temperature. Radiation fog can be very dense, and under the right conditions, it will stack up to a considerable altitude.

Earlier in the afternoon of that same day, Stub Morrison, on his way to Anchorage with a passenger, encountered the same radiation fog that trapped Sheldon. Morrison's plane was found totally demolished after it impacted in an extreme nose-down attitude among the dripping spruces and cottonwoods on that windless autumn night. Both Morrison and his passenger perished instantly. The date was October 4, 1951.

After spending the night at the mine, Sheldon landed at Talkeetna the next morning, in the bright sunshine that had burned the fog away. The news of Morrison's death numbed him, and he became obsessed by the realization that he himself had escaped the same trap by mere minutes. Had he not unloaded the cargo of drill casings alone, he most certainly would have finished early, taken off before the fog formed, and been trapped en route to Talkeetna.

With the jovial Irishman's death, Don Sheldon had lost one of his closest friends, and in addition, an astute business partner. Lena Morrison, who was now the sole owner of Stub's share in the struggling Talkeetna Air Service, knew she could rely upon Sheldon in the matter of running the business. This is not to imply that Lena Morrison shied from the making of decisions. Her common sense backed by a will of iron has been demonstrated on many occasions just as forcefully as it was one cold night at the Cache Creek Bar, across the river from Talkeetna, where she and several local citizens were enjoying a few drinks. A member of the party, a regular customer of another nearby flying service, lost his bout with the bar liquor and fell from his stool unconscious. The rest of the party decided that his condition warranted a rush trip to the hospital in Anchorage, and the next logical move involved a quick call for Sheldon. Lena, who was watching the sour weather and darkness outside, heard Sheldon's name mentioned, and with her interest in Talkeetna Air Service firmly in mind, put her foot down hard and said, "He's Hudson's customer sober, and he's gonna be Hudson's customer drunk." It can safely be said that Lena Morrison was a diplomat only when the situation warranted.

Her faith in Sheldon's ability to manage the charter service was well founded. Since Stub Morrison's death, he has never taken on another partner.

"I didn't need another partner then and don't need one now. Airplanes are just numbers, really. First you get yourself acquainted with the original cost of the airplane. These are numbers. Then after you fly it for a while, you get acquainted with what it will really do performance-wise. These are numbers. Then you might find out that a sandbar 200 feet long is too short to take off from. This sometimes means big numbers. Aircraft are a lesson in economics, a rich man's hobby, and unless you can find a specialty-flying job, you can't support a couple of airplanes, let alone a whole fleet of the things."

After Sheldon's meeting with Washburn, the barest glimmer of an idea had begun to shape itself. That glimmer would become reinforced almost on a daily basis as he looked north at the looming summit of McKinley and northwest at Mount Foraker, the peak that is sometimes called "Denali's Wife." Since Washburn's departure, Sheldon's thoughts had often strayed to these mountains, which were only a brief 30 minutes from Talkeetna by air. As ambitious as it sometimes seemed, he never seriously doubted that he could back up his decision to do the long-term flying for Brad Washburn's mapping expedition.

"I'd been hunting grizzlies up to about the 4,500-foot level during the years from 1948 till the time I met Washburn, and I had the new retractable skis on one of my Cubs. They were the second pair that the Federal Company made, and Terris Moore up at Fairbanks had set number one."

During those years prior to his meeting with the Boston scientist, Sheldon had become proficient in making soft-snow landings on the new retractables, and he remembers Washburn's delight when he discovered that Sheldon was so well equipped.

Sheldon's meeting with Washburn could not have come at a more opportune time, for with Morrison's untimely death, he was suddenly faced with making all of the decisions that related to the business. He knew that the fledgling business was doomed unless he could offer what he now terms "specialty flying," and as he and Washburn talked that day at the foot of the Ruth Glacier, he began to get an inkling as to what that specialty might be.

"Washburn had some good bait to offer for the survey. He had looked at all of our fine new airplanes, all well maintained and polished up, and he said, 'I want to know first if you're interested in the flying for this project.' I said, 'You bet I am. I've got paper on most of these planes, and right now the only thing I've got going is the road contract in the park. Other than that, I'm putting a lot of time in the air for what I'm making.' Later, in a letter, he [Washburn] said they were pretty well funded and could offer me $100 a landing on the upper glaciers. With this my ears stuck out two feet, and I began to think about buying a five-wheel truck to haul the greenbacks to the bank! After the survey work resumed in 1955, I remember making eight separate landings on the Ruth Glacier in one day, and when I touched down after the last one, foxy old Washburn was waiting for me. He knew now, and I did too, that at this rate I would soon break the Boston Museum of Science, so we adjusted the rate accordingly. Washburn said, 'Suppose we make it $50 a *new-area* landing and then revert to your regular $25 per hour charter rate?' I agreed that this would be an equitable arrangement, and that's how we set the fees for the rest of the survey."

And so it was that Don Sheldon's education in landing airplanes on the forbidding glaciers of Alaska began, an education that progressed through the following years and reached the postdoctoral level many years ago. Crosson, Nieminen, Reeve, and the others had proved that landings could be made on glaciers and Washburn would provide invaluable technical expertise, but the rest Sheldon learned the hard way, through trial and error, bent and sheared landing gear, the total loss of an airplane, and a tremendous expenditure of both money and personal effort. That he has become expert at accomplishing glacial landings is testimony to his ability and explains why his "specialty" is unique the world over. It is interesting to note that Sheldon defines an expert as a "local boy in his own backyard." Then he grins and summarizes his thoughts. "This doesn't apply to me, because I live here."

By way of describing his first glacier landing, Sheldon offers the following brief account: "Hell, it was no big thing. I already knew that you had to look the area over before you landed, and had to do it in good light. The landing area had to be steep enough to slow you down as you landed uphill and assist you when you took off downslope. It had to be smooth enough to keep you out of the crevasses and offer enough room for an overrun. After that, I just went ahead and did it."

Unless the light that Sheldon speaks of is just right, the character of the snow is impossible to see. One of the very first things that Brad Washburn taught Sheldon was that the only time to see what the surface of a given glacier was like was during the very early morning or late afternoon of a sunny day, for at such times, the shadows would tell the story. These shadows could indicate a drifted surface, and more important, would show the very subtle indentations that spelled crevasses, the often bottomless fissures hidden beneath the smooth snow surface—some of them big enough to engulf a freight train as well as a tiny Super Cub. The snow that overlays these awesome chasms is sometimes but a few inches thick, and the repercussions of even one mistake are brutally obvious. Also, the overrun area that he so casually mentions can mean the difference between enough room to stop the forward momentum of the brakeless airplane or a plunge to oblivion over a snowy precipice in an airplane that is moving too fast to stop but too slow to fly.

Another factor that Sheldon has not mentioned is the lack of depth perception while flying over a pure-white and featureless field of unmarked snow, particularly on a sunless, cloudy day. The unwary pilot suddenly finds that he can no longer judge his height above his intended landing surface because there is absolutely nothing to assist the eye in estimating the distance above the snow, which is so very critical. Over the years, Sheldon has developed his own method of coping with this illusion. Prior to a flight that will terminate in poor light or over snow that is questionable, he packs an armload of spruce boughs behind his seat. On the first pass over the area, he drops them at regular intervals, then swings around and lines up again. Now he has some objects before him to which his eyes can relate, and he can judge the critical separation between plane and stark-white snow. On more than one occasion, he has removed his cap and jacket and asked his passenger to do the same. Then he uses the clothing as hasty substitutes for the spruce boughs.

Perhaps a bit of feeling for the dangers inherent in any glacier landing is found in Sheldon's reaction to the question that has been asked of him countless times over the long years: "What was your hairiest landing?"

"That's a question I can never really answer because I've made hundreds of 'em. Most glacier landings are hairy, in their own way, I suppose. The toughest landings on glaciers are almost always made at the very high altitudes.

"When I had the Institute of Arctic Biology [University of Alaska] research team with Professor Morrison up at 14,300 feet on the West Approach of McKinley, each and every landing was a skin-of-the-teeth, seat-of-the-pants deal because of squirrely winds. I'd

Talkeetna during the Cache Creek gold era, 1919.
The Bucket of Blood Bar is the first building at the left,
and Belle McDonald's store is the first building on the right.

Bob Reeve at his Valdez mud-flat "airfield" with his Fairchild 51,
geared up for glacier operations, 1934.

Bob Reeve and Don Sheldon at the Reeve home in Anchorage prior to the pilot's marriage to Bob's daughter Roberta.

Roberta Sheldon operating the Talkeetna Air Service base radio.

The old and the new. Sheldon's original red frame hangar (left) and the bigger metal one he built in 1973.

Photos by the author

A pair of expensive retractable skis on Sheldon's current Cessna 180. Notice the blankets on the cowling and the heater cord, necessary for cold-weather starts.

Sheldon on the
Cessna 180's wing,
performing his
decades-long ritual:
filtering the plane's
gasoline through
a chamois skin.

Sheldon on the radio
in his Cessna 180.

Barry McWayne

One of Sheldon's unbelievable flight schedules,
like uncounted others he has managed singlehandedly for many years.

Sheldon's hexagonal mountain house set high in the magnificent
amphitheater of the Ruth Glacier.

Bradford Washburn

Opposite page (top): Devil's Canyon from 2,000 feet. The Susitna River appears docile compared to the late spring conditions under which Sheldon made his hair-raising rescue.

Opposite page (bottom): Sheldon receiving a citation for his flight to locate the downed Air Force C-54 on Mount Iliamna. Presenting the award is General Necrason.

The Sheldons at home in Talkeetna. Seated in the venerable jeep are Don, Roberta, and the "Bippies"—Robert (left), Holly (center), and Kate.

Photo by the author

The last flight of Sheldon's Cessna 185 in 1971. Badly bruised, he points to the wreck—on Hayes Glacier—with an ice ax.

come in on a given approach at 15,000 feet—glide slope all set up, airspeed on the peg—and all of a sudden hit a thermal that would literally toss me 1,000 or 2,000 feet vertically up or down. It ruins your aim. It just depends upon what is meant by hairy when you're talking about a glacier landing."

Sheldon's work at the top of the world was perhaps best summed up by Pete Haggland, a bush pilot of no small repute in Alaska. "Even routine landings that he [Sheldon] makes would raise hair on a frozen orange."

After Washburn's massive survey got under way—a mapping study that would include not only Mount McKinley but many of its sister peaks, such as Mount Hunter, Mount Brooks, Mount Silverthrone, Mount Tatum, two peaks on the flanks of McKinley named Mount Carpé and Mount Koven in honor of the two men who lost their lives there in the early thirties, and the impressive Mount Foraker—there was also considerable interest focused on the Wrangell, Chugach, and St. Elias Mountains, many miles to the southeast of Mount McKinley National Park.

The Bering Glacier, which is born in the Chugach and St. Elias Mountains, is the largest glacier in the state of Alaska; and in the early fifties, this great mass of rotted, slowly moving ice was of particular interest to Dr. Maynard Miller, a geologist with the U.S. Geological Mineral Mapping Survey. Dr. Miller conducted a study of the surface of the glacier in an early attempt to locate petroglyphic shales thought to occur there. At Katalla, a tiny coastal settlement about 30 miles to the northwest of the point at which the Bering Glacier enters the Pacific Ocean, considerable oil seeps were found in 1902. These seeps occurred in beach shale and drained into Prince William Sound. As a result of their presence, it was thought that oil-bearing shale might be found beneath certain glaciers of the area. The Bering Glacier was selected as a prime study area by the U.S. Geological Survey.

Dr. Miller was based at the tiny coastal hamlet of Cordova, a fishing village 30 miles from Katalla. He had contracted with Cordova Airlines for transportation to and from his research sites on the Bering Glacier. His pilot was Herb Haley, a highly competent airman. On a blustery day in October 1955, Haley was killed in a crash while en route to the Indian Mountain strip, 300 air miles northwest of Anchorage. He was carrying a load of dynamite, which, strangely enough, did not detonate on impact.

During late spring of 1956, Sheldon was called south by Merle ("Mudhole") Smith, then president of Cordova Airlines, to take over where Haley had left off. The Talkeetna pilot spent the summers of 1956 and 1957 flying air support for Dr. Miller's research team "to all quadrants of the Bering Glacier." Sheldon made more than 50 separate landings on the glacier during this period, all of them below 8,000 feet and all without incident.

Coincidental with the U.S. Geological Mineral Mapping Survey, the U.S. Army Ordnance Division had sent Major William Hackett to Alaska from the more sunny climes of Fort Ord, Virginia. Major Hackett was in charge of Arctic Cold-Weather Testing for the Army, and he would concentrate his efforts on developing the cold-weather clothing and military footgear that were tested on Mount Logan, a peak in the St. Elias Mountains. Hackett, who had climbed McKinley's West Buttress with Brad Washburn in 1951, was an expert in the art of mountaineering and would lead a crew of 13 experienced climber-researchers. The jumping-off point for the expedition was the tiny mining village of May Creek, near McCarthy, in the St. Elias Mountains. Sheldon would do the flying, and in the process, would also do a lot of learning about the practical aspects of high-altitude landings on glaciers. Sheldon and Hackett selected an area at the 10,000-foot elevation that offered a short but adequate landing site for Sheldon's tiny Super Cub, but they both miscalculated the prevailing wind. Because of this oversight, Sheldon was forced to make repeated downwind takeoffs. In later years, under similar circumstances, Sheldon would use a five-place Cessna 180, but even this airplane has its disadvantages. With its 230-horsepower Continental engine, it can haul up to 900 pounds of cargo, but since it weighs about one ton empty, it requires a much longer runway than does the Super Cub. In addition, engines become much less efficient at higher altitudes.

"The standard loss of power in nonsupercharged engines is equivalent to about ten horsepower for each thousand feet of elevation above sea level. So at 10,000 feet, even the 230 Continental shrinks performance-wise to a much less respectable 130 usable horsepower, not enough to raise the heavy Cessna from the snow without a steep takeoff run."

The Super Cub, on the other hand, with its much smaller load capacity and lower empty weight, can become airborne from extremely short high-altitude strips. In addition to the loaded-weight and horsepower-loss factors, Sheldon has to consider the ever-present wind, which unfortunately blows down a glacier under normal conditions. A down-glacier wind on landing is the pilot's friend, but it can kill him in a carelessly planned takeoff, for not only must the aircraft be accelerated to a safe flying speed while going downwind but it must reach a ground speed high enough to overcome the velocity of the wind. On Mount Logan, Sheldon consistently made takeoffs with ground speeds well in excess of 70 miles per hour with relation to the ground. To abort a takeoff at this velocity is to court disaster on a grand scale.

These were the factors that Sheldon was forced to consider in depth on Mount Logan while flying the Super Cub and servicing the Hackett Expedition. From 1953 through 1958, Sheldon worked with Hackett, both in the Wrangells and on McKinley in the Alaska Range. One of the products of Hackett's research and Sheldon's flying is the white-rubber inflatable bunny boot that has saved many GIs and mountaineers the agonies of frostbite wherever extremely cold temperatures are encountered.

A Hell of a Good Pilot

The twin trails left by the wolves as they ascended the pass looked like long undulating strings of beads on the immaculate upsweep of windblown snow. Sheldon had spotted the tracks from 500 feet above the sun-dazzled surface of the Kahiltna Glacier. The altitude here in the pass was 10,320 feet above sea level, and to see sign of wolves at this elevation pricked his curiosity. He began a slow descent over the tracks to determine the direction the wolves had taken and quickly discovered that they were climbing up into the pass ahead of him. He was en route to a landing at the camp of a scientific party located between Mount McKinley and Mount Foraker, and since the wolves seemed to be going his way, he followed.

In seconds he overtook the animals, which were just topping out on the ridge between the Kahiltna and Peters Glaciers, gateway to the North Approach to McKinley's crown. The lanky gray animals glanced upward as the Cub's shadow flitted over them, and the gusting wind rippled their coats as they stood a few feet apart in chest-deep snow. The books say that wolves usually inhabit the dense spruce thickets and low ridges of interior Alaska. Sheldon knows differently, for he has seen them on several occasions at altitudes in excess of 8,000 and 10,000 feet.

"I have located tracks and have often seen not only wolves but grizzly, lynx, and black bear at the high elevations."

Sheldon is an avid observer of Alaska's wild-game populations. In his extensive travels and countless hours in small aircraft over the sprawling area that is now the 49th state, he has assimilated a wealth of knowledge relating to the creatures that inhabit the bush. For instance, in the barren snows above 10,000 feet, one would hardly expect to see, let alone be harassed by, birds that are common residents at sea level, yet there is one the pilot has seen at these altitudes.

"Ravens are a constant threat to the food supplies of mountaineers, for they fly effortlessly to extreme altitudes. I've seen them circling at elevations up to 17,000 feet in the rising thermals over McKinley. These characters are equipped with a heavy beak and a one-track mind and are the scourge of the climbers. Anything short of a metal canister will not protect the mountaineers' food, and the standard procedure for airdropping rations to climbers includes the packing of all foodstuffs in five-gallon metal cans and securely wiring and taping the lids down. Even so, I have on many occasions seen the dents in these, where the ravens have made concerted efforts to get into them. What's more, the birds don't stop at attempting to vandalize unattended supplies that have been dropped from an airplane but will boldly enter the camps of mountain climbers in their constant search for food. Cardboard and canvas are absolutely useless, and the ravens go through either like it was cream cheese."

As has already been mentioned, Sheldon is also addicted to beautiful scenery, a fact that is immediately obvious to anyone who flies with him. He delights in providing a running commentary on any and all points of interest that pass beneath the wings, spiced with exclamations of constant wonder at the beauties of his own personal Alaska. When he first saw the Wrangell Mountains and Mount Logan in the St. Elias Mountains, he was inspired.

"Mount Logan, at 19,850 feet nearly as impressive as McKinley, stands slightly inside the Canadian border. Logan and the Wrangells are spectacular. There are many lesser peaks, with tremendous icefalls and rugged glaciers."

There are places in Alaska that are special to the aviator. One of these is the Wrangell Mountains-Copper River country in south-central Alaska—an area of brooding mountains, fickle weather, and great silt-laden rivers all rushing to the Gulf of Alaska. He has spent considerable time in this land of towering rock outcrops, and in the process, has garnered a wealth of historic fact, which he is fond of relating.

It was at the tiny village of Chitina, near the Wrangell Mountains, that Sheldon met the team of 14 climbers from California in 1953. The UCLA team had expressed their desire to climb several of the peaks in the Mount Logan-Mount Lucania country, at the source of the Chitina Glacier. The pilot from Talkeetna was building a solid reputation servicing scientific expeditions in the Alaskan mountains, and to his delight, word of his abilities was beginning to spill over into the world of sport climbing. After the war, there had been a noticeable increase in the number of climbers interested in the North American peaks, especially McKinley and other Alaskan prominences. The UCLA team was Sheldon's first major sport-climbing contract, and because of his burgeoning interest in the art, he had looked forward with keen anticipation to working with the Californians.

The expedition left Chitina for the landing strip at the mining village of May Creek. Due to the ruggedness of the area in which the group would climb, Sheldon had no choice but to go with his reliable and "highly tuned" Super Cub. He knew from the start that he faced a "super-endurance contest," for it would require a total of 15 round trips to place the team on the surface of the Anderson Glacier, 16 air miles north of Mount Logan. Each round-robin haul from the tiny strip at May Creek to the Anderson was an impressive 180 miles.

"The Super Cub is not known for its speed. It is primarily a short-field, high-performance airplane and only does 100 miles an hour loaded."

After lift-off with his first passenger and some of the gear, he pointed the nose of the Cub toward Mount Logan. His objective was the upper source of the Anderson Glacier and the suitable landing area that he hoped it would offer. If he were successful, he would be able to place the team within striking distance of 14 separate and heretofore unclimbed peaks. To date, these isolated prominences at the southwestern fringe of Canada's Yukon Territory had "only been seen from afar by occasional passing bush pilots."

"The airlift went smoothly, and the weather was ideal, with high blue skies and unlimited visibility. From past experience, I knew that it wouldn't last. The conditions over coastal-mountain areas, especially this one, run in definite cycles. For a day or at the most two, you would have bright, ideal weather for flying, and then either a layer of stratus clouds or a cumulonimbus deck would move in, and you'd get high winds or precipitation in the form of rain or snow. This kind of thing happened almost without fail, so I was planning accordingly."

Because of the number of people in the expedition and the large amount of gear that he had to relay to the Anderson, Sheldon had decided to make the airlift in nonstop fashion, a practice he swears by. He hoped to avoid the possibility of getting caught by a week of bad weather with only half of the crew on the mountain.

"I knew right at the start that I was in for a tremendous amount of flying, because of the 15 round trips I had to make to get the climbers into position. In addition to the actual flying, there was, as always, a lot of time involved loading and unloading the airplane. Also, the first trip into an area that is at all unfamiliar and the first landing are always the most critical. But everything went like clockwork, and I found a smooth but steep area where I could land that offered a good location for the base camp. The airlift continued all day and then all night."

In good weather conditions and on a familiar landing strip, Sheldon can make night landings with "precision accuracy."

"The weather still held good during the second day, and I continued to push the Super Cub and move climbers, all the while watching the skies to the southeast. Sure enough, during mid-afternoon, the weather began to deteriorate, and by nightfall of the second day, it went overcast. I found myself flying in rain-squalls and gusting winds. Needless to say, I could've used some sleep, but I'd learned from past experience that I could go for several days and nights without it."

Sheldon was eating a candy bar and gassing the Super Cub from a cache of drums at the May Creek strip as the last of the afternoon began to slip away. He had four round trips and one very important decision left to make. With the skies now heavily overcast, the darkness of the approaching night would be almost complete. As the last of the red 80-octane gasoline swirled through the chamois filter and into the wing tank of the Super Cub, he made up his mind.

"I was quite desperate to get those last four loads moved. I knew that as it got darker and the air temperature dropped at the upper elevations, it would begin to snow in the high peaks."

Icing is a well-known flight condition, and as it got colder, it would become more of a factor. During the hours of daylight, structural ice is a force to reckon with, and Sheldon was well aware that if he encountered it on the flights he was about to make that night, it could spell disaster.

"With the airplane loaded, the first of the last 4 trips got underway, but after about 45 minutes in the air and approaching the Anderson, I knew I was in trouble. I began to have serious problems negotiating the passes through which I had to fly because it was darker here in the mountains than I had expected. I had instructed the crew on the glacier to soak newspapers in kerosene and arrange them along the edge of my landing strip. They were to light these flares so I could make my landing.

"As I dropped into the long pass of the Anderson Glacier, I saw the first of the flares being lit. I was on a long straight-in final approach and was getting set up to land the airplane when suddenly the flares went out."

The black curtain of the rain- and snow-peppered night completely obscured his vision. Sheldon knew that he was flying between high ridges on his right and left and that he was now well beneath these ridges, flying gradually upslope. Now he suddenly found that there was no escape. He could not turn 180 degrees and get out because he could not judge his distance from the wet rock walls of the steep canyon through which he flew, nor could he climb ahead toward the tantalizing dimness of the cloudy night sky because the gradient of the slope exceeded the rate at which the loaded Super Cub could climb in the low-lift air at 10,700 feet.

"After the last flare winked out, I knew that I was on a one-way trip that would either end up with a landing on the ice ahead or somewhere beyond in a heap on the glacier. I frantically began to blink my landing lights to indicate that I needed the flares. When the lights went out, I held the plane in a constant attitude and had no alternative but to go to my magnetic compass to hold my course.

"At about five miles from touchdown, several flares winked on. It was spooky as hell, and I realized that the gusty wind and rain were making the flares difficult to light and even harder to keep lit. Just as I began to breathe a little easier, the flares all went out again, and I glued my eyes on the compass."

Sheldon was caught between the proverbial hard spot and a rock. Time was now critical, for his glide slope was carrying him inexorably to the steep glacier surface. Two more flares appeared, and it was now or never. If these feeble torches were blown out ahead of him, there would not be enough time left for more to be lit. Sheldon's breathing stopped, and his pulse throbbed in his head as he applied full power, raised the nose of the Super Cub, felt for the glacier surface with the skis, and was down. He was soon surrounded by the jubilant climbing crew.

"Needless to say, we corrected the problem of making the flares light and burn more reliably. I took off and made the final three landings, which continued through the night in light snow and rain, without incident."

With the coming of the cold, rainy dawn, his last landing on the Anderson Glacier was completed. Sheldon wearily made his way back to refuel at the May Creek strip.

"Two days and two nights are almost too much, especially with that kind of flying. I decided to refuel at May Creek, return to Talkeetna, and get some sack time."

After landing at May Creek, Sheldon set his five-gallon chamois strainer on the wing, and using a hand-operated barrel pump, began to fill the tanks from a 55-gallon drum of gasoline.

"I was standing on the drum working the pump, and this is the last thing I remember. The next thing that I was aware of was a dull ache all over. I was soaked in gasoline, covered with insects, and I thought for one horrible moment that I had crashed."

Gagging from the fumes of the raw gasoline, Sheldon struggled to a sitting position.

"I knew I wasn't dead, because there couldn't be that many mosquitoes in heaven. I found that I had been lying beneath the airplane, a light rain was falling, and I deduced that I had gone to sleep while gassing the Super Cub, fallen, struck my head on the rocks, and in the process, pulled the five-gallon strainer can from the wing. It had spilled over me, and I was drenched from head to foot. My head ached horribly from its meeting with the cobblestones.

"This ended the possibility of returning to Talkeetna, so I rolled out my faithful Woods down sleeping bag under the wing of the Super Cub. I'll never forget waking up at six o'clock that evening. It was worse than regaining consciousness after the fall from the gas drum. Swarms of mosquitoes were hovering over me, and the temperature was 95 degrees. The procedure was to come to the top of the sleeping bag, grab a breath of fresh air, and then be driven back to the bottom by the damned mosquitoes. Between the 95-degree temperature, the heavy down sleeping bag, and the mosquito treatment, I was wringing wet with sweat. I bailed out of the bag, stowed it in the plane, finished gassing up, and in a cloud of bloodthirsty Alaskan mosquitoes, beat a hasty retreat to Talkeetna."

About five weeks later, Sheldon returned to the Anderson Glacier to retrieve the UCLA team. One of the expedition members was a woman whom Sheldon remembers well. Her name was Barbara Lilley.

"Barbara was a Hughes secretary, weighed about 90 pounds on the hoof, and was a tremendous climber. She had shining blond hair and later made a very successful Mount McKinley climb. Barbara was dainty as a flower, yet she always packed her own weight on any crew she climbed with."

In 1953, Sheldon also flew for the Harrer Expedition. Heinrich Harrer, an Austrian engineer, was a climber of vast experience, gained in such exotic places as the famed mountains of Tibet, Kilimanjaro in Africa, and the Andes Mountains of South America. He had called Sheldon in Talkeetna via transoceanic cable and indicated his intense desire to scale Mount Deborah, a most formidable Alaska Range peak of 12,340 feet, located 90 air miles east of McKinley Park Station. Named in 1907 by James Wickersham, an early territorial judge, in honor of his wife, Mount Deborah is a prominent feature on the horizon near Fairbanks, and its South Face boasts a sinister icefall that tumbles more than 6,000 vertical feet beneath the mountain's serrated summit. In spite of the fact that the experts evaluated Deborah as a magnificent climb, no one had as yet succeeded in scaling the mountain, a fact primarily dependent upon the existence of this great icefall, the birthplace of the Yanert Glacier.

Harrer arrived in Talkeetna accompanied by Fred Beckey and Fred Meybohm, both American climbers with extensive experience in rock and ice work. Sheldon flew the trio from McKinley Park Station to the 7,000-foot level below the great icefall. Due primarily to Sheldon's growing ability to handle such landings with the almost casual finesse that would become a hallmark of his later mountain operations, all of the landings on the 18-percent grade below the precipitous icefall were made without incident.

Three weeks later, he picked up the three-man team and found them greatly elated at having succeeded where others had failed. They had attained the summit of a peak that was considered by the world's climbers to more than equal the difficulties encountered on McKinley, and had thus captured a coveted first. In fact, Harrer and his companions were so elated that they decided to go for broke and attempt the first ascent of another Alaska Range peak—14,570-foot Mount Hunter, in the McKinley Group. They would attempt the ascent via the West Ridge, an amazing series of precipitous snow slopes and extraordinary cornices.

Due to a warm winter in 1952–53 and the abnormally tepid summer that followed, the snow at the base of the West Ridge of Hunter was in very poor condition and almost flat. Sheldon remembers the place and the circumstances clearly.

"Three landings were made there, in a very confined place, and I was hindered by the lack of pitch on takeoff. But all of the gear was finally brought in."

After the last load was stacked on the slushy snow, Harrer blew into his hands, squinted against the glare from the patchy sheet ice that overlaid the rotten snow, and said to Sheldon, "We will be a month, maybe six weeks on this climb. Can you pick us up when we're through?"

The crow's-feet at the corners of Sheldon's eyes crinkled with a skeptical grin. His face was burned to a deep mahogany. Like his clients, he had spent many hours beneath rarefied mountain sunlight that summer.

"Fellas, in six weeks from right now, there won't be enough snow left around here to cool a mint julep."

Harrer, Beckey, and Meybohm, after a herculean effort, became the first to scale the West Ridge of Mount Hunter, thus adding another prominent jewel to Don Sheldon's crown of mountaineering assists.

Because of Sheldon's ominous prediction relating to the lack of snow for a ski landing, which proved to be more than accurate, the Harrer party decided to walk out to Talkeetna. They were equipped with skis, which they planned to use as long as they could on the descent and then abandon. Sheldon followed the slow but methodical progress of the group on both the climb and the descent. All seemed to be going well, and the climbers finally disappeared beneath the canopy of spruce and downed timber on the flats south of the mountains. The weather had gone from bad to poor as the group retreated from the flanks of the range, and rain and sleet scoured the snow from the more exposed ridges, ulcerating the drifts between them. The rain continued for almost the entirety of the long and demanding hike to Talkeetna, and Sheldon finally sighted the climbers again in the area of Cache Creek, not far from the site of the old Jenkins Mine of his earlier years in the Territory. There was a landing strip nearby, and he dropped in. Harrer and his two companions were more than happy to accept a ride the rest of the way to Talkeetna, a distance of about 60 miles. In describing their odyssey, they told Sheldon that the actual climb had been quite easy when compared with the perils of their return. They had encountered numerous grizzlies at uncomfortably close range and had managed to fall into a profusion of crevasses that were concealed by thin roofs of deteriorating snow. The party did not carry a firearm.

The winter after Sheldon's activities with the Harrer Expedition was a mild one, but predictably, the month of February was ushered in with a series of storms. High winds in the Alaska Range and the vicinity of Talkeetna brought warm weather accompanied by heavy, wet snow, and the combination bore all the elements that make flying at such times particularly hazardous.

During the morning of February 4, an urgent radio message was received at the headquarters of the Tenth Rescue Division, U.S. Air Force, in Anchorage. A military C-47, flying inbound to Anchorage and about 70 miles north of Talkeetna, reported extreme turbulence and heavy icing conditions. They were flying a low-frequency-range course, and after making a position report, went off the air and could not be recontacted. Sheldon clearly remembers the events that led to his involvement in the incident.

"A railroad maintenance crew chopping ice from a track switch in the vicinity reported hearing the heavy snarl of engines somewhere high overhead in the blinding blizzard—then nothing. Tenth Rescue initiated a search, but they were badly hampered by the storm and contacted me late in the afternoon. They figured the plane had gone down, and I made a quick note of the position they gave me. It looked to me like they had to be up around Curry, and after making a quick check on the weather, I wondered if I had any business going up there for a look."

High winds were still buffeting Sheldon's parked airplanes, and the low layer of leaden clouds that blocked visibility in all quadrants promised more of the heavy, wet snow that had been falling for several days.

"By now, the C-47 was long overdue, and I had bad feelings about the outcome of this one. Because of the weather the night before, I had visions of heavy rime ice on airplane wings, but I gassed the Cub and got ready to go."

Sheldon took off late in the afternoon, following the Susitna River north and flying low to maintain visual contact with the ground 200 feet below. In the area near the position at which the military plane had been last reported, he blundered through the haze and falling snow and was forced to make two emergency landings in rapid succession to wait for local visibility to clear.

"She was just too thick to plow, so I went home. I hated to do it, but you can really get your tail bent in that kind of stuff. On skis, you're pretty well fixed, but my problem was that I couldn't see 200 yards in front of my nose."

Sheldon hangared the Cub out of the freezing rain that had now started to fall. Then he began the pilot's ritual of resigned waiting for the weather to clear. It took the rest of the day and night, and by noon on February 5, it began to look as if he could make another try. During the night, a foot of wet, ice-mixed snow had fallen.

"After I got the hangar doors and ramp shoveled out, the weather started to break a little, so I headed north, glad to be looking again after being tied down in the soup. There were still line squalls in the area and about every kind of front known to man—warm fronts, occluded fronts, and what have you—but at least for the moment, I could see fairly well. After about an hour and a half, still plowing through the tail end of a line squall, I was in the high country about 60 miles north of Talkeetna and working my way south. I was negotiating heavy turbulence and carrying my share of structural ice. At 5,000 feet, over some low mountains near Chulitna Pass, I broke out in a thin spot and something caught my eye."

Stretching down a snowy slope was a long string of fresh tracks. Sheldon circled. His visibility was going as quickly as it had improved, but he knew that these were not the marks of a traveling band of caribou as he had first suspected. He did not dare get closer because of the turbulence, so he flew downslope. It was here, about a thousand feet lower, that he got the better look he needed.

"There were three trails that converged into one at 4,000 feet, and I could now see that there was a lot of blood in them. I continued to follow the trail downhill. At the 2,000-foot level on the slope, I saw two guys dragging a third one, and I knew that they had to be from the lost plane."

Sheldon quickly looked for a place to land. The only possibility was about 1,500 feet farther downslope in the scrub spruce. Still circling the downed airmen, who had now stopped and were looking up at him, he hastily scrawled a note on a brown paper bag, weighted it with some stones that he carries for that purpose, and dropped the bag on a low pass. The red surveyor's ribbon that was attached to the bag fluttered as the note fell, and in moments, the men had picked it up. They continued downslope in the deep snow as Sheldon banked away and headed full-bore for Talkeetna, where he knew that the Air Force had a flight surgeon waiting.

Back in Talkeetna, Sheldon picked up the surgeon, two medical bags, two cases of survival rations, a big bundle of wool blankets, and a gallon of hot coffee. He jammed all the supplies into the Cub's boot.

"We went roarin' up there, and when we got back to the spot where I intended to land, the survivors were about 150 feet uphill and heading for it. We'd timed it just right. I hauled off and landed, and the flight surgeon bailed out. We both put on snowshoes and went tearing over to see what we could do with the injured man."

By the time Sheldon and the medic reached the struggling men, the snow had again begun to fall heavily. One look told the surgeon and pilot that the injured man was in bad shape.

"He'd almost bled to death and was cut from the back of his neck to the rear of his left foot and was just barely conscious. You know, a guy's only got about 2½ quarts of blood in him, and it looked like he'd lost about 15. The doctor went to work right there on the spot in the falling snow, and the other guys began to build a lean-to. I figured what with the light going as fast as it was, we were in for a night here, and I couldn't fly anyway because the visibility was down to almost nothing."

Sheldon slipped his ax from the Cub and began to cut spruce boughs. In a short time, they had a crude but serviceable shelter erected. Some of the GI blankets were used as a roof. Then with an almost unreasoning perversity, the weather got even worse. Wet snow mixed with rain began to fall and froze on contact, the whole system pushed by increasing winds. Sheldon spent the entire night "beating the ice off the airplane with spruce boughs and a rope."

"After we got the lad who was hurt into the tent, the flight surgeon put him to sleep and went to work sewing on him. Before long, he had him sutured from ankle to ears. He was a boy from Georgia, and when he came to, he began to tell about 'big dogs with yellow slanty eyes and bushy tails' they had seen while coming down the slope after the crash. I listened for a while and then informed the GI that what he'd seen couldn't be dogs and were undoubtedly wolves. When this fact hit him, his mouth dropped open, and I thought for a minute he was going to pass out. I had apparently spooked the wolves when I made my first pass over the three men."

During the night, the survivors told the chilling story of what had happened to their airplane, and it became obvious to Sheldon that the fact that there were any survivors at all was indeed a minor miracle. The heavy turbulence had twisted the big C-47 and severed its tail section. The three crew members had been sucked out of the plane. Two of them had barely managed to pull their rip cords before they hit the mountain. The injured man had not been able to open his chute until just before hitting the ground, and his back had been horribly lacerated on rocks.

"They had been vacuumed out of the plane like ants. When I asked these guys if any others had gotten free, they didn't know, but they thought that some of the others in the plane might have escaped as they had."

The weather did not improve till the following noon, and then Sheldon was finally able to get the men off the mountain in four separate relays. While he was transporting the four men to safety, the Air Force had gotten a helicopter into action. When it arrived at the crash scene, three more survivors were found near the wreckage. The balance of the crew of ten had perished.

"The concussion ripples on the fuselage of the plane looked like ocean waves, and it was obvious that the turbulence at 12,000 feet, where the plane had broken up in midair, had been tremendous. They found all of the crew except one, a British colonel who was a cold-weather test expert. This bugged 'em. Here was a luminary from the Canadian Cold-Weather Test Program and a real hearty type, and they couldn't find him. The military said that in view of his tremendous capabilities, he might somehow have escaped like the others and still be alive somewhere on the mountain. They wanted to find him real bad.

"Man, we looked like you wouldn't believe. I flew a grid pattern over that mountain till I knew the first name of every rock and spruce tree on it. We were working under ideal conditions, and I noticed as I crisscrossed the wreckage that there were an increasing number of fox tracks in the fresh snow around the wreck. Then a light went on."

Sheldon advised the military to "look where the fox tracks led them, and sure enough, two days later, under the snow about half a mile away lay the colonel. He was dead."

With the completion of the rescue, Sheldon returned to Talkeetna and was later presented with the first of a series of military citations that confirm his unadvertised alliance with the military in Alaska, an alliance that through the years would be mutually beneficial.

A Red Fox and
a Black Leather Bag

After a hectic summer, the deepening snow and short days of yet one more Alaskan winter descended upon the interior, and the 1954 season became a discarded pile of cardboard flight schedules. Sheldon, both by choice and necessity, was becoming far more than just another flatland bush pilot. He did, however, continue to cater to all comers: the homesteaders, trappers, and others who are annually isolated by deep snows and frozen rivers during winters of seven months' duration. Though his choice of specialty flying was reaching what some might define as obsessive proportions, to assume that he disliked the milk runs to points often not more than 15 minutes from his own doorstep would be highly inaccurate. Sheldon was, and always will be, a man completely enamored of all phases of aviation. On those rare occasions when he could not fly due to illness or long spates of sour weather, he could be found seated in one of his airplanes, idling the engine under the guise of checking the oil pressure or a magneto or just moving the airplane so the winter sun could melt a slight accumulation of snow on the wings in a more expedient manner.

Winters are usually a time of inactivity for all bush pilots, and so when Sheldon was offered a contract to fly the son of a prominent Anchorage fur buyer on a hopscotch itinerary of northern Alaska, he accepted eagerly. Such fur-buying trips in small airplanes were the rule rather than the exception. Each winter, around the first of the new year, the fur buyers in Anchorage, Fairbanks, and other population centers hired bush pilots to fly their representatives to interior and northern native villages that were known collection points for skins. Wolverine, marten, and seven- and eight-foot-long wolf pelts, and in the high Arctic, white fox, polar bear, and seal pelts were brought in by trappers who either sold them to a local buyer or awaited the arrival of the flying fur dealer. Sheldon met his client in Anchorage late on a January afternoon.

"We were soon engaged at an old market in the Anchorage area, buying food for a north-coast flight. Our plan was to fly over the Alaska Range to our first stop at the village of Ruby, on the Yukon River. It was going to be a good night for flying, about 30 below, with no forecasted ice fog. We took on a big stock of survival-type food, such as milk and oranges, all of it selected because it's still edible after being frozen and then thawed out. We also bought cheese and bologna, which made great snacking on the long flights."

Sheldon has become a confirmed snacker. He carries odds and ends of such foods as cheese, fruit, and jerky with him on all flights and prefers to "eat on the run." He attributes his excellent physical condition to this habit, and he is probably correct.

Daylight lasts a mere two or three hours in central Alaska during early January, but these short days are a luxury compared with the almost total darkness of the northern Arctic. In addition, the coastline of the Arctic Ocean, where the pair would fly, is a producer of weather miseries that defy belief. High winds of hurricane proportions drive the snow parallel to the frozen earth and produce the condition that is innocuously referred to as a whiteout. The airplane Sheldon had selected for the trip was a Super Cub equipped with a magnetic compass and DG (directional gyro).

It is interesting to reflect that Joe Crosson and the legendary Carl Ben Eielson before him flew Alaska's bush country long before the advent of navigation equipment, Eielson making the trip to McGrath in an open-cockpit De Havilland that did not even boast a magnetic compass. Eielson navigated by moonglow, watching the paths of the frozen rivers below him, and he often made the trip at night in weather that disoriented trappers in their travels on the ground.

Because there were few banks in the isolated native settlements of the bush, a fact that rendered cash payments for furs highly desirable in a hand-to-mouth economy, Sheldon's airplane became a flying bank vault. Stowed in the baggage compartment was an old doctor's satchel containing $40,000 in cold cash. Before the two

110

travelers could become airborne on that frigid January night, this satchel would become about as popular with the Talkeetna flyer as a dead mouse in a punch bowl. With a chuckle, Sheldon clearly remembers how this came about.

"The fur buyer's son, Perry, said to me, 'You take care of the satchel, and I'll take care of the groceries.'"

Sheldon, well aware of the extent of his own responsibilities, carefully declined.

"After our shopping was finished, we caught a cab out to Merrill Field. It was a beautiful, cold moonlit night, and we quickly loaded the gear and supplies into the plane. I was priming the engine, when Perry suddenly said, 'Hey, where's the satchel?'"

With detached calmness, Sheldon replied, "You were taking care of the satchel; I bought the groceries. Remember?"

After a hurried search, they called another cab and rushed back to the store. It was closed, but there was a light burning inside.

"We beat on the door, and after about three minutes, two patrol cars skidded to a stop behind us. The cops began to load us up for what was going to be a quick trip to the Anchorage pokey."

Sheldon, this time with no hint of his original calmness, managed to get in a quick explanation of what was happening. By the time he got around to mentioning the lost satchel, the cop was beginning to lose what little patience he had. But when Sheldon came to the part about the satchel containing $40,000, the cop's nightstick beat a fast and formidable tattoo on the front door of the store.

Fortunately, the storekeeper, who had summoned the police to stop what he thought was an attempt to break into his store, was still there. Once they were inside, they quickly located the satchel —to Perry's infinite relief. Now the question arose as to where the unlikely pair had come by the fortune in the old black leather bag. Perry quickly phoned his father, who corroborated the origin of the money and vouched for its intended use. The police then escorted the pair back to Merrill Field for a midnight takeoff. As Sheldon gained altitude and turned northwest, he looked back at the field.

"The patrol car was still there as we flew into the night, and I have often wondered how long the two cops sat there discussing the weird circumstances that would cause someone to casually leave that huge bag of bills in a grocery cart."

The villagers of Ruby knew that the fur buyers were due, and they had waited up. At 3:30 A.M., Sheldon made a low pass over the cluster of cabins squatting in the snow-muffled silence, their windows glowing like coals in a dying campfire, and landed on the frozen surface of the Yukon River. It was much colder here, and a layer of wood smoke hung like a translucent curtain in the windless night. After tying down and extracting the bag of cash from the rear of the plane, the two made their way up the riverbank to the old Olson Roadhouse, which they entered in a cloud of frozen vapor as the warmth of the inside met the biting cold of the Arctic night. Everyone inside was in good cheer, and after old acquaintances were renewed, Sheldon and his partner sat in on a panguingue game that was in progress. Panguingue, no longer in vogue, was played with at least eight decks of cards and was a forerunner of the game of rummy.

It should be mentioned here that Don Sheldon is a stout devotee of only two things other than flying—fresh milk and card games, in that order. Because the white stuff is hard to get in the bush, he has also developed a taste for honey-laced tea. Games of chance with the cardboards have always been as popular in remote Alaska as booze, and such a game was in full swing in Ruby at 3:30 on that frozen January morning in 1955.

Later, under a weak sun, with the plane's fuel tanks topped and a couple of hours' sleep under his belt, Sheldon tipped his wing at the group of miners and other "local luminaries," who waved from the powdery, knee-deep snow on the riverbank, and the Super Cub howled in the cold morning air. Ruby had been an "overnight rest stop," but the only time Sheldon really rested was when someone else was dealing.

"We continued to the coast of the Bering Sea and eventually made all of our required stops, including such places as Moses Point, Nome, Shishmaref, Kotzebue, Kivalina, and Point Hope. By now, we were flying in almost perpetual darkness and munching on frozen bologna and cheese. We finally arrived at the village of Point Lay, about 180 air miles from Barrow, the continent's farthest north settlement."

Point Lay was near a DEW-line site, one of a series of radar installations that fringed the north and west coastlines of Alaska. These sites were manned the year round, and though the employees were well supplied with all of life's comforts, including a wide variety of good food at each meal and a paycheck of $2,000 or $3,000 each month, they craved new faces. The tiny airplane that materialized in the lightly shifting snow promised respite, however brief, from the enforced loneliness of their job. Another thought crossed the minds of those who eagerly watched the Super Cub taxi to a stop. Maybe these two guys could play poker.

Shortly after their arrival at the DEW-line site, the pilot and his fur-buying partner learned that all of the pelts in the area were stored in a warehouse at the tiny village of Wainwright, 100 miles farther up the coast. Their informer, a grizzled old Eskimo, also indicated that to buy this considerable quantity of fur, one would need the official blessings of both of the Wainwright village elders, one of whom was known to be away on a caribou hunt. Since it was already late in the day, Sheldon and Perry opted to stay the night at the DEW-line site, and to the delight of the station employees, were soon sitting in on a poker game that would last well into the following morning.

After a deep purple half-dawn at noon, Sheldon lifted the Super Cub from the snowy strip at the sandspit village of Point Lay and headed up the coast toward Wainwright. The two had cornered the stakes in the card game, and it was a far richer fur dealer who settled his already weary south half in the airplane's tiny rear seat. After about an hour of flying and a landing at Wainwright, Perry closed the deal on the warehouse full of luxurious furs. The second elder had returned that same morning and placed his official blessings on the sale. The skies were deceptively clear in most quadrants, and the aurora was a building smudge of pastel to the southeast as Sheldon and Perry finished packing the pelts for shipment to Anchorage via air parcel post. This was the cheapest way to ship a large cargo.

The next stop would be Barrow itself, and Perry was anxious to be gone. But as Sheldon stood on the brittle-packed snow of the street and surveyed the weather, he was not at all happy about leaving the comparative security of Wainwright. Wise in the ways of coastal weather, he noticed the shifting whiteouts that still slithered over the pressure ridges to the east, and the northeast wind that moved them was a sure sign of degenerating weather.

"Perry was insistent and wouldn't take no for an answer. He was also paying the bills, so I formulated a plan. I would fly 10 minutes on a north-northwesterly heading, tell Perry that the whiteouts ahead made the trip an impossibility, and then make a 180-degree turn and come back to Wainwright."

Ten minutes out, it was not difficult to convert Perry's thinking, as he peered ahead into the thickening white wall that separated the black night sky from the featureless landscape, and Sheldon rolled the Super Cub into an easy 180-degree turn toward the sea. As he banked, he felt the gusting wind tug at his wings, and the plane lurched in the turbulence before he could level it and set a course back to the village.

"I flew on the reciprocal heading for 10 minutes, which soon became 15 and finally 20, and would you believe, I couldn't find Wainwright. I might mention here that this close to the pole, compasses of the magnetic variety are somewhat less than accurate. I had taken this fact into account, but somehow I had goofed, and it really rattled my cage. We were in trouble. It was 50 below zero outside the cabin, with a chill factor that must have been around minus 75 degrees with the wind that had begun to blow. I had no alternative but to reverse my course again and head toward Barrow.

"We flew for about 45 minutes along the coastal pressure ridges, and most of it in partial whiteout conditions, which was lucky. In a full-fledged whiteout, all a guy can do that is constructive is to hold his altitude and heading and keep the plane level. Negotiating one is somewhat like flying through a tall glass of milk. There is no up, down, or sideways. The visual disorientation is so complete that the only way you can tell if you're right side up is to trust the attitude instruments."

Sheldon flew for about 45 minutes on the possible course to Barrow. Then through a fleeting thin spot in the blowing snow, he saw movement.

"Suddenly, both Perry and I saw a flash of something reddish-brown above the wing tip, and I immediately began to ease the plane upward in a very cautious climb. Perry said, 'Was that a fox?' and I said, 'It sure was.' We were flying about 10 feet below the north-coast pressure ridge, which in most places isn't more than 60 or 70 feet high. I climbed the plane about 100 feet, then leveled off. The fox, crossing the lip of the pressure ridge, had saved our bacon, for had I banked even a couple of degrees, I would have hit the ridge."

After the encounter with the fox, Sheldon held the Super Cub level above the pressure ridge, which he could see sporadically

114

through the swirling snow in the diffused and almost nonexistent light. His only hope of spotting Barrow was to fly by what little visual reference to the ground he could get, but he soon flew past the pressure ridge and was once again in the limbo of an Arctic whiteout.

"I guessed that I must by now be in the vicinity of the lagoons. I knew that I should be at least 75 miles out of Wainwright, near Barrow."

As if to confirm Sheldon's appraisal, a ghostlike line of scrub willows, like the ones he knew fringed the Barrow lagoons, loomed out of the white darkness below.

"I flew on, and in a few minutes, I saw what looked like a band of caribou moving over the tundra, and I hauled the throttle back and put on full flaps. I aimed the nose straight in toward the animals, for I would have to land close in order to use the caribou to gauge my height above the snow, and yet try not to hit one of 'em. Just before the skis hit, I realized my mistake. The gray blobs that I'd thought were caribou were in fact sled dogs, which were attached to a sled carrying an old Eskimo. Fortunately, my skis missed the old hunter and his dogs by only a few feet."

Sheldon taxied the airplane back to the dog team and cracked the door on the plane. The Eskimo cautiously walked beneath the wing and squinted from the frost-rimmed wolf parka ruff with astonished disbelief.

"Where the hell you come from?"

His words, in puffs of vapor, were almost lost in the humming wind, which was now buffeting the airplane and causing it to sway drunkenly on its landing gear.

"From Wainwright," Sheldon yelled. "Where are you going?"

"I go for my rock house."

And with this, the old-timer looked to his mukluk-swathed feet, as if to ponder one of life's deepest mysteries.

Since he was now completely lost, a fact that no pilot, especially Sheldon, likes to admit, he made the Eskimo an offer that he couldn't resist.

"Tell ya what. I'll trade you a case of milk, if you'll lead us to your rock house."

Both Sheldon and Perry were acutely aware that the ancient Eskimo and his 12 gaunt huskies represented their best hope for survival. In the severe cold, Sheldon knew the utter futility of starting his engine if it were to be shut down or if it quit because the fuel had run out. The two plumber's stoves that he carried would be of little use.

The Eskimo stoically reached with mittened hands for the milk, loaded it aboard his sled, and without a word or gesture, started slowly on his way.

"I followed him with increasing difficulty. The snow here was ridged, and we were taxiing in a high wind with our landing light on. It was a nightmare, and I found myself hoping that the old guy's rock house was not far away."

Suddenly, and without warning, the sled team accelerated, and it soon became painfully obvious to Sheldon that if he tried to keep up, he would ruin his landing gear or nose the airplane over on its spinning prop.

"We finally got on a flat spot in the snow, and I gunned the engine enough to overtake the sled and get in front of it. I shoved the door open against the wind and the slipstream and told the old man that he was going too fast."

The Eskimo, who cared nothing about the intricacies of airplanes, had little appreciation for Sheldon's predicament.

"It gettin' late. I got to go for rock house."

Ahead of him were 12 half-wild dogs of indistinct parentage, and a better compass cannot be found. They were headed unerringly toward a meal of dried fish at the old man's rock house—the sled and the Eskimo were only incidental.

Sheldon thought fast, for he was now fully aware that the old man did not completely understand what he wanted.

"Which way to Point Barrow?" yelled Sheldon.

After a long hesitation, the Eskimo finally pointed into another quadrant of the swirling white darkness.

Over the noise of the idling engine and the prop blast, which was being accelerated by the howling wind, Sheldon said, "How long have you lived around here?"

"Sixty-nine years," replied the old man.

Sheldon asked, "Which way is Wainwright?"

This time he took a peek at his magnetic compass as the old man pointed the way toward the distant settlement. Then Sheldon adjusted the directional gyro to coincide with the magnetic instrument.

"How many miles?" asked Sheldon.

"Maybe 60 miles Wainwright," mumbled the oldster in exasperation.

"Okay," shouted the pilot. "We are going to Wainwright. In case anyone else comes looking for us, tell 'em where we went."

With this, Sheldon closed the door against the burning wind and firewalled the throttle. He felt the Super Cub fairly leap free of the snow as it nosed into the 40-knot head wind.

"As soon as I was airborne, I glued the gyro to the magnetic course. I flew the airplane for about 45 minutes and was about to settle for the fact that my gamble had failed and I had goofed for the third time that night when suddenly ahead and off my starboard wing, I spotted the lights. It was Wainwright."

Sheldon and Perry were delighted to see the place they had left several hours before, and Perry was more than content to spend one more night at the village before continuing to Barrow. Since it was now midnight, the village's light plant had closed down for the night. Sheldon knew that his engine would need heat throughout the night if it were to start the next morning. He negotiated with the manager of the light plant, who agreed to restart the generator for a fee of $12 an hour. The plant manager also threw in five 200-watt light bulbs to show that his heart was in the right place. The five bulbs were placed beneath the airplane's cowling, which was then wrapped with a quilted cover, to keep the Lycoming engine warm enough to start with ease.

At 6:00 A.M., Sheldon paid a bill for $96 and started to taxi. The plane had barely begun to move when it weathervaned, and Sheldon found it virtually impossible to hold it in a straight line. Without shutting down the engine, he alighted and walked to the rear of the plane, where he discovered that during the night, someone had removed the tail-wheel return springs to use as part of a dog-sled brake. Without them, the tail wheel became free-castering and very difficult to control. Muttering darkly, the pilot walked to the general store and purchased two screen-door springs, made hasty repairs, and was en route to Point Barrow before Perry even began to shiver.

Perry purchased another load of furs at the village of Barrow and arranged for their shipment. Then they began retracing their tracks across the north coast of Alaska.

It was March 8, on a stormy afternoon, when they reached Kotzebue, a large village located to the north of the Seward Peninsula. They had been on the move for a month, and Perry had about $9,000 of the original $40,000 still safely cached in the old leather bag. In spite of the fact that he had spent virtually the whole of the past four weeks driving his airplane through some of the meanest weather that the Arctic coast could cook up, Sheldon was in high spirits. The airplane had performed well, and they were headed home. They had landed under a lowering ceiling of scud, which had closed in minutes after they touched down on the bleak strip at Kotzebue.

The new Rotman Hotel, on Kotzebue's main street, had been completed shortly before the pair arrived. As they entered, they smelled drying paint and fresh wood and heard the unmistakable sounds of yet another game of chance in progress. The din came from room five, and the game was poker, one of Perry's favorites. A decision to sit in on the game was made before they shed their parkas.

After about an hour and a half, Perry, his instincts tuned to a high pitch during the past month, had command of the game. Several of the players—two polar-bear hunters, a guide named Leon Sheleberger, and one of the town locals—had dropped out, while Perry, Sheldon, and two others continued to play. Sheldon had "made a couple hundred," and he describes what happened next.

"Perry hit a hot streak and had the loot cornered in the poker game when one of the players left the room. Shortly, he returned with a small check issued by the Bureau of Indian Affairs. Along with the check, he brought a set of dice. The poker game soon degenerated into a game of four-five-six, a move that suited Perry no end because though poker was one of his better games, he fancied himself expert at bouncing the dice. I dropped out, and though Perry had most of the resource from the previous game, I figured he now was in trouble.

"I noticed that he [Perry] seemed to be pulling in only the smaller pots, while one of the other players, a guy by the name of O'Conner, was attracting the big ones like a magnet. I made mention of what I was seeing, and the dice were changed. Since I was keeping track of what Perry was winning and losing, it soon became obvious that he was not doing well, to say the least. He had lost $3,500, and then, since the game was a no-limit affair, he began to double his bets. I winced.

"By three the following morning, I was looking through tired eyes at what was left of our fur-buying stake, and it had shrunk considerably. Instead of nine grand, we had about two, and the rest was in O'Conner's pocket as he suddenly announced that he had to leave. It seemed that his wife was expecting him, and besides, he said he needed some rest."

Outside, a heavy storm was now in progress, and the wind roared down Kotzebue's main street. Glancing through the frost-scalloped window, Sheldon noticed that he could barely see the glow of a lamp in a cabin window across the street.

"Suddenly, we heard an aircraft engine start somewhere in the black and bitterly cold night. Before we had recovered from our surprise, there was a roar, and the plane took off to disappear into the storm-laced night. Needless to say, it was O'Conner, who, we now realized, was from out of town. We later found that he went to the village of Noatak, where he paid off the mortgages on his airplane and a small house, both of which the bank was about to foreclose."

Sheldon and Perry cooled their heels in the Rotman Hotel until the weather stabilized and eventually arrived in Anchorage, poorer but wiser. The pilot shrinks inwardly when he considers the reaction of Perry's furrier father when he discovered the large shortage in the receipts that remained in the old black leather medical bag.

Layer Cake and Lemon Drops
and a 300-Pound Lady

At noon on Thursday, March 31, 1955, Brad Washburn and Don Sheldon sat on a small rocky ledge adjacent to the Ruth Glacier, eating their lunch in the warmth of a windless and sunlit day. Somewhere off to their right and below their line of vision, an eagle screamed, the piercing sound echoing thinly in the brittle air. Washburn described that idyllic day at 5,300 feet in his diary.

"Up at seven, and Don Sheldon arrived at 10:30 A.M. He and I took off at 11:25 for the valley adjacent to Cook's fake peak. We landed there about 15 minutes later, and the weather was absolutely perfect. It was clear, windless, and smooth. We consulted the pictures from Cook's book and decided that our little pass at the head of this valley was precisely the spot where Cook took his '15,400-foot' picture, 10,000 feet below where he alleged it was taken."

In 1906, Dr. Frederick A. Cook published pictures to support his claim that he was the first to reach the summit of McKinley. He said he had accomplished this feat in less than two weeks. Three years later, Cook claimed to have beaten Admiral Robert Peary to the North Pole. After an investigation proved that Cook had actually been nowhere near the Pole, people began to doubt that he had really climbed the continent's highest mountain. The suspicions were confirmed when Cook's climbing partner, one Edward Barrille, signed an affidavit that Cook's claim was fraudulent.

In 1910, Herschel Parker and Belmore Browne produced photographs that were identical to Cook's "summit picture." Only their pictures were of a tiny rock outcrop at the end of Ruth Glacier. The outcrop was 19 miles to the south and east of McKinley's true summit—and only 5,300 feet high.

Today, Washburn remembers that noon as one of the most pleasant he has ever spent on any mountain.

"Don and I sat down in the warm sun, without a breath of wind, and had a delightful lunch together. It was just a plain picnic. With the airplane parked a couple of hundred yards away, we could look up to the magnificent south side of the Moose's Tooth, which is composed of tremendous granite cliffs, or look down to the other side of the pass and the prodigious drop down to the Buckskin Glacier. It was a very fascinating and beautiful spot, and one of the few times that I have ever been able to sit down with any pilot in a completely relaxed state, with flawless weather conditions, and do nothing more than eat lunch. After we had eaten, I backed and filled around in the pass to get exactly the spot where Dr. Cook had taken his picture, and after I took my duplicate of his picture, I'll never forget walking back the dozen feet from where I was to where Don was sitting munching his lunch. Right before me, wedged among the rocks, was a one-pint fuel tin, precisely similar to the ones we later found at Dr. Cook's camp at Glacier Point the following summer, and also an old food bag, that had doubtless been left there in 1906—49 years before."

By 1955, Sheldon was well on his way to becoming highly proficient in the art of landing an airplane on glaciers, a skill which he was further developing in direct proportion to the concerted effort that Washburn was now putting into the mapping project.

During the early spring of 1955, Sheldon did a lot of work for Brad Washburn, who was completing the map survey of the Ruth Amphitheater, at the foot of the Southeast Face of McKinley. Sheldon made a number of risky, but extremely well-coordinated, glacier landings and takeoffs. The planning of all of these and subsequent Sheldon-Washburn operations included the maintenance of continuous high-quality radio communications between Washburn on the mountain and the pilot at his base in Talkeetna. Over the years, this factor alone enabled them to avert a tremendous number of difficult situations and some near disasters.

Quoting from his extensive diary, Washburn recalls some of the happier but infinitely meaningful events that firmly cemented his respect for Don Sheldon.

"On Wednesday, April 13, 1955, we had a call on the radio from Don, and he said he had a friend down there that he would like to bring up, just for a visit. Grant Pearson, a member of the four-man [Lindley-Liek] team that made the second successful ascent of Mount McKinley in 1932, came in with Don about eleven o'clock."

Pearson, an old friend of Washburn's, stayed for two hours and chatted.

"Don never sent us a bill for such things as this. On another occasion, he unexpectedly dropped in and brought a huge lemon layer cake. That night we ate the cake, topped with canned peaches, and enjoyed an unheard-of luxury in a high mountain camp."

Sheldon, who perhaps better than most men has come to know the severe dietary disciplines that must be imposed in order to subsist in the high peaks, takes great pleasure in dropping such delicacies as a quart of peach ice cream (his favorite) from the window of the Cub. On one occasion, during a break in foul weather that had lasted for several days and kept him grounded, he dropped a huge bucket of fried chicken with all the trimmings to a group of climbers who had literally existed on lemon drops for five days after their supplies ran out. The chicken had come from the old-fashioned wood stove of Caroll and Verna Close, proprietors of the Talkeetna Road House. Sheldon's thoughtfulness does not stop with the professional mountain climbers. On many occasions, he has done the same for sheep hunters and fishermen.

Also during the 1955 season, Sheldon assisted Washburn in the task of photographing the Great Gorge, just below the huge amphitheater of the Ruth Glacier. An immense, bowllike depression, the Ruth Amphitheater is one of Washburn's favorite places, and in his diary, he recalls his impression of the place.

"In late spring of '55, we had promised Augie Hiebert, of KTVA in Anchorage, and Ward Wells, an Anchorage photographer—both of whom we had known for years—that if we really did get a beautiful day sometime during the course of the trip, we would just devote the whole of it to getting some photographs in the Great Gorge of the Ruth Glacier. It is a sight that one just has to see to understand the magnificence of Alaskan mountain scenery at its best. The Moose's Tooth, on the east side, and Mount Dickey and its satellites, on the west side, make this, in my opinion, the most awe-inspiring mountain gorge anywhere in North America. In fact, it is the most magnificent thing of its sort that I have ever seen. The surrounding peaks—particularly those on the east side of the gorge and Dickey and its neighboring peaks on the west side—tower 5,000 feet from the 4,000-foot surface of the gorge floor, as deep as the Grand Canyon in one virtually perpendicular cliff, and if one were to remove the Ruth Glacier from the bottom of the mile-wide gorge, the entire thing would be a thousand feet deeper than the Grand Canyon at its deepest point. Since the entire gorge is composed of snow, ice, and the spectacular granite cliffs, it is a superlatively thrilling scene."

Mount Dickey, a peak 9,545 feet high, is located one mile east of Pittock Pass on McKinley's flank. First climbed by Bradford Washburn and David Fisher in 1955, Mount Dickey was named for William Dickey who, while prospecting in the area in 1896, was responsible for naming Mount McKinley and for making the first estimate of its height (20,000 feet). Today, Washburn says that Dickey's estimate was "a damned good one."

Because of the idyllic location of the small bench of rock at the head end of the Ruth Amphitheater, where Washburn's key survey station was located, and an adjacent year-round snow surface free of crevassing and with just the right amount of pitch, Sheldon would later build a hexagonal mountain house here. It was a labor of love for the aviator, who shuttled most of the lumber and materials to the location in his Cessna 180. Some 16-foot-long pieces of lumber were brought to the site tied to the Super Cub. A newly appointed inspector for the CAA reprimanded Sheldon for these flights: "If I ever see you hauling even a set of moose horns on the outside of your Cub, I'll revoke your ticket." Shortly after he delivered this ultimatum, the budding inspector was transferred, and Sheldon considered "Alaska saved."

Glazed on all sides, the mountain house affords a view so magnificent that it defies description, for the soaring white summit of Mount McKinley is a scant ten miles away. The house is simply constructed and is equipped with benches and a small fireplace. On his travels to and from the mountain, Sheldon drops firewood off at the site because nothing but lichens and moss grow at this elevation. Sheldon brings his friends and others who appreciate the ultimate in mountain scenery here, and he has often laconically remarked that "it's the only place where the ladies can step out of the powder room and fall 6,000 feet."

After arriving with Sheldon and Haakon Christensen in a pair of

Talkeetna Air Service's two-place aircraft, Hiebert and Wells, with Washburn's help, secured the pictures they wanted so badly. Washburn clearly remembers that it took a full three hours in the fluffy snow of the gorge to get the sound movies and recordings for television.

The following day, Sheldon removed Washburn and his crew from the mountain just ahead of weather that was curdling fast. Gray, milky cirrus clouds flooded down the sky and obscured McKinley as the Super Cub lifted from the glacier surface for the last time. It was April 16, 1955. The survey work for the season was completed.

Washburn returned to Boston to spend the balance of the year sorting out his data and integrating the huge mass of information with that which had been secured during preceding years. More information would be acquired in following seasons, and the culmination of the survey would come in 1960 with the publication of the first comprehensive topographic map of the McKinley Group, in the Alaska Range. Bradford Washburn, now in his 64th year, is still mapping the inhospitable regions of North America, this time the Grand Canyon of Arizona.

The year was only partially over, and already Sheldon had done more mountain flying and made more risky landings than many pilots do in a lifetime. It was during the summer of 1955 that Sheldon got involved in a very unusual rescue.

In the near vicinity of Talkeetna and draining into the Susitna River are numerous headwater streams that become the temporary home of untold thousands of salmon and other migratory fish during late spring, summer, and early autumn. The fishing here has long been some of the very best to be found anywhere and ranks on a par with Alaska's famed Bristol Bay country to the southwest.

A Fairbanks bush pilot of no small repute, who shall remain nameless for reasons that will soon become painfully obvious, made a quick trip south in a floatplane to a point where Chunilna Creek empties into the Talkeetna River, about six miles upstream from the village of the same name. With him were two passengers, one of them a jolly red-haired woman of ponderous bulk who owned the small Fairbanks Hotel.

After landing the float-equipped airplane on the Talkeetna River, the three proceeded to catch an impressive number of salmon and oversize rainbow trout. The fish, along with some river water, were placed in the compartments of each of the airplane's floats. This practice, though a very common one among airplane drivers in the Far North, was frowned upon by those persons who are charged with enforcing regulations designed to keep the business of flying safe, namely the CAA. The reason for the rule relating to the transport of oversize trout in airplane floats has to do with overloading the plane and changing its center of gravity. In all fairness to the aviator, it must be pointed out that in addition to the load of fish in the floats, the woman's weight, which Sheldon swears was in excess of 300 pounds, contributed to the events that followed.

With everyone and everything aboard, the pilot began to negotiate what would later be viewed as an epic attempt to become airborne. Carrying its heavy load of people and fish, the plane accelerated downriver with the current. Soon two miles of river had slipped beneath the floats, which were still firmly planted upon the boiling surface of the Talkeetna. At this point, an evil-looking switchback turn in the river loomed into sight, and the pilot desperately horsed the wheel back into his lap in a last-ditch attempt to get the bird airborne—he was almost successful. But because it was getting quite dark and raining steadily, the hapless pilot did not see the approaching sandbar, located exactly where the river made its sharp, 180-degree turn.

The tops of the moose-browsed willows on the sandbar later bore mute testimony to the fact that the plane did leave the water. That it did not leave the water *soon enough* was evident. In a steaming cacophony of shearing metal and snapping struts, the plane crashed into a mass of tangled stumps and snags on the other side of the sandbar. From here, what remained of the fuselage skidded to rest in the middle of the shallow but fast-flowing river, and parts of the plane rained into the trees on the far bank, 50 yards from the point of impact.

At three o'clock the next morning, Sheldon, returning from a circus with a group of local citizens, flew into Talkeetna from Anchorage. Because it was pitch dark, wet, and very windy, he decided to land at the 4,000-foot CAA field on the other side of town rather than use the unlighted 900-foot dirt strip in his own backyard. As he entered the flight-operations room, he was met by the pilot of the plane that had come to grief earlier in the evening on the river above town.

"He was soaked to the skin and had 90 percent of his pants torn off, his elbows stuck out of his concussion-ripped jacket sleeves, he sported a knot on his head the size of a large tangerine, and the whole thing was topped off by a nasty black eye."

In a tight voice, he explained to Sheldon what had happened: "After the plane hit, it was all I could do to get out of it. I swam to shore, and when I looked back, it was too dark to see anything. I don't know if the passengers got out or not. I hope to God they haven't drowned."

Sheldon quickly replied, "Let me get another airplane and go take a look. I'll get the Cub, pick up Pedro, and we'll hop over there."

Pedro was the nickname of Lynn Twigg, an ex-railroad worker who was flying for Sheldon at the time.

Sheldon stowed three sleeping bags and a box of food in the space behind the Cub's rear seat, and with the sleepy Twigg aboard, was en route to the crash area. It was about 3:30 A.M., and the false dawn of the rainy July morning was just beginning to cut through the shifting fog patches over the river.

As they neared the area the pilot had described, Sheldon stared in disbelief through the fingers of rain that fanned upward across the windscreen in the prop wash of the Super Cub. On a narrow sandbar in the middle of the river, jumping up and down and waving her arms frantically, was the huge proprietress of the Fairbanks Hotel. What made the sight totally incongruous to Sheldon was the fact that she was "naked as a jaybird and resembled a white elephant. One thing that could be said—she would have been hard to miss, even in the poor light of a rainy morning. She was waving her clothes at us, and after recovering from our surprise, we made three passes over the tiny sandbar. It was only about 10 feet wide and 30 feet long, and Pedro managed a direct hit with only one sleeping bag. The food and the other bags ended up in the river."

Sheldon then made the short hop back to Talkeetna, landing at 5:30 A.M. The light was getting better, but it was still too dark to land the four-place floatplane on the river.

"At 7:30, the weather had improved and we took off. Again we overflew the sandbar a couple of times, and I decided to land on the stretch of river above the stranded woman, because of the current and the sharp bend downriver. Once on the water, I had to taxi backward downstream to get her."

126

Over the slipstream of the idling Continental engine, the woman wailed, "I'm sure damned glad to see you."

Her teeth chattered between blue lips, and she had the wet sleeping bag loosely draped over her ample shoulders.

"Hop aboard, and we'll have ya back in Talkeetna in a shake."

On their arrival, Sheldon happily learned that the third member of the fishing party had staggered into town after wandering all night through the wet mosquito-infested brush.

Back in the Fairview Inn, still wearing the sleeping bag at half-mast and nothing else, the big woman from Fairbanks bought drinks all around, and Sheldon recalls that "they were even dragging people in off the streets to help celebrate." Setting her drink on the bar long enough to readjust the wet sleeping bag, she invited Sheldon and the rest of the town of Talkeetna to Fairbanks.

Sheldon remembers the pickup of the 300-pound lady as being one of the most amusing rescues he has ever made. Later that year, he would be involved with one of the most harrowing exploits of his flying career.

Devil's Canyon

The Susitna River was first explored in 1834 by a Russian named Málakov, who recorded it in his field journal as the Sushitna, a word meaning "sandy river" in the gutteral dialect of the Tanaina Indians of the southern interior. When he saw it, the river, like a tattered ribbon of gray satin, sought the sea 260 miles from its source at the foot of a vast crevasse-scarred glacier in the then unnamed Alaska Range. Its fresh though silty waters mingled with the North Pacific in a broad maze of stinking tidal flats, 24 coastal miles from a place that would someday be called Anchorage.

With the exception of spring, when the flow becomes bloated with snow runoff, black drift logs, and rotted ice, the river is placid enough, and its journey to Cook Inlet is half over as it passes the village of Talkeetna. Here, it is already braided with countless side channels and split by willow- and driftwood-covered islands of scoured gravel. The river's deceptively slow current is accentuated by roiling boils, the occasional rhythmic slapping of some bankbound sapling, and the monotonous splash of collapsing silt bars. The riverbed, like the desert, changes with each passing minute of every year.

In most places below its confluence with the shallow and swift Chulitna, five miles above the approach to Sheldon's backyard airstrip, the river, known to Alaskans as the "Big Sue," is at least one-half mile in width. There is, however, a place 65 miles above Talkeetna where this generous breadth shrinks to a measly 50 to 70 yards between vertical rock palisades. Here, during late spring, the Susitna's 6,750,000-gallon-per-minute flow attempts to surmount itself in a roaring dervish of hissing gray spume. The U.S. Army Corps of Engineers is planning to construct a power plant in this five-mile stretch of turbulent waters called Devil's Canyon.

A rank profusion of pink fireweed and blue lupine nodded on the high cutbanks of the river near town, and countless tons of salmon were moving upriver. Sheldon had been almost content with the transport of itinerant fishermen, miners, and homesteaders during the weeks that had followed his rescue of the nude woman from the Talkeetna River.

The arrival of the northbound train, an event of regular though transient interest, took on new dimensions one July afternoon in 1955. Sheldon noticed that a crowd had gathered on the planking near the station almost before the engine jarred to a stop and braked against the slight grade. Resting on a special flatcar like some huge landbound ark was a bright yellow boat, with its bow decked over and two formidable-looking engines in its capacious stern section. The detachment of U.S. Army scouts that presided spelled property of Uncle Sam.

As the 50-foot boat was being off-loaded, Sheldon joined the group of curious spectators and found that little if any information was being offered by the Army as to why the boat was there or what it would be used for. Speculation was the order of the day, and Sheldon had already heard several rumors when he spotted a casual acquaintance—a lieutenant with the Search and Rescue Section at Fort Richardson in Anchorage. The lieutenant was busy checking a sheaf of dog-eared papers.

"Hi! How've ya been?" grinned the pilot.

"Good, Don. How's yourself?"

"Great. Hey, what's the deal here? You guys goin' fishin'?"

The officer glanced once more at his paperwork and allowed that the boat was to be used in an attempt to chart navigable watersheds in the Susitna Drainage.

Sheldon was incredulous. "Hey, you don't mean you're going to attempt to run this thing up the Susitna and through the canyon?"

The lieutenant, who had never seen Devil's Canyon, missed the surprise in Sheldon's voice. His reply was curt and precise.

"That's exactly what we plan to do, and the sooner we can get under way, the better."

There wasn't time for Sheldon to appraise the real chances of such a mission on such short notice, and even if there had been, he was sure that the officer was not particularly interested in his home-spun opinions. He did, however, have a very vivid picture of Devil's Canyon and had serious doubts about the possibility of the mission's success.

"Lookee, I've got a heck of a lot of fishing traffic up that way in the next few days. I'll check on your progress from time to time."

With the boat successfully launched, the small detachment of eight scouts that comprised the crew cast off. The powerful engines churned the current-roiled river, and the boat disappeared from view around the first upstream bend. Sheldon had flown over the five-mile stretch of boiling water in Devil's Canyon many times. It was a very familiar landmark to the pilot. From the air, the canyon's sheer rock walls, rising to 500 and 600 feet, produced an awesome corridor, the bottom of which is always in shadow. Above the canyon, the air was characteristically turbulent.

"The current here is so swift and heavy that even the salmon get beat to death trying to swim upriver."

The day after the scouts started up the Susitna, Sheldon flew over the river to make a casual check on the progress of the boat, but he did not see it. On the second day, he was curious, a trait that to date has accounted for not only his promptness in times of trouble but his own personal safety as well. This time, with two elderly fishermen aboard his Aeronca Sedan en route to Otter Lake north of Talkeetna, he deliberately flew up the Susitna. As he reached the flume below the fast water, he banked sharply to the left and rolled the portly Aeronca Sedan up on its ample side. Something at the periphery of his vision caught his attention, and he made a second swing to get a better look. What he saw made his skin crawl.

"I was shocked to see pieces of yellow wreckage floating down the river. I had a feeling this was a fresh wreck, and they'd really gotten clobbered. I saw barrels of gasoline bobbing around here and there. The wreckage was strewn downriver to a point almost 25 miles below the canyon, and it consisted mostly of bright yellow chunks of the boat's hull and other debris—but no people."

Sheldon continued the ten miles to Otter Lake, off-loaded his passengers, and quickly retraced his path to the tail of the Devil's Canyon rapids. He dropped down to a point just above the jagged rim of the canyon. After making several passes in the seething air, he spotted a group of men huddled on a narrow ledge of wet rock in the shadows at the base of the north wall. Even from his vantage point, he could tell that they were in bad shape and in desperate need of assistance.

"They were in a terrible condition—cut up and barely managing to cling to the shelf of rock. Their clothing was literally torn off, and a few of them still had life jackets on. These were also in shreds. They had apparently floated down about 60 percent of the canyon, a distance of roughly 3 miles."

Because he knew the place so well, Sheldon could rapidly appraise his chances of retrieving these men, and they looked poor. The canyon walls at their top were but a scant 200 yards apart, and the river was a succession of hissing combers broaching over house-size boulders in the river bottom. His chances were not only poor but probably nonexistent, for the Aeronca weighed only a scant 1,400 pounds empty and would be tossed like a tiny cork even if he somehow managed to land it on the surface of the river below, a feat that at the moment looked impossible. To drop onto the surface of the rapids here would be suicide because the floats needed a flat surface upon which to dissipate the forward momentum of the airplane. Sheldon needed little or no imagination whatsoever to visualize the results of running headlong at 65 miles per hour into any one of the tumbling white crests of water that surely towered up to 6 feet above the surface of the river.

"There was no place to land below them; it was just more of the same terrible rough water. I did a 180-degree turn, and about a quarter mile above the guys, I spotted a slick, high-velocity stretch of river that looked like it might be big enough. I made a couple of passes to try it on for size and then set myself up for an up-canyon approach to the place. It looked mighty small."

As Sheldon dropped the Aeronca below the tops of the canyon's walls, he found himself flying in a narrow alleyway of wet spruce and vertical rock. The plane rocked with the turbulence produced by the unstable air of the canyon, and he carefully adjusted his glide path. The floats were causing the airplane to respond to the controls in a delayed manner, due to a lowered center of gravity. This reaction is normal and in a routine landing produces no problems. But in this case, control of the airplane was everything, and Sheldon hitched forward as far as his seat belt would allow to gain every last inch of forward visibility.

Even before the floats touched down, spray and mist from the river surface were streaking the Plexiglas windshield of the Aeronca.

Sheldon fought the compulsion to firewall the throttle plunger and climb away from the terrifying spectacle of the gray water. Then he was down.

Sheldon was landing against a 30-mile-per-hour current, and the airplane decelerated at an alarming rate. When an airplane is moving through the air at an airspeed of 90 to 100 miles per hour, the control surfaces—ailerons, rudder, and elevator—work at optimum efficiency because the forward motion of the plane through the air and the slipstream blast of the rotating propeller produce the rush of air over the wings and tail surfaces. An airplane out of its design element and on the ground or water is much more difficult to control, primarily due to the fact that only the rush of air produced by the propeller provides forward velocity. In addition, an airplane on floats is infinitely less maneuverable than one on wheels or even skis, and as a result, the Aeronca became an unresponsive death trap as it almost immediately began to accelerate downriver with the current.

"The nose wanted to swing in about every imaginable direction, but somehow I managed to keep it pointed upriver with the throttle. I was floating backward at about 25 miles an hour, the windows were fogged, and I couldn't see where I was going."

Sheldon was certain of one thing—that behind him was the beginning of the heavy stretch of boiling rapids he had seen from the air only seconds before. At that moment, he was like a blindfolded man rolling backward toward a cliff in a brakeless car he could not steer. Sheldon will never forget those moments that elapsed so rapidly they precluded panic.

"As the plane backed into the first of the combers, I felt it lurch heavily fore and aft. It was like a damned roller coaster. The water was rolling up higher than my wing tips, beating at the struts, and I could barely see because of the spray and water on the windows. All of a sudden the engine began to sputter and choke, and I knew it was getting wet down pretty good. If it had quit, I'd have been a goner, but it didn't."

Suddenly, through the Aeronca's side windows, he saw the Army scouts on the small rock ledge. They stared, openmouthed, as the airplane backed past them. And now the most critical and delicate aspect of the entire rescue began.

"After spotting the men, I had to stop the airplane's backward motion, which I did with full throttle, but I knew my problems had only begun. Without damaging a wing on the rocks, I had to get the airplane close enough to the ledge for the guys to jump out onto the float and get aboard. If they missed, in their condition, they'd drown for sure. I jockeyed around and finally got the wing angled just enough to get one of them on the left float and still keep myself from turning downstream."

Once aboard the float, the grateful GI managed to balance-walk long enough to get into the cabin of the Aeronca while Sheldon was already making his next move.

"Because of the heavy current and extremely rough water, it was impossible for me to taxi upriver, let alone take off in that direction, so all I could do was continue to float backward as I had been doing. It was a mile and a half downstream to the end of the rapids, and that first trip was one of the longest rides on a river that I've ever taken."

Once below the rapids, Sheldon was able to turn the plane and make a downriver takeoff. He would make three more of these landings for there were still six men on the ledge, and he could only remove two at a time due to the need to keep the plane as light as possible for maximum maneuverability.

After miraculously returning to the rapids three more times, without damage to the airplane, himself, or the stranded scouts, he turned his attentions to the search for the eighth man.

"I flew upriver, looked and then looked some more. I still saw a lot of debris but no eighth man. I was just about ready to go back for another load of gas when I finally spotted him. The guy had dragged himself out of the river, and he was about 18 miles below the canyon. He had floated all that way hanging onto a piece of debris, and when I got to him, he was a shock case and could barely crawl aboard. The water was about 55 degrees, and he was all skinned up and bruised but had no broken bones."

The rescue at Devil's Canyon had been a marvel of efficiency. It was but one of many such feats that Sheldon would perform over the years. Many would be of a milder cast, while some would exceed the events that had transpired that day at Devil's Canyon. Today, Don Sheldon is well aware of the part that luck played in the four landings and subsequent takeoffs, for not even he could gauge the depth of the water as it plunged over the jagged rocks in the floor of the Susitna, yet somehow his floats missed them all four times.

Sheldon neither expected nor received financial compensation for the rescue. The U.S. Army, in a formal ceremony, awarded him a citation, which stands as a constant reminder of his close association with the military organization. It reads as follows:

ALASKA CERTIFICATE OF ACHIEVEMENT

TO

Mr. Donald Edward Sheldon
Civilian Aviator—Talkeetna, Alaska

The Alaska Certificate of Achievement is awarded for meritorious achievement while assisting in the evacuation of an eight-man patrol of the United States Army on the 9th and 10th of July, 1955. Mr. Sheldon, having information that a patrol was operating in the area in which he was flying, and knowing the treacherous nature of the rapids on the Susitna River, made an aerial check to determine the patrol's progress. Spotting debris in the water, and realizing that the men might be in trouble, he continued his search and located the patrol upstream on the bank of the river. At possible risk of life, Mr. Sheldon guided his aircraft between towering canyon walls and landed in the river. He then proceeded to fly the first group to Talkeetna, so that an injured man could be given medical attention. Returning to the river three times, he continued the evacuation of the patrol in semi-darkness to bring the last member to Curry at 0300 hours in the morning. His humane efforts prevented possible exposure and extreme difficulties for the members of the patrol. Seeking neither acclaim nor reward, Mr. Sheldon had willingly and voluntarily pitted his skill and aircraft against odds in behalf of the U.S. Army personnel. His intrepid feat adds lustre to the memory of those stalwart pilots whose rare courage and indomitable spirit have conquered the vastness of Alaskan Territory, and merits the deepest respect and admiration of every member in the United States Army Alaska.

Today, when asked which aspect of the entire Devil's Canyon episode he remembers best, Sheldon smiles thinly.

"I guess it would have to be the expressions on those guys' mugs as they crawled aboard my old floatplane."

134

"The Famous Last Ride
of 55 Xray"

As the 1950s drew to a close, Sheldon's name and reputation were well known in mountain-climbing circles the world over. During the months to come, he would be described as "Alaska's most celebrated bush pilot" in the pages of *Life* and *Sports Illustrated* and would be sought after for interviews by the nation's press, whose members, in the time-honored manner of reporters everywhere, were soon busily engaged in hurling adjectives and catch phrases. The droll aviator from the obscure Alaskan village of Talkeetna was being described as one of the world's truly "natural-born pilots." Sheldon's own definition of his prowess was and is considerably more prosaic: "Anybody can fly an airplane. You just jump in, crank her up, and get with it."

Sheldon takes great personal pride not in his ability to land airplanes where others fear to fly but in the lesser-known fact that during 33 years of flying, he has never killed a passenger. True, he has had a number of what he innocuously calls close scrapes, a few of which must be more accurately described as terrible brushes with sudden death. Yet these have been few when one considers that for many years, he has logged at least 800 hours in the air each year. At the date this is written, Sheldon has tallied each single hour he has flown during his long career in small airplanes. All but a few hours of his time in the air has been spent flying over the uninhabited expanse of Alaska, our largest state, which, to Sheldon's constant delight, is studded with an almost continuous profusion of rugged mountain ranges.

Sheldon is a product of the proverbial school of hard knocks. His success in this highly competitive business of bush aviation is based on experience fortified by an endless amount of ambition and an almost staggering quantity of imagination and raw guts, the latter always tempered by cool calculation and practiced caution.

Cool—either assumed or genuine—is the byword for both the sweaty-palmed greenhorn on his first solo cross-country hop and the seasoned pro making an instrument approach. Sheldon's casual running commentary on the passing scenery and other splendors of the Far North gives calm assurance to his passengers that all is under control in the left seat. He has become a veritable master in the subtle art of passenger comfort; even the hapless hunter who must straddle his own caribou antlers because of space limitations is never totally unhappy. Often, mountain climbers suffer the ride to the peak they are about to ascend buried under a pile of their own gear. To the legions of mountaineers who have voluntarily trusted Sheldon's judgment, the expedition flights are one of the highlights of each climb.

Luck is a factor that most people prefer to minimize in the interests of image, whether they fly an airplane or not. Sheldon believes that most good luck is the natural product of advanced planning and careful recognition of contingent factors, two of which take absolute precedence—mechanical condition of the airplanes and the weather, in that order. An FAA-rated mechanic, with both Authorized Inspection and Airframe and Engine certifications, the flyer services his own planes whenever possible, and a mere routine oil change becomes a ritual. Nothing is ever left to chance. If the manual for an engine boasts a 2,000-hour useful life between major overhauls, Sheldon arbitrarily halves this and does the job himself at 1,000 hours.

He is meticulous in the care of the costly Sensenich and Hartzell aluminum propellers that he uses today. Nicks that mark the blade edges, and are a trademark of a bush airplane, are surprisingly rare on Sheldon's props, even though they drive airplanes that seldom know the luxury of a paved landing surface. He dresses the occasional burr that thrown gravel produces with a fine mill file, for he knows that these insidious flaws can, on occasion, suddenly produce a growing crack under stress, causing the tip of one blade to break away. Then the runaway unbalanced prop will tear the engine from its mounts. Fortunately, this phenomenon rarely occurs, but if it does, it will almost always happen in flight when there is no time to chop the throttle. The whole event, as Sheldon is fond of saying, "usually ruins a guy's whole day."

Though he leaves nothing to chance where the airplane is concerned, he is always the potential victim of vicious weather. In the Alaskan mountains, the weather is so changeable that it often undergoes a complete reversal during a routine 45-minute round-trip flight. As a result, and by necessity, Sheldon has become his own best weatherman, especially in the vicinity of the ponderous McKinley.

Sheldon's virtues and the nature of those ever-present factors beyond his control are graphically illustrated by an incident that occurred not far from Talkeetna at a place in the Talkeetna Mountains called Yellowjacket Lake.

Some high-country streams are spring-fed and flow from the lower ends of lakes that have reasonably constant year-round water levels, but most streams are transient, making their appearances in the rocky gorges only after the spring thaw or heavy rainfalls. At the upper end of such streams, in obscure valleys often far above timberline, are shallow, rock-strewn basins holding token quantities of water during dry years. The lake at the head of Yellowjacket Creek is 6,000 feet high, and when the ground willows of its basin are blood-red with first frost, it normally holds barely enough water to feed the tiny stream that empties into the Talkeetna River far below.

Sheep hunters are mountain climbers only by necessity and have come to expect the pilots they hire to place them and their gear at the highest elevation possible. Over the years, Sheldon has learned not only where the sheep of interior Alaska live but how to place his many clients for maximum success. The tiny lake that feeds Yellowjacket Creek has long been a favorite, though precarious, landing site for such operations.

Sheldon had taken a sheep hunter named Wally Grubb, an Anchorage plumber, to the lake, and after five days, he returned to bring Grubb back to Talkeetna. The Cessna 180, with its 230-horsepower Continental engine, had a trivial 100 hours of flight time logged on its tachometer and had been purchased only three months earlier. Though barely broken in, this float-equipped plane was Sheldon's current favorite.

On this particular day, he landed into a stiff wind, which ruffled the surface of the tiny lake at one of its ends, and taxied into shallow water along the shore. Though Sheldon had already made nine successful landings at this same spot during the early fall, he was, as always, highly suspicious of taxiing, for with a sudden gust of wind blowing off the lake or the slightest application of power at the wrong time, the fragile aluminum floats, which cost more than $6,000, could be run onto sharp rocks and holed.

Sheldon planned to make two separate trips, one to remove Grubb and his trophy sheep horns and a second to pick up the hunter's tent and other gear. Both would be light loads for the Cessna, even here at 6,000 feet.

"This takeoff, the famous last ride of 55 Xray, was spectacular. The wind was still blowing from my left on leaving the lake. All of my other successful operations from this particular lake were done in no-wind conditions, with the exception of one occasion when I took off into a direct head wind."

Sheldon has refined the art of getting into the air with a float-plane to its highest degree. His method is to aileron-roll the plane onto one float after an adequate speed over the water has been acquired. This subtle action reduces drag friction caused by the water and allows the airspeed to increase rapidly to the point at which the airplane will fly. The plane becomes airborne at the slowest speed possible, however, and he must be extremely cautious about turning until a safe flying speed has been built up.

"As I cleared the end of the small lake, turbulence increased noticeably, and I could feel the plane sink."

Grubb, though not a pilot himself, was also aware of the strange sensation, which was beginning to resemble a landing rather than a takeoff. "I think the damned wind changed or something," he said to Don.

"He was dead right, and what had happened was that we had run into a freak and very abrupt tail-wind switch just after takeoff. It had been a barely quartering crosswind as we lifted off, and I was holding the plane in a slightly nose-high attitude in order to miss some large rocks at the end of the lake."

The Cessna continued to balk at the idea of flying. What had been a crosswind and slightly quartering tail wind of no major concern had suddenly increased and become a lift-destroying, direct tail wind. Just after lift-off, the powerful Continental engine became incapable of holding the airplane in level flight, let alone enabling it to climb. The plane was headed for a field of rocks and boulders, usually safe beneath the surface of the water but now looming ominously in front of the limping plane.

"I had already gone through a great obstacle course while I was still on the water, and as the plane lost altitude, I found myself back in it."

Sheldon dared not haul back any farther on the wheel, for he knew that to do so would cause the airplane, which was barely flying now, to stall and plunge nose down.

"Two huge boulders loomed ahead, and all I could do was aim for the space between them. It wasn't wide enough, and I lost both of the wings at exactly the same time."

When asked to describe the crash, Sheldon winced and waved his hands in a gesture of futility. Then he immediately referred to the terrible and all-inclusive noise that is always part of any crash.

"Right after the wings hit, I lost both floats, and the plane broke off at the tail on final impact. We figured this out after the dust settled, and we also noticed that the engine had torn itself loose and had been thrown about 50 yards ahead and to the left. The sheep hunter, myself, and the two seats landed upside down in the bottom of a deep crevasse among the rocks."

Grubb's ears still rang horribly as he tripped the release on his seat belt with a shaking hand. In the absolute postcrash silence, he whispered, "Are you all right?"

"I wiggled around. Nothing seemed broken, and it turned out that we'd hit so hard that neither one of us had a scratch. The only casualty, other than my brand new $40,000 Cessna, which was a total loss, was the right horn of the sheep. It was gouged."

With Sheldon and his passenger out of sight in the crevasse, the first search plane over failed to spot them and returned quickly with a "no survivors" report. The two were later brought back to Talkeetna by an amazed chopper pilot who flew in for the "bodies."

Sheldon, in the disaster at Yellowjacket Lake, had been the victim of a freak wind reversal aggravated by turbulence. Wind is generally a desirable flight condition, but turbulence, which usually consists of vertical air movement—either up or down or both at the same time—is not. Sheldon normally encounters turbulence when flying in mountainous terrain and considers it an acceptable fact of a flyer's life. He has learned to predict the presence of certain kinds of turbulence, one of which is aptly called shear turbulence. Occurring at high altitudes on clear blue days, shear turbulence has downed a number of the big commercial jetliners and is a constant danger among the high peaks. On Mount McKinley, it usually announces its presence with certain visual clues, which Sheldon watches for constantly.

"When the big mountains are turbulent, the peaks often show a lens-shaped or banner cloud around their summits. On McKinley, the winds on such days reach velocities of over 100 miles per hour."

The winds that Sheldon refers to are vertically opposed, and there is little or no calm air between the wall-like layers. The condition might be likened to the tremendous force generated by the passage of two trains, each traveling in opposite directions at breakneck speed. All one can do is pity the pilot who unknowingly enters these invisible corridors of speed. The effect, as its name "shear turbulence" suggests, is one of awesome shearing force, and total destruction often ensues.

Like any skilled pilot, Sheldon has learned to use the invisible forces of moving air to increase the lift capabilities of his aircraft. In the dense air at sea level, a plane functions best. As the plane enters the thin air at higher altitudes, the engine must work harder to maintain adequate lift. The Super Cub, which has become Sheldon's home away from home, is rated as a high-performance aircraft and gains prominence mainly through its built-in ability to take off and land in extremely short distances. However, like most other small aircraft, the Super Cub, with its present 150-horsepower engine, is limited in the height to which it can climb, due mainly to the simple fact that the engine can produce enough speed for lift only to a certain altitude. The absolute ceiling listed by Piper Aircraft Corporation is, coincidentally, 21,300 feet, just 20 feet lower than the South Summit of McKinley. To fly over the peak, a feat that he has routinely accomplished in his Super Cub, Sheldon has learned that if he quickly finds a rising thermal wind and applies full throttle, he will get a free elevator ride over the top.

"The best procedure is to circle the peaks to establish exactly where these thermals are, then use them to assist your altitude-derated engine performance. From 14,000 feet, full throttle will be necessary. Care should be taken against close proximity to peaks, as downdrafts and squirrely pockets of air might decorate the scenery with your aircraft."

Sometimes, however, the wind works against Sheldon, as evidenced by the crash at Yellowjacket Lake. On another occasion, after surmounting McKinley, he attempted to lose altitude by advancing the throttle and guiding the plane into a dive attitude. Although he was getting red-line readings on his airspeed indicator, he realized that he was not moving. An unseen wall of uprushing air caused the plane to remain motionless with relation to the ground below.

With each such experience, the man who singlehands it at Talkeetna Air Service enlarges his knowledge and skill. Occasionally the lessons have been costly.

"I've owned a lot of planes, 45 at last count, and I've demolished a few, but I've never lost a single passenger."

This fact somehow makes it all worthwhile.

Senator Boecher's White Bear

At midnight, 1958 became history, and the arrival of the new year was celebrated in Talkeetna with the consumption of an inordinate quantity of bar whiskey at the Fairview Inn and with the snow-muffled discharge of various shotguns by those still conscious enough to see what time it was. The shots were immediately answered by the discordant howling of sled dogs on the outskirts of town. Sheldon had celebrated his 37th birthday in the November just past. During the coming year, the first ascent of the Western Rib of Mount McKinley's South Face would be accomplished, in June, by a four-man party led by John ("Jake") Breitenbach, a very close friend of Sheldon's. Jake would later lose his life on Mount Everest. Talkeetna Air Service was still alive and well, and Sheldon's comings and goings had assumed the almost unnoticed regularity of a ticking clock.

That the presence of the pilot and his airplanes in the village by the Susitna would become a matter of less concern than the daily trains that pass between Fairbanks and Anchorage was predictable. Today, as then, rare is the morning that he is not airborne long before the rest of the town is alive, especially during the summer and autumn months. More times than not, darkness has descended before the plane's winking, red anticollision light announces his return. The townspeople of Talkeetna, in a somewhat disappointing manner, seldom mention his comings and goings, for they assume that everyone knows he flies an airplane for a living. Yet he is a legend in his own time everywhere else in the state, and in the smaller states to the south, he is, at the very least, known as "that guy in Alaska who lands on mountains."

Sheldon was busy during the 1959 season, flying many climbing crews to McKinley. By the spring of 1959, the South Summit of McKinley had been successfully scaled 14 times.

In addition to his flying activities for climbers, Sheldon flew for hunters. In 1947, he became a registered big-game guide and had conducted many hunts throughout Alaska, almost always with the aid of his airplanes, but he has also operated riverboats on the Susitna and other rivers for the same purpose. By the winter of 1959–60, Sheldon had flown and guided his share of polar-bear hunts, most of them in the Point Hope area.

Polar-bear hunting, be it with airplanes or Eskimo dogsled, is always a chancy business because the ice pack is a continually shifting mass. With temperature fluctuations, wind, and tremendous internal pressure, the ice pack heaves and buckles, throwing up jumbled ridges 50 to 60 feet high. The floes separate and rejoin in a never-ending northeasterly circuit of the North Pole, and these movements, which often occur over a span of minutes, leave the monotonous white of the ice pack scarred with jagged jade-black leads of steaming open water. This supercooled seawater of the Arctic Ocean requires temperatures well below 32 degrees to freeze. To fall into these smoking leads is to die suddenly, for the human body, even wrapped in fur and down, can tolerate but brief seconds of this total exposure.

The problems encountered in the operation of aircraft on this unpredictable frozen sea are manifold. The shifting ice is a constant hazard, and incidents of suddenly opening leads that have trapped resting airplanes are legion. Even the best landing on the smoothest surface to be found can strain landing gear, remove tail skis, and destroy propellers.

In addition to the physical nature of the ice itself, there are the numbing cold and the winds that suck the breath from all who venture here. Sometimes in less than half an hour, the chill factors in this area can cool engines that have foolishly been shut down, making them impossible to start. Besides bringing along spare parts, wise pilots carry tentlike cowling covers and plumber's stoves or Thermex heaters to maintain the engine's heat so the crankcase oil will not solidify, or they drain the crankcase while the oil is still liquid and heat it on a stove the following morning.

In the summer of 1959, Sheldon had received correspondence from State Senator Roy Boecher, of Kingfisher, Oklahoma, an avid conservationist who had been instrumental in the revamping of his state's game laws. Senator Boecher wanted to hunt a polar bear. His enthusiasm was shared by Howard Driggs and his two sons, who ran a considerable dairy operation in Palmyra, Michigan, and so they decided to make it a foursome. In February 1960, they flew to Point Hope, on Alaska's northwest coast, by commercial airliner and were met there by the pilot from Talkeetna and a half-Eskimo friend of Sheldon's named Floyd Wheeler, who had agreed to fly cover for Don on the hunt. Earlier, Wheeler, now an FAA mechanic in Kotzebue, had purchased the plane he flew from Sheldon. The weather was good, and the hunt got off to what appeared to be a good start.

"After two days of hunting, one of the Driggs boys killed a big bear that squared a shade over nine feet. Then a strong southeast wind sprang up. I knew from past experience that this kind of a blow is bad news in this corner of the Arctic, so we canceled the hunt for the following day."

In 1960, the village of Point Hope was not known for posh accommodations, and Sheldon with his four clients were lodged in a small Quonset hut.

"After the storm hit, the wind began to build at a fast rate, and we retired to the Quonset for a game of poker. The game continued for the rest of that day, all night, and into the early hours of the following morning."

Probably nowhere else on earth can be found storms of wind and driving snow that compare with those of Alaska's Arctic coast. After an uninterrupted race across the flat coastal forelands, the wind reaches the sea at hurricane velocities and drives the sandy snow ahead of it horizontally. Quonset huts had been specifically designed to shed rough weather, but the dilapidated condition of this one made it a poor shelter for the game in progress. The alternately roaring and keening wind, which barely changed course as it cleared the curved roof, created icy drafts around the loose-fitting door and sifted snowdrifts into the corners behind the players.

"At about three o'clock in the morning, there was one tremendous crash, and Wheeler looked at me and said, 'I bet that was your airplane.'"

The great Riccardo Cassin takes a serious look at his adversary, the unclimbed South Face of Denali.

Sheldon landing his Super Cub at Cassin's first base camp on East Fork, Kahiltna Glacier. Flags mark the 8,000-foot-high "runway."

Above (left): Three members of Cassin's party near camp at 11,000 feet on McKinley's South Face. Left to right: Gigi Alippi, Jack Canali, and Luigi Airoldi.

Cassin's Italian crew were experienced rock climbers. Above (right): A member of the expedition crossing a couloir of ice. Below: The team nears the end of the second couloir, at 13,000 feet.

A storm forced Cassin's party to remain lashed to this portion of the
South Face (above) for nearly three days before resuming the "impossible"
ascent. Below (left to right): Cassin, Annibale Zucchi, and Sheldon
after the last flight to remove the victorious climbers from McKinley.

Sheldon with members of Helmut Raithel's party at their 4,000-foot base camp on Chedotlothna Glacier. Left to right: Sheldon, John Dillman, Siegfried Gebel, Raithel, Peter Hennig, and Robert Goodwin.

Opposite page (top): Raithel's party became the first to reach the summit of Mount Russell. Left to right: Klaus Ekkerlein, Peter Hennig, Robert Goodwin.

Mount Russell, the mountain conquered by Helmut Raithel.

Bradford Washburn

The Northwest Approach to sinister Mount Huntington,
Lionel Terray's route to the summit, was named French Ridge
after his successful climb in 1964.

Don Sheldon and the great Lionel Terray at Talkeetna prior
to the first ascent of Mount Huntington.

Mary Carey

Photos by Dr. George Wichman

The first winter climb of McKinley was made in 1967. Above, the team at Talkeetna, ready to depart. Left to right (standing): Shiro Nishimae, Jacques Batkin, John Edwards; (seated) Dave Johnston, Gregg Blomberg, Dr. George Wichman, Ray Genet, Sheldon. This was Sheldon's first meeting with Genet (below, left), who has climbed to McKinley's summit more often than any other man.

The success of the climb was marred by Batkin's death. Below (right): The team brings his body down the mountain.

Alex Bertulis

A typical Sheldon "landing strip," amidst innumerable crevasses:
The arrow indicates the site and direction of a near-miss takeoff by
the aviator during an expedition to Mount Foraker in 1968. Note the climber
partially obscured by the small peak in the center foreground.

Sheldon's airplane had been securely tied down to 15-foot whale ribs that had been frozen into the ice in the lee of several of the sod buildings which abound in Point Hope. He was reasonably sure that *his* airplane had not broken loose—yet.

"Wheeler," said Sheldon, "I bet it was yours."

The two pilots dashed to the door, opened it, but went no farther. There in the enclosed hall-like entrance alley to the Quonset hut lay the cause of their concern.

"The alleyway had been struck by a flying doghouse. A gale-force wind, that by now was blowing full drums of diesel oil up and down the beach, had picked up the doghouse and hurled it into the entranceway to our little hut. They never tie a dog to his house on the north coast."

Sheldon grimaces as he remembers that the ice which gradually builds up around doghouses in Eskimo villages is sometimes accidentally mixed with other ice, melted, and used for tea.

Three days later, the storm that had roared from the southeast over Kotzebue Sound finally chased its tail out over the ice pack of the Arctic Ocean. The poker game stopped with the storm's passing, and Sheldon checked the weather forecast. The wind had streaked the barren landscape with hard knife-edged drifts of snow, and as he looked out over the ice pack to the west, he saw a number of new open leads.

"It looks good—I think we're in business," he said, ducking back inside.

"We resumed the hunt, and everybody was glad to be on the move again. Senator Boecher was next on our list for a go at a bear. The telephone company that he owned and operated back in Kingfisher had presented him with a fancy Weatherby rifle in commemoration of his trip north. Then he had a gunsmith friend hone the trigger for a very light pull. I fired the gun a few times when they were sighting it in, and in addition to the touchy trigger, I noticed that the rifle only held two cartridges in the magazine and one in the chamber. Thinking this a bit unusual, I had mentioned it to the senator, and he had not been able to explain it either, so it was temporarily forgotten."

With the breaking weather, Boecher boarded the idling Super Cub. As Sheldon prepared to taxi for a takeoff, the senator prodded his shoulder with a mittened hand and announced, "I just remem-

153

bered I left a cartridge in the chamber of my rifle. What should I do?"

Sheldon blanched as he remembered the hair trigger on the big rifle and quickly said, "Jeez man, make sure the safety is on or else unload it."

Luckily, the door of the airplane was still open, for the tremendous explosion and shock wave that followed an instant later almost deafened Sheldon and filled the cabin with acrid gun smoke. Fortunate too was the fact that the rifle, when it discharged as the senator fumbled with the safety, was pointed at the floor.

"Over the crazy ringing in my ears, I heard the senator gasp and say, 'By damn, I just shot my left foot off.' "

In honor of the hunt with Senator Roy Boecher and the Driggses, which had been in the planning for about six months, Sheldon had contracted with an old Eskimo lady in Point Hope to make five pairs of sealskin mukluks. He had presented four pairs to his hunters on their arrival and kept the fifth pair for himself.

"These mukluks are quite waterproof, and they are about the warmest thing there is for the Arctic. When the senator said he'd shot his foot off, I shut the engine down and told him to get out if he could, and we'd look at it. He sat down on a piece of frozen whale rib, and I could see that the big 200-grain slug from the Weatherby had sliced down the back of his left mukluk. He had huge feet, size 14 as I recall, and as he started to pull the sealskin boot from his foot, neither one of us was anxious to look."

After the mukluk was off, the caribou-hide sock, which was also split by the bullet, had to be removed. Sheldon took out his knife and cut the sock the rest of the way around and gingerly tugged it from Boecher's big foot, while the senator complained about how numb his foot felt. With three sets of heavy wool socks to go, Sheldon had as yet seen no blood.

"After I got the socks off, I noticed a heck of a big welt along the tendon of his left heel. My mukluks had saved him."

In due time, a much-relieved senator from Oklahoma, shod with a new pair of mukluks and glowing with restored optimism, made a fresh start with Sheldon. He got his polar bear and returned to the warmer states happier and considerably wiser.

Sheldon had found the polar-bear operations lucrative additions to his annual income, especially since they were conducted during

154

late winter and early spring, when the air-charter business is usually slow in Alaska.

"Truthfully speaking, we were a bunch of mercenaries—we were paying off airplanes and could make $3,500 for five hours of work."

It is also quite true that he enjoys the Arctic and the special challenges it offers a pilot. He is more than content with the solitude of being aloft, and except for the big mountains, the lonely wastelands of the coastal Arctic are among his favorite places. He can fill his eyes to the brim with the beauty of a low sun at noon and the purple twilights with their promise of the aurora. Like Carl Ben Eielson and others before him, Sheldon considers flight over the trackless snow and the ice leads, which almost glow with green fire when the sun's angle is just so, an endless delight.

But in 1960, it was somehow different. The powerful scenery of the high Arctic had lost none of its appeal, and the old familiar urge to head out over the endless ice just to see what could be seen was still there. But there were fewer bears.

"There was no doubt in my mind that the bears were getting scarcer in 1960, and I was just as sure that the airplane was responsible to a large extent. In later years, it became legal to hunt only with a dog team, and that's the way it should have been in 1960. Even with a dog team, a client takes his chances, and the chances are numerous. The high winds and long stretches of terrible weather can leave a party isolated, and the danger of being split off from the mainland by a separating ice pan is formidable. With aircraft, we too had our problems, but we were mobile. As a rule we flew two planes; one flew low and followed tracks, while the other stayed at a higher altitude. The bears were not hard to spot and catch up with, and if a bad landing occurred, the pilot who was still aloft could lend a hand. The general practice was to pick a suitable day, fly out of one of the places like Shishmaref, Point Hope, Kotzebue, or Barrow, and look for tracks. Once you spotted them, you followed, and usually in a few hours of hunting, the great white hunter would be on his way home with a trophy."

Sheldon decided to quit guiding polar-bear hunts because of his growing disenchantment with the method. But many others were not possessed with his insight and continued to use planes to chase the long-necked bears. Finally the use of the airplane for such hunts was banned completely. Sheldon believed it was about time.

Today, the law is even more restrictive, and it is illegal for anyone except the Eskimo to pursue the white bear.

After the hunt with Senator Boecher and the Driggses in 1960, the last hunt for the white bears that he would ever make, Sheldon flew home. It was mid-March as he crossed the Alaska Range, the days were lengthening, and the sun was warm as it streamed through the green Plexiglas canopy overhead. As he added the last notch of flaps over the still-frozen Susitna, he could see his small frame hangar building through the slight blur of the prop—the building with the red paint, tar-paper roof, and the sign that still said Talkeetna Air Service—Morrison and Sheldon, Big Game Guides.

Mount McKinley's "Highest Airport"

By 1960, Mount McKinley had become a popular place, and to some climbers, it seemed that there were few major scraps left on the bone of discovery in this newest state to the Far North. They were wrong. The year would witness more successful ascents of the mountain and its sister peaks than any previous one. By the end of the normal climbing season in late July, the difficult North Summit had been scaled for the 6th time by a Japanese team, the more accessible South Summit saw its 19th conquest, and East Kahiltna Peak and Mount Crosson had been climbed for the first time. In perhaps the most interesting feat of all, two intrepid Japanese climbers had actually camped overnight on the corniced brow of the South Summit, where previously men had tarried just long enough to plant the banner of their expedition before retreating from their humbling and highly debilitating vantage point.

As the decade began, climbing in the McKinley Group was attaining a decidedly international flavor. Today, as in the past, Sheldon estimates that 15 percent of the climbers he caters to come from Japan. The laughing, mostly non-English-speaking groups of Oriental climbers have become commonplace on the gravel main street of Talkeetna. Sheldon's tiny front-porch office is festooned with expedition flags of Japanese origin, and a huge unopened bottle of sake reposes in a remote corner of the desk that holds his base radio gear. He seems to have an instant rapport with the Orientals. Like magic, he finalizes the complex logistics and liaison arrangements for expeditions without speaking a word of Japanese and is even able to joke and laugh with the climbers over subjects of mutual interest. On the wall near his desk is an outdated calendar issued by the Mitsubishi Aircraft Company of Tokyo, and he is fond of pointing to the picture of the sleek twin-engined plane on its cover and grimacing in mock disdain, a tenuous attempt at humor that Sheldon always brings off with perfection.

During the spring and early summer, the sagging plank floor of the Talkeetna Air Service hangar is strewn with the unrolled sleeping bags of transient climbers and piles of additional gear in the process of being sorted. It is the temporary home of Sheldon's clients, and the subject of mild criticism by other business people of Talkeetna, especially those who own motels. The hangar affords a large area in which to sort ice axes, crampons, jumars, pitons, carabiners, climbing ropes, expensive down clothing, handmade boots, daily food rations, and other seemingly endless items of gear that are essential to all mountain-climbing expeditions. Best of all, the hangar, called the "Talkeetna Hilton," is free of charge. Mountaineers, who usually operate on tight budgets, really appreciate Sheldon's hangar hotel. And with the climbing crews close at hand, Sheldon can assemble them for a fast departure when the weather breaks in his favor.

In 1960, Talkeetna was fast learning to accept the climbers. True, they were a motley lot of mixed extraction, but unlike the average tourist, they exuded a professional sincerity. These men often got their first look at McKinley from Talkeetna's main street. Impressive at any time, the view is especially awesome when the mountain, reflecting the sun's rays from its snow-covered surface, glows pink against the pale-blue evening sky. With few exceptions, the huge mountain to the northwest signified the happy termination of long planning, meticulous preparation, and high expectation, and they were now anxious to accompany Sheldon on the second-to-last step toward their goal.

The enigma of the mountain climber is virtually insoluble. These men with the sparkling eyes and sun-crinkled features share one common bond—the desire to reach out and grasp the ultimate challenge. To the climber, the higher and more difficult the mountain, the more desirable the challenge becomes.

That they go to the mountain with full recognition of the risks involved is a fact of life totally beyond credibility to the nonclimbers of the world, and critics have mumbled about the need for bonding all climbing parties as insurance against the expense of retrieving them from the mountain. Usually mere record breaking has little part in what makes them tick, but in the history of climbing, there have been men who admittedly seemed more interested in getting there fast than in enjoying what happened on the way. John Day was such a man.

John Day's lifelong ambition was to be recognized as an Olympic-class athlete, but he had always just barely missed his goal. Earlier, guided by the legendary Hal Waugh, he had spent a mountain of effort and a river of money trying to shoot an Alaskan brown bear of world-record size. He had failed.

Afflicted with a slightly crippled back, the wealthy owner of the Gold Rey Ranch, near Medford, Oregon, was 51 years old and in excellent physical condition when he arrived in Talkeetna in mid-May. With him was his hired climbing crew, consisting of the Whittaker twins, Jim and Lou, from Seattle. Jim Whittaker three years later would establish his name in the top rank of the mountaineering world by becoming the first American to stand at the summit of Everest. Both of the tall, rugged Whittakers were active mountaineers and guides on Mount Rainier in their home state of Washington.

In 1957, Day had been badly bitten by the climbing bug. It mattered little to John Day that this was a job for professionals, most of whom spend their lifetimes learning the techniques of survival in this most demanding vocation. In 1958, Day convinced the Whittakers to accompany him on a whirlwind climbing tour among the seven "majors" of the South 48. The climbing of these prominences would be a feat in itself, but Day wanted more. He wanted to top the peaks faster than anyone else in the history of mountaineering. John Day and the Whittakers succeeded. They climbed Mount St. Helens on August 26, followed by Mount Adams on August 27, Mount Rainier on August 30, Mount Baker on August 31, Glacier Peak on September 2, Mount Olympus on September 3—all in Washington State—and Mount Whitney in California on September 10.

And now, with these successes behind him, Day was consumed by an unreasoning desire to up the ante. McKinley beckoned, and he convinced the Whittakers that the speed binge they had all been on could be continued on the highest of the North American peaks. An additional climber, like the Whittakers also from Seattle, agreed to make the trip. He was Peter K. Schoening, an engineer and veteran of the Himalayas. Schoening, now 46 years old, has been selected to lead a 12-man climbing team on an ascent of Lenin Peak in the Soviet Union. This will be the first authorized American team to mount a climb in Russia. Prior to the Day Expedition in 1960, Schoening was a member of a 1953 team that failed in an attempt to scale K-2, the world's second highest mountain, in the Karakoram Range of Kashmir. Day, the Whittakers, and Schoening came to Sheldon, who would place them at the starting gate for their race to the top of the mountain that towers into the cold, pale-blue Alaskan sky almost 14 times the height of the Empire State Building.

A damp chill hung in the early-morning air of May 13 as the silver Cessna 180 became airborne over the small dirt airstrip in Sheldon's backyard. For a number of years, Sheldon has ordered most of his Cessna 180s from the factory at Wichita, Kansas, without paint, because of the 25 or 30 pounds of weight it adds. The powerful silver planes are another of the pilot's many trademarks. The Cessna's aluminum retractable skis, now spattered with rain-puddle mud, reflected the orange of the rising sun. Sheldon automatically monitored the plane's early performance as he banked over the sprawling river to set a northwesterly course toward Mc-Kinley. All was well. The six-cylinder Continental power plant, giving off the faintest odor of warm engine oil and high-octane aviation gasoline, was smooth and alive; oil pressure was "in the green"; and the other engine gauges looked normal. Perhaps most encouraging of all was the weather. Through the scrupulously washed Plexiglas windscreen, the early morning sky promised fair weather, and the vast mountain to the northwest slumbered in reflected light.

As Sheldon watched his airplane smoothly make course for the south slopes of McKinley, he listened to the casual banter of his passengers and felt the well-controlled undercurrent of professional excitement that filled the Cessna's cabin. He also became even more convinced that though the Whittakers and Schoening seemed less enthusiastic than Day, here indeed were men who were truly committed to their earlier-stated objective, that of a record-speed climb to the South Summit of McKinley.

Tugging at the corners of Sheldon's mind was the tenuous nature of the official permit that Day had secured for this climb. All expeditions that are airlifted to points on the mountain within the geographical borders of Mount McKinley National Park must be conducted under scientific permits issued by park authorities. Most authorizations are awarded for scientific studies in fields such as geology, cosmic-ray analysis, or entomology. Somehow, Day had secured authorization for a "photographic" expedition, a marginal category only occasionally acknowledged by authorities. However, once permission, regardless of its basis, is granted, Sheldon is exempted from any consequences.

At an indicated airspeed of 120 miles per hour, the 60-odd miles between Talkeetna and the South Face of McKinley quickly slipped beneath wings that now reflected the subtle shadings of a carpet of green spruce, meandering streams, and countless small lakes. Leaving the wooded lowlands, Sheldon applied climb power to establish his approach to the 10,200-foot level near Kahiltna Pass. When viewed from the air, Kahiltna Pass appears as a long, steep alleyway of snow, bordered by rocky crags that cast their shadows across its floor. The overall effect is one of highly deceptive gentleness, and on clear days such as this one, when the winds are calm, an aura of peaceful solitude prevails.

Until 1956, the favorite approach to the South Summit was over the Muldrow Glacier. But the surface of the Muldrow Glacier had undergone a change in the winter of 1956–57 that can be described accurately by only one word—cataclysmic. Glaciers, or more descriptively, ice rivers, steadily respond to the constant tug of gravity and flow toward sea level in a lethargically slow manner. During this winter, the vast Muldrow, which moves in a northeasterly direction after it is almost doubled in size by the marriage of the Brooks and Traleika Glaciers, surged in a most extraordinary manner. It roared and thundered into the valley ten miles below. Before returning to a more docile state, the glacier had sunk vertically 250 to 300 feet below its original height. This phenomenon rendered its surface so rough that it was impossible to climb for three full years—thus intensifying interest in Sheldon's "private" Kahiltna approach.

With his landing spot in sight, Sheldon's right hand made a smooth throttle adjustment, which gentled the engine. With the lessening of engine noise came an awareness of the sound of the wind rushing by the aircraft. All eyes were forward watching the surface of the glacier. From a distance, the floor of the glacier looked like an undisturbed carpet of snow, but the surface actually consisted of countless ridges of varying size, sharp outcroppings of rock, and numerous blue-green crevasses up to several hundred feet deep. Sheldon knew how to land here. At 80 miles per hour, the Cessna responded, and with a slight hissing sound and a series of moderate bumps, the skis found the glacier surface, and the plane's tail dropped.

At 10,200 feet above sea level, the climbers stepped into a brilliant world of sun and snow that seemed thousands of miles from the summertime of Talkeetna, a brief 30 minutes in the past. Almost immediately, the Day party was ready to begin its assault on McKinley's South Summit via the West Buttress. John Day was anxious to grapple with the mountain, and the four-man expedition departed after bidding a terse farewell to Sheldon. They started their climb immediately without even setting up a base camp.

After turning the plane and taking off downslope, Sheldon returned to Talkeetna. Four hours later, on a support flight for another group, he overflew the pass and was surprised to see that the Day party was nearing a place called Windy Corner, 3,000 feet above their starting point. Sheldon rolled the Cessna into a steep bank for a better look.

"They were at 13,200 and still climbing at a rate of 800 feet per hour with heavy packs. In addition, they weren't climbing on dry rock and gravel, but on powder snow. They had been using snowshoes and crampons alternately, and in view of this, I was flabbergasted. The air temperature must have been in the mid-60s, and to make the time that they were was really cuttin' the mustard."

At the time the Day party began their rush toward the South Summit, there were three other groups on the mountain: a five-member team from Waseda University in Japan, a larger Japanese expedition from Meiji University, and a five-member crew climbing under the banner of the Mountaineering Club of Alaska. Slightly ahead of the Day party, this group, all from Anchorage, consisted of Mrs. Helga Bading, Paul Crews, Andrew Brauchli, Dr. Rodman Wilson, and Charles Metzger. Sheldon had taken both Japanese teams as well as the Anchorage group to the mountain and was flying supply drops to all three.

The group from Anchorage, led by Paul Crews, had been taken to the 7,000-foot level, since they were climbing without a scientific permit. They had started a week earlier than the Day party, on May 7, and by May 16, were camped at 16,400 feet, just above the crest of the West Buttress. Radioed reports from this position had been encouraging, even though the climbers had experienced difficulty adjusting to the lower oxygen content of the air at that altitude. Temperatures were ranging between minus 17 and plus 17 degrees, and wind velocities had been reasonable. They expected to reach the summit "the next day."

Both the Anchorage team and the John Day party attained the South Summit of Mount McKinley on the afternoon of May 17.

Helga Bading, who could not adjust to the low oxygen levels at 16,400 feet, had stayed in camp while the balance of her party climbed the last leg to the summit. On a whim, the Anchorage team brought along their tiny transceiver so they could broadcast from the summit.

The group from Anchorage reached the South Summit at 7:15 P.M. and were closely followed by John Day's crew. Both parties shook hands, planted their expedition flags, and took the usual pictures. The meeting of the Day Expedition and the Mountaineering Club of Alaska team represented the first time in the history of McKinley climbing that two teams stood at the South Summit simultaneously. After spending a half hour at the highest of all vantage points on the North American continent, the Anchorage team began their descent. John Day and his companions stayed a while longer to take more pictures.

By 9:30 P.M., the Anchorage climbers were in 18,200-foot Denali Pass. They noticed that Day's crew had already started down and was "about 40 minutes behind them," descending a steep, crevassed section of the mountain. Then without warning, the mountain turned victory to chaos. One of Day's crew had become careless and slipped. The others had allowed the rope that joined them to become slack, and one by one, they were all pulled off their feet, to begin a plunge of 500 feet down the steep face of the mountain. As they fell, they futilely attempted to arrest their plunge with ice axes, but their descent had become a deadly game of crack-the-whip.

The Anchorage team, a considerable distance away, heard muffled shouts from above but did not see the actual fall. When they were finally able to pinpoint the trouble, they saw only that the Day crew was piled in a heap at the foot of the sheer wall. By shouting questions, they were able to ascertain that there were injuries and that the Day team wanted a tent. Paul Crews, who was less exhausted than his comrades, ascended to the site of the accident with a

Logan tent, which he slit across the bottom and erected over John Day, who seemed to be the most badly injured. It was at this point that the tiny radio transceiver became critically important, for it was their only communication link with the outside world.

At 6:00 A.M. on May 18, after a night of exhausting effort to do what they could for the Day team, Paul Crews sent a message to Tenth Rescue in Anchorage. He indicated the extent of the injuries suffered in the fall. (Day had badly torn ligaments in his left leg, and his hands and feet were badly frozen.) Crews requested an air evacuation for Day and fresh radio batteries for the tiny transceiver. An hour later, Crews detailed the worsening condition of Helga Bading. Sheldon was alerted by Tenth Rescue. He gassed the Super Cub and placed emergency medical supplies, more radio batteries, some food, sleeping bags, and a Primus stove behind the front seat. Sheldon knew that the Day party would need additional supplies if they were forced to stay on the mountain for any length of time.

After donning a light down jacket, his knit watch cap, and his ever-present felts and overshoes, he departed Talkeetna in the Super Cub and by plan flew to the North Face of McKinley. As he had expected, this side of the mountain was still wrapped in clouds and was shielded somewhat from the abating 100-knot winds of the past 3½ days. Calling upon his superb knowledge of cloud formations around the mountain, he climbed through multiple layers to an altitude of 19,000 feet above the North Face and finally topped out of the thick, swirling cloud layers. Using his Scott portable oxygen equipment, he flew the tiny Super Cub just west of the North Summit and then crossed over the South Summit and spiraled downward for a break-through-the-clouds look. As he lost altitude in the multilayered clouds, he was able to hold the course he wanted by reference to his compass. Finally he broke through the bottom of the lower layers.

Sheldon had done an uncanny bit of flying and navigating. He had pinpointed the accident scene exactly. Banking the Super Cub gently, he grimaced as he viewed the broken trail left by the tumbling Day team. The ugly scratches streaked the snow slope down the 40-degree face of the West Buttress for a good 500 feet, from just below the crest of Denali Pass nearly all the way to the small level plateau behind the 17,230-foot crest of the upper step of McKinley's West Buttress.

164

"Refrigerator-sized chunks of snow had been ripped out by their axes as they fell, and I could see that someone had erected a small tent at the foot of the steep face."

These sightings and appraisals occurred in a matter of brief seconds. Before leaving the area, Sheldon was shocked by one last horror. Approximately 200 yards from the scene of the fall lay the charred and "still-steaming" wreckage of a plane, identifiable only by the upthrust tail assembly and skeletal shape of the incinerated wings. Sheldon would later learn that the plane, a Cessna 180, had been flown by William Stevenson, an Anchorage contractor. Stevenson had been flying over a lower climbing camp, and curious, had climbed upward to see what was occurring at 17,200 feet. But the area over the accident site was too confined for the Cessna. Trying to turn in the tight confines of the basin, he had stalled his airplane and spun to his death. The plane had burned immediately, and Stevenson's passenger died with him. Technical Sergeant Robert Elliott, a climber and cold-weather test expert with the Air Force, had flown with Sheldon on three expeditions, one to Mount Logan in the St. Elias Mountains and two to Mount McKinley.

Sheldon was revolted at the horror of the scene. He had had his much-needed look, and now, glancing upward to the wing-root bubble gauges, he realized that he would soon need fuel. Making one final circle, Sheldon popped the door upward, admitting a frigid blast of air, latched it to the wing, reached behind him, and dropped the extra supplies, which were recovered by the Day party. Then, he radioed home.

"Talkeetna base, this is 8898 Delta. I'm at 18,000 and there's been bad trouble here. Some guy piled a 180 up, and it burned. I'm going to Summit for gas en route Talkeetna."

Sheldon placed the Super Cub in a steep, spiraling climb and retraced his route over McKinley's North Face. Free of the oppressive clouds, he set course for the FAA station at Summit, on the Alaska Railroad. Here he found two Army jet helicopters fueled and ready to leave for the scene of the accidents. As he alighted from the Super Cub, one of the chopper pilots approached him.

"We're on our way in and would appreciate it if you could show us the way on a chart."

"You betcha I can show you the course on your chart," answered Sheldon, "but you'll never find it because of the heavy cloud layers.

Lookee, if you'll let me refuel, I'll be glad to take you guys to a position above the area."

Declining the offer, the Army pilot said, "We appreciate it, but we're too fast for you, and you wouldn't be able to keep up."

The pilots started their engines and took off. Their rescue attempt would graphically prove that Sheldon's intimate knowledge of the mountain was the undisputed key to success. One helicopter would develop electrical problems and limp back to the Summit strip 2½ hours later. The crew of the other became lost after seeing nothing but fog and rocky crags. They made an emergency landing near Kantishna and radioed back for fuel. Since Sheldon's departing look at the cloud conditions on the mountain had convinced him that an immediate return to the disaster scene would be sheer folly with any aircraft, he refueled and returned to his base at Talkeetna, 75 air miles to the south.

Crews' radioed report from the mountain on May 18 had alerted the world to the multiple tragedy. Climbers from Anchorage, Seattle, Portland and elsewhere on the West Coast had begun offering their services for a rescue effort that would dwarf any before or since. Several of the large commercial airlines brought these climbers to Anchorage free of charge, and the Army ferried many of them to Talkeetna. Almost overnight, Sheldon's red, sag-roofed hangar building had become the temporary home of almost 100 rescuers. Sheldon, between flights to the accident scene, ferried these men to the base of the mighty Kahiltna Glacier on McKinley, the main staging area for the rescue efforts. Due to the onset of ugly weather, Sheldon had decided that even though he could not land at the disaster site with his Super Cub, he could saturate the lower levels with climbers, who might, in a concerted effort, reach the ill-fated Helga Bading and the John Day crew.

On Thursday morning, May 19, 5 rescue parties of 6 men each had passed the 12,000-foot level and were climbing slowly. Since these climbers were still a long 5,000 feet below the disaster area, they would need, at the very least, another full day to reach it. At this point, the U.S. Army Rescue Coordination Center in Anchorage issued a press release which stated that two HO43-B turbine-powered helicopters were being dispatched to Alaska. These craft had recently set altitude records by attaining 30,000 feet. After their arrival, however, they were unable to land at the 17,000-foot level due to the wind conditions and terrain limitations on the mountain.

The Rescue Center announced that all subsequent use of the Army's helicopters would be abandoned.

By noon on May 19, the dense cloud layers above 2,000 feet had slowly begun to recede. Sheldon continued methodically relaying climbers up the mountain, but it was excruciatingly slow work. He also overflew the accident site and made a second airdrop of supplies.

That evening, the wind increased in velocity, and there was little sleep for the Anchorage team in their whipping tents. The hours crept by with agonizing slowness. Helga Bading's condition had become much worse during the two days that had elapsed since she had opted to stay at the lower level while the rest of her companions went to the South Summit. She was now incoherent and could not keep food in her stomach. Oxygen, a supply of which had been airdropped the night before, could not overcome the terrible effects of the weak air, and she was being rapidly consumed by a condition called cerebral edema, known simply as altitude sickness prior to late 1960. (The syndrome was formally described several months after the Helga Bading rescue.) Her deteriorating condition forced another decision. Her companions knew that if she were to live, she would have to be moved soon to a lower altitude, where the oxygen content of the air was higher. It was late evening of May 19 when they radioed the increasing seriousness of her condition.

Tenth Rescue called Sheldon to ask if he could meet the stricken woman near the 14,000-foot level on the mountain the next day. Sheldon said that he would try. After making this commitment, he felt the first stirrings of the strange loneliness that he has experienced so often during his life. All subsequent decisions would be his alone. Those decisions would affect both his own life and Helga Bading's life, which was now almost totally dependent upon him.

No one, including Sheldon, had ever made a landing near the 14,000-foot level on McKinley. He knew that pilots who fly at these heights, unless properly equipped, suffer hypoxia, the insidious disease of oxygen starvation. In the anemic air at this altitude, the engine of any fixed-propeller aircraft would lose about 45 percent of its total power capabilities. In addition to the lower power capabilities of the airplane, the pilot must exercise extreme care in selecting a landing site that will allow for a reduced-power, gravity-assisted takeoff with the added load of a bulky passenger. The powerful, unpainted six-place Cessna would not meet this challenge due to its high empty weight, and the only choice he had left was the small two-place Piper Super Cub, upon which he had depended so often before.

"The Super Cub is powered by a 4-cylinder Lycoming engine, which develops 150 horsepower. Its greatest single advantage lies in the fact that it is an extremely light airplane. Fabric-covered, it only weighs a bit over a thousand pounds and is a frail bird of very high performance."

Finely tuned, the Super Cub would be the only tool that Sheldon could use to answer this plea for help. His next thought automatically shifted to the weather.

"After May 17, the weather began to go ape and was shifting into a tremendous storm cycle. The wind of the past 3½ days was still in the process of blowing itself out on McKinley."

Sheldon knew that he would have to stifle his natural desire to leave immediately. He would have to endure the terrible waiting, which is the bane of all pilots even when there is no emergency at hand.

Standing upon his dirt strip in Talkeetna, with the warm 70-degree breeze from the west carrying sounds of the children playing and birds singing among green leaves, he had to project his thinking to appraise a seemingly impossible rescue mission at 14,000 feet in gale-velocity winds, with the accompanying vortices of snow and multilayered clouds. On McKinley, a mere 60 land miles away, the air temperature could be near zero, with an accompanying chill factor that would plunge the temperature still lower.

In the almost 24-hour daylight of the Alaskan spring, Sheldon could look northwest at virtually any time of day and view the weather near McKinley. As he stared at the mountain on the evening of May 19, he could see that he would have to continue to control his impatience. The entire lower two-thirds of the peak was socked in, and the gray scud seemed to cling there without motion. Sheldon watched continuously until late that night, slept for a few hours, and was back keeping his vigil early the next morning.

On the morning of May 20, Sheldon was up at about 4:00 A.M. as usual, after a brief three-hour nap. He found that the weather had broken substantially, and the sky around the mountain was now relatively free of clouds. He made his move at midmorning.

"On the 19th, Jack Wilson of Gulkana, Jim Gibson of Kenai, and

168

George Kitchen along with Ted Huntley, both of Anchorage, had flown in to lend a hand. The thought of landing at 14,000 feet didn't particularly bother me, though I knew I would have a weight problem with the Super Cub. I also knew that I had a power problem with it. I had flown over the top of McKinley in it on many occasions, so ceiling was no consideration, but performance at high altitude is mainly dependent upon the weight you're carrying. I had to haul my own oxygen gear and survival equipment in case I didn't get there in one piece. I asked George Kitchen to fly cover for me for the same reason."

After carefully stowing these bare essentials of equipment, along with a generous bundle of fresh spruce boughs and willow wands, in the rear of the Super Cub, Sheldon began to think about gassing the plane. This consideration would be most important. He knew that too much gas in his tanks might negate a high-altitude takeoff, especially with a passenger in the airplane. Too little fuel could leave him stranded with a dead engine somewhere between the mountain and Talkeetna.

"A landing above 14,000 feet was no sweat, providing I could find a decent piece of steep snow-covered ice to do it on. It was the takeoff that was the big problem. All of the basics of glacier landings would apply, but even with the loss of power I knew I'd get up there, I had to play the weight factor real close. I figured what would be the best fuel load and gassed her up. I filtered the gas carefully through the chamois because the last thing I could afford was ice particles on this deal."

All aviation gasoline has small quantities of water no matter how well it is filtered. If this water, which is liquid in air that is above 32 degrees, is present in great enough quantities, the ice crystals that form as the temperature drops can plug a fuel line or filter. This fact has been learned the hard way by scores of pilots the world over, especially in the Arctic. Sheldon is so meticulous that he filters each and every drop of fuel he uses, even when he gasses up at the Anchorage International Airport.

"As soon as everything was ready, Kitchen and I blasted off. On the way, I noticed that the weather up to 17,000 feet looked pretty good, and I kept thinking about what Washburn had told me over the phone."

Brad Washburn and his wife Barbara first heard about the situation on McKinley while listening to the radio news in their Boston home on the hot sultry evening of May 19. As Washburn remembers the situation:

"To our astonishment, they were reporting an accident on McKinley and telling of John Day having been injured. We knew that the Day party was up on the mountain, because he had been in Cambridge earlier, and I had shown him some pictures of the route he would take and discussed the climb with him. I remember remarking to Barbara that John was, indeed, in a hell of a bad situation. I knew the place well, and to be isolated there with a badly broken leg was an appalling thought. I telephoned Talkeetna direct. I was lucky. Don was there, and I asked him about John Day. Sheldon said, 'Right now, he's not our main concern. They're going to bring Helga Bading, an Anchorage climber, down the mountain from 17,000 on a sled, and she's got a bad case of altitude sickness. Is there anyplace I can land at about 14,000?'

"I thought for a moment and then replied, 'There's a shelflike basin immediately south of the West Buttress, near where we camped in 1951. It's at about 14,000 feet, and I'm certain that you can get in there with no trouble, but I can't say about coming out. Get 15,000 feet of altitude as you fly up Kahiltna Pass and fly due north until you're over your strip at 10,000 feet. Now, turn your airplane exactly 90 degrees to the right, and directly in front of you will be a large triangular pyramid of granite rock. Fly directly toward it until you are really close, drop some power, pull on your flaps, and fly around the right-hand side of the pyramid. Right in front of you will be your landing spot.' "

These directions were repeating themselves in Sheldon's mind as he glanced ahead through the white haze that hung over Kahiltna Pass. He looked to his right and could see Kitchen flying slightly above and behind his position.

"The Cub was purring like a kitten, and as I made the sharp right turn over my strip at the 10,000-foot level, I began to look for the granite triangle. It wasn't hard to spot, and I put the nose of the airplane on it and flew. Washburn had said to get close, as close as possible, before making my last turn, and I could count the rocks, as I finally rolled into it. Just as I throttled down and began to pull on the flaps, I saw it. Jeez, I was sweating like a champ, and it was the Devil's Canyon bit all over again. The spot looked mighty small and had a brisk slope, but I figured I could make it."

170

Sheldon's landing site had every right to look small, for it was situated on a tiny, shelflike field of snow that tilted upward to the east. It ended abruptly at the foot of a steep slope leading to the top of McKinley, and its lower end deteriorated into a broken jumble of evil-looking crevasses, followed by a staggering cliff. The entire usable surface was only about 2,000 feet long—but it was steep and smooth, and it was where it was needed.

Reducing power slightly, Sheldon flew lower over the tiny area and dropped a line of spruce boughs along the surface upon which he would land. These dark branches would be critical in the actual landing during the next go-around, for he would not be able to gauge his height above the unblemished snow without them.

"The worst part was that this had to be a one-shot deal—no second chance, no nuthin'. Once I lined up on short final here, I would be committed to a landing, like it or not. I knew that I'd have to paint it on or slide backward into the crevasses."

Fortunately, there was little turbulence, and as Sheldon lined up the Super Cub, he had the spooky feeling that he was on a collision course with the mountain, which filled his entire field of vision and rose high above it. Then he reached the point of no return, and his eyes watered with intense concentration.

"I sucked in my breath and played the lower end of that little slope against the crevasses I could see. I knew I had to get every available inch out of the landing surface or risk spreading my airplane and myself all over the side of McKinley."

Sheldon also knew that after he was down, he must continue upslope under full power, for his turnaround must be made just scant feet short of the near-vertical buttress.

During the next few fleeting seconds, with the Super Cub under full power, time stood still. As the shadowy crevasses flickered beneath his skis, he pulled the nose up sharply to match the angle of the snow surface that leaped upward before him. The Super Cub screamed in protest in the thin air as he felt for the snow surface with his skis. Then they touched with a metallic hiss, and he was climbing upslope. The plane bounced gently, and with the steepening face of the buttress leaping toward him, Sheldon kicked hard on the left rudder. The Super Cub turned abruptly, and he pulled the throttle back to idle. Sheldon was now parked crosswise on the slope, his left wing pointing downward at a severe angle. His skis held the plane, and he reached up to flip off the master switch.

Then, to the popping sounds of cooling metal, he began to consider other pressing matters, such as drawing a deep breath.

Don Sheldon thus became the first man to ever land at the unprecedented altitude of 14,300 feet on the western flank of McKinley. Within an hour after touchdown, and sweating profusely with the heavy exertion of snowshoe-packing the fluffy snow, he had the tiny airfield flattened and flagged with orange survey tape and willow wands that he had brought with him. He then got Kitchen, who still circled above him, on the HF radio and told him to "come on in."

"Kitchen was an old flight instructor, and I had told him he had to make the landing with full power on. This is tough to do, because in a normal landing, the power is reduced just before touchdown. In spite of my suggestions, his instincts made him drop some power, and he hit without enough thrust to climb the steep grade and began to slide backward. Luckily, he stopped just short of the crevasses."

It then took Sheldon and a crew of six mountain climbers who happened to be in the area three hours of punishing exertion to push the plane, at full power, upslope to the takeoff position. Just as Kitchen's Super Cub was finally placed on the high end of the short slope near Sheldon's, Paul Crews and Chuck Metzger, on the verge of total physical exhaustion, arrived on the scene pulling the sleeping-bag-swathed Helga Bading on a fiberglass sled that had been airdropped earlier by the Army. They had made the descent, over highly difficult and steep terrain, in 5½ hours and arrived at Sheldon's landing site during midafternoon.

Though she had regained consciousness because of the increased oxygen in the air at 14,300 feet, one glance told Sheldon that Mrs. Bading was in a condition very close to death, in the grip of what the press would term "moaning hysteria." Her skin showed the typical shadings of blue and green that accompany the condition that would soon be recognized as cerebral edema by the medical profession. That she was still alive was a credit to the efforts of both Dr. Rodman Wilson and the two team members who had brought her down to the 14,300-foot level. Dr. Wilson had cared for the woman with limited supplies at the 16,400-foot level, and though still in desperate condition, she was improving at the lower altitude.

After Sheldon and the others had gently loaded the woman aboard the Super Cub, he turned the plane to point it downslope and firewalled the throttle. He knew that this would be another one-shot affair. If he failed to get enough airspeed on the downhill run to fly the airplane, he would plunge into the crevasses or over the edge of the cliff beyond.

The tiny plane grudgingly gained airspeed, hurtling him toward the crevasse field. After what seemed an eternity, the Super Cub's tail came up. Easing back on the stick, he raised the plane's nose just as the last orange marker strip flitted beneath his left wing tip. He was airborne.

With the most difficult part of his first operation at the 14,300-foot strip accomplished, Sheldon set his course for Talkeetna. And now a final figure emerged out of the place from which these momentary heroes come—the obscurity of everyday life in Alaska. His name was Link Luckett, an employee of Hughes Helicopter Service in Anchorage. After returning to Talkeetna with Helga Bading and watching the Air Force medics load her aboard a military aircraft for the trip to Anchorage, Sheldon found Luckett waiting. The balding chopper pilot, flying one of his boss's Hiller two-place copters, had come to render aid and was heading for McKinley.

"Will you fly cover for me?" asked Luckett, after explaining what he had in mind to Sheldon.

"Yowsah, let's put the burn on her."

Luckett's tiny rotor-powered craft was assumed to have an absolute operating ceiling of 16,000 feet, and to assure maximum performance, he had off-loaded his battery (after starting his engine) and all of his emergency gear and had gone light on gasoline, allowing just enough fuel to reach the Day party and attempt rescue operations. Sheldon would accompany Luckett to 17,500 feet, and as they ascended above 10,000, he knew that Luckett had the throttle of his tiny Hiller to the stops. The chopper reluctantly gained altitude, and after what seemed an impossible time period to the circling Sheldon, Luckett miraculously set his fragile craft down on the snow near Day's camp. With this landing, at 17,230 feet, he established an altitude record for this tiny chopper and was the first rescuer to speak personally with the members of the ill-fated team. It was 7:00 p.m. on May 20.

Luckett found that the four men were indeed "fortunate" to be alive. Day's left leg was immobilized by badly torn ligaments, and his hands and feet were badly frozen. The leg had been neatly splinted by Dr. Wilson. Schoening's fingers were puffy and black with frostbite, and he had suffered a severe concussion in the fall. As a result of this concussion, he would remember little of the incident and would suffer memory lapses for some time. One of the Whittaker twins had also received head and neck injuries, and the other suffered frostbite and contusions. All of the men's faces were blistered by exposure, and the injuries had rendered the party immobile. Until this moment, they had been at the mercy of the mountain they had "conquered."

Luckett then instructed the climbers on how to pack down and mark a landing pad, after which he took off empty. Later, at 9:30 P.M., he returned to the scene, and watched by Sheldon who circled overhead, loaded and removed John Day. The climber who had raced with Denali rode uncomplaining, though in excruciating agony, to Sheldon's 14,300-foot landing strip.

Early in the morning of May 21, Luckett made his third and final landing at the top of the world and plucked Pete Schoening from the snow for the relay to 14,300 feet. Meanwhile, the Whittaker twins climbed down to the 14,300-foot level under their own power. Sheldon then relayed the four members of the Day party down to 10,200 feet. Though both Sheldon and Luckett had slept briefly the night before, both were still in a state of near exhaustion, their faces burned by the rarefied sun that was now shining through the clouds.

Although fatigued and weakened by the long period of superhuman effort, during which he had averaged only two or three hours of sleep per day, and the repeated exposure to the oxygen-weak air in which he had worked, Sheldon continued to remove 13 rescue climbers from the 14,300-foot strip and relay them to 10,200 feet. To accomplish the evacuation, he made a total of 18 landings between 3:00 A.M. on May 20 and noon of the next day. Prior to the marathon, he broke for one of his short naps between midnight and 2:00 A.M.

There followed a massive effort with both military and private aircraft to remove the remainder of the rescue teams from the mountain. Thus ended what the news media would herald as "one of the most daredevil and selfless feats in the long history of Alaskan aviation." Today, Sheldon returns only on certain occasions to his 14,300-foot airport on the desolate flank of McKinley's West Buttress. Because of regulations, he uses it only as an emergency landing site, for it is well within the park boundaries.

The June 6, 1960, issue of *Life* carried a full account of the entire rescue, along with pictures taken while it was in progress. Entitled "Intrepid Men vs. Mighty Mac," the article was a precursor of many stories to come, and Sheldon's name would become even more well known as the years passed. The pilot has also flown for numerous movie and television productions, including *Bold Adventure, Ice Palace, The Sourdough Sky,* and the highly controversial release, *Wolf Man.*

Recently, Sheldon has been much sought after for magazine and newspaper interviews. When asked to authenticate what has been written about him, he smiles modestly.

"Don't believe a word you read. Most of it's a pack of lies."

It was over. The long sleepless nights, the tension, and the depressing weather that had been Sheldon's constant companions during the long and arduous rescue were finally at an end. During what he succinctly calls the "Day-Bading Calamity," Sheldon had felt an oppressive weariness that he had not experienced before, though he is fond of passing if off as "something he got rid of with a good night's sleep." During the many years of mountain flying prior to 1960, he had, however inadvertently, trained for the rescue of Helga Bading. The harrowing landings at places like the Anderson Glacier with only burning newspapers to mark his landing site, and the sleepless days aloft between them . . . the heart-stopping horror of spinning to earth among the giant cottonwoods en route to Anchorage, and the strange elation of walking away to fly again—these and many other no-way-out situations, coupled with "routine" flying that most experienced pilots would not try even on a one-shot basis, have prepared Sheldon for the unique task of aiding the Helga Badings of this world. Don Sheldon is not a totally modest individual, but neither is he a showman. Incredibly, he considers his line of work as much a routine as does a professional skier or fireman. Many of the stories that people tell about his flying are exaggerations, but because the facts are unbelievable, even the most accurate of these fabrications falls short of describing what Don Sheldon really does.

During the 1960 season alone, while flying and servicing 15 major expeditions, Sheldon spent more hours on Mount McKinley than in

Talkeetna. Since that year, it is a rare season that does not see the pilot singlehandedly do the flying for at least that many mountain crews, along with countless other trips that are made in behalf of fishermen, hunters, miners, homesteaders, and sight-seeing tourists. During the 1973 season, he flew 22 climbing parties, with a total of more than 200 men and several tons of gear, in either his new turbo-supercharged Cessna 180 or his tiny yellow Super Cub. Sheldon is still capable of performing within the tightly controlled boundaries of his self-imposed minimums, and the sometimes-stated pilot's adage of growing old at a mile a minute seems remote.

Almost as if by prior arrangement, the balance of the 1960 season and the year that followed would be a relatively quiet period for Talkeetna Air Service. A normal season's activity has always been described as a "Chinese fire drill" by Sheldon, but he chuckles as he says it and would be disappointed were it any different.

In 1960, notwithstanding the "Day-Bading Calamity," even the mountains were kinder to the relatively small number of climbers that came to the Alaska Range. In late August, Brad Washburn's highly detailed map, which Sheldon described as "the most accurate in the world," had been published in Switzerland. As a result of his leadership in the survey that produced this map, Washburn has become known throughout the world as the leading expert on the physical aspects of Alaska's mountains, especially those of the McKinley Group. Mountain climbers of all nations constantly have sought out Washburn for detailed information and advice on the feasibility of ascent routes.

In 1957, Brad Washburn had published a lengthy article on McKinley in *The Mountain World*, the bible of alpine climbers. Profusely illustrated with large aerial photographs, the article not only described in great detail the major routes that had been climbed on Mount McKinley but it also listed in considerable detail the unclimbed challenges for the expert mountaineer.

The last paragraph states: "Last and probably the most difficult and dramatic of all potential new routes on Mt. McKinley is the great central bulge in the fabulous 10,000-foot South Face of the mountain. While expert alpinists may argue that most routes on McKinley are difficult because of their length, the cold, or their isolation, *this* route may be classed as unequivocally excellent climbing from start to finish."

The South Face was obviously Alaska's greatest mountaineering opportunity. Riccardo Cassin, one of history's greatest mountaineers, read this article and rose to the challenge. He wrote Brad about his plans. For months, letters and pictures went back and forth between Boston and Italy.

Finally, in July 1961, when Alaskans were "roasting" in the heat of 85-degree days and the big mountain to the northwest of town was all but lost in the swimming heat mirage that rose from the lush lowlands at its feet, Cassin and his team arrived in Talkeetna to attempt the "impossible" climb. The small flamboyant 52-year-old Italian, who was a sporting-goods and mountaineering-equipment manufacturer from Lecco, Italy, led a crew of seven, five of whom were professional rope artists. Sheldon was shocked to learn that only one member of the Cassin Expedition, Bob Goodwin, of Fairbanks, had ever actually seen McKinley. On many occasions, Sheldon had studied the route with which Cassin would do battle, the Central Rib of McKinley's unconquered South Face, and nowhere else had he felt the overwhelming sheerness of the mountain so vividly. When he flew along the towering, near-vertical wall of jagged, snow-swept granite pinnacles, he felt like a tiny gnat, and the bleak loneliness that he experienced on those occasions had been crushing. The South Face, with its scarlike Central Rib running like a distended artery to the summit, was the creator of high-altitude shear turbulence. It was an evil place, this South Face, this home of powerful and unrelenting winds. That Cassin could succeed where all others had feared to try was a possibility that Sheldon could accept were it not for the fact that the man knew little about the mountain.

For many years, Sheldon had been in the mountaineering business just as surely as were the men who clung to fixed lines as they fought their own battles with oxygen starvation, cold, and high winds. He knew the intricacies of the art, and he knew climbers.

The five Italians who accompanied Cassin were veterans of the peaks of Europe and the Himalayas. They had been selected by the 8,000-member Alpine Club of Italy from the elite 15-member Spider Group. Of the three Americans who joined the Italians, two had so exaggerated their abilities in preclimb letters to Cassin that he would later, at 11,000 feet, request Sheldon to remove the almost totally incompetent pair from the mountain. To fill out his crew, Cassin had written the American Alpine Club for their recommendation of one climber, and the name that came back was Bob Goodwin. Goodwin later left the expedition at 17,000 feet because of prior commitments. So only the six Italians would ultimately attempt the South Summit via the South Face approach.

The Italians knew rock climbing in all its forms. Their physical qualifications could not be faulted, and they were well equipped. Cassin manufactured the finest sporting goods and mountaineering gear in all of Europe, and he spent $10,000 equipping his crew. For morale purposes, he had even provided two complete sets, one blue and one red, of sweaters and socks as climb "uniforms." When Goodwin agreed to become a team member, Cassin requested his measurements so that he could completely outfit Goodwin with custom-made gear. In addition to all this, Cassin brought 300 cans of beer and a supply of wine and cognac, a sure sign that no expense was being overlooked. These liquid "essentials" for a truly enjoyable climb were "rationed" to a can each for climbers returning to camp on hot days. Finally, Cassin and his countrymen often spent "all afternoon in base camp preparing gourmet-quality spaghetti with all the trimmings."

There were few aspects of high climbing that were strange to the Italians, but on the awesome South Face, they would find one they had not yet encountered—the merciless weather fluctuations and chill factors of Mount McKinley. In the years to come, other groups would also learn from bitter experience to account in their preparations for McKinley's extreme cold, produced by the combination of low ambient air temperatures and wind. Sheldon, knowledgeable in the weather phenomena on the mountain, broached the subject to the confident Italians while they camped on the skirt of his runway in Talkeetna, but he could not persuade them to supplement their preparations with more suitable footgear.

"In Europe, they climb differently than in Alaska, and the tremendous chill factors encountered here are not found over there. European climbing shoes and other types of leather footgear are designed to protect your ankles and not for warmth. I knew that even a moderate wind of say 30 miles per hour could produce temperatures on the skin of 10 degrees below zero at 16,000 feet. But Cassin was confident that the weather would be good to them on the climb."

And so, with the talking done, Sheldon took the Italians to the mountain, and the epic assault of the South Face began.

"After camping on a 3-foot ledge at 14,000 feet, where they had to tie themselves to the face so as not to roll into space during the night, they climbed to the 17,000-foot level in moderate weather conditions and were experiencing no particular problems. They had just a shade over 3,000 feet to go before they reached the South Summit, and this approach was extremely steep, and so sheer that even hardened climbers, looking down at it from the summit edge, shook their heads in awe. Many mountaineers of international fame had looked upon the South Face of McKinley and counted it as an impossibility. It was just too steep to climb in the kind of weather that the big mountain was famous for."

But Brad Washburn and Riccardo Cassin felt differently.

The Cassin Expedition had been climbing almost straight up in alternate areas of jagged granite and ice and were like tiny flies clinging to the side of a stucco building. At 17,000 feet, the weather became a force to reckon with. The wind had been building for some time and now began to gust heavily, buffeting the climbers as they inched their way upward. They were employing the classic techniques of hard rock and ice climbing, using pitons, ice screws, and all the other specialized tools of the trade, in the use of which they were expert, to secure fixed lines as they progressed. The pitch was so steep in many places, that they climbed barehanded and used rope ladders; this was "direct-aid climbing." Even the wind, which was becoming severe, could be endured, but there was one phenomenon that could not—freezing rain. With its coming, visibility dropped, clothing and leather footgear became wet, and the face of the mountain was soon encased in glasslike ice. Then the temperature plunged, and the wind reached the intensity of a full gale.

"Riccardo Cassin and his crew were caught in a murderous storm that lasted three days and three nights. With the wind roaring across the South Face, the chill factor was 10 to 30 degrees below zero in spite of the fact that it was mid-July. Throughout the duration of the storm, the climbers, in an unbelievable display of superhuman will, clung to the face of the mountain, roped together and tied to driven rock pitons. They would not go down and could not go up. On the third day, the wind died, and with its passing, the air temperature rose. Some of them were, by now, badly frostbitten. I was highly concerned and was continually watching their progress. I knew that they were in trouble but could only watch from the cockpit of the Cub. It was a frustrating experience."

Sheldon had experienced this frustration often. He is as much the slave of the mountain, perhaps even more so where weather is concerned, as those who climb it. Even in the event that an emergency was declared and somehow transmitted to him, he could not help Cassin now. This situation has often arisen. Because of the Park Service rule, only in cases of dire emergency can a landing be made within the park boundaries to rescue members of a noncertified party; that is, one climbing without a scientific permit. There were no alternatives now, for if there were, Cassin and his crew would not be clinging for their lives with frost-blackened hands to the South Face.

"When the storm broke, the wind moderated and I figured they would have no alternative but to come back down. I didn't see how they could make it, because I knew they were in bad straits. As I came in for another look, I couldn't believe my eyes—*they were going up.*"

Sheldon would later describe this ascent as one of the most amazing feats he had ever witnessed on any mountain under any conditions, and he watched, fascinated. Bradford Washburn later cited the climb as "the greatest achievement in American mountaineering history."

"They continued up the face, but at an extremely slow rate. After what seemed like a week, they reached the summit, to become the first men to ever scale the great South Face of the mountain."

Cassin had conquered the unconquerable, but the excruciating pain he and his party suffered on the ascent almost completely obscured the joy of victory. Their faces were cracked and charred with advanced frostbite. The feet of all but one member were frost-swelled, some to grotesque size, and their hands were almost useless with the blue cold. One crew member, whose boots had remained drier than others during the ascent rain, gave them to another whose feet were badly frozen (Jack Canali) and somehow made the descent in his socks. In the wretched air at 20,320 feet, all exhilaration that their success might have afforded under other circumstances was numbed as they faced the reality of the descent, which must now be made—and quickly. So desperate were these men that the simple act of setting up the numerous commemorative expedition flags at the summit was an ordeal, and no pictures were taken. Standing as they were, on the high end of the short, wind-compacted ridge that is the South Summit, they were isolated from any and all help. They must return the way they had come—on the fixed lines stretching downward almost two miles to the base of the South Face of McKinley—or perish.

"How they made it, I will never know, but they slowly retraced their steps, and when they came off the rope just above 11,000 feet, I was waiting. It had been an endurance test that made the hair on my neck stand straight out. They looked like walking dead men, but Cassin had won. They had one guy named Canali on a sled when I got there, and I had to carry him from the plane to the ambulance in Anchorage. They named the route of the great South Face in Cassin's honor."

Later, Bob Goodwin would recommend that Cassin be voted an honorary member of the prestigious American Alpine Club, and as a result, the Italian became one of a handful of men to whom this honor has been accorded. The route that bears his name is a fitting additional tribute for the durable Cassin and his crew. There have been few since that 19th day of July 1961 who have been tempted to climb the South Face. Of those who have, two have died. Jerrold R. Smith and John Luz were killed in a fall from the 13,500-foot level on the West Rib of the South Face on April 29, 1970. At the time of the first ascent of the South Face by Cassin, the South Summit of McKinley had been attained no less than 23 times via other more accommodating routes. The South Face route via the great Central Rib was the last of the true challenges offered by Denali.

Though Sheldon's part in the ultimate success of the Cassin Expedition was minimal, he was the only man alive to observe the entire ordeal at close range. That he was impressed with the skill he saw demonstrated there on McKinley's South Face would be a gross understatement, and he was awed not so much by the successful accomplishment of the first ascent of McKinley's most dangerous approach but by the raw courage that Cassin and his crew had needed to pull it off. Sheldon is no stranger to courage, and because of this, he will never forget the intrepid Italians and the year 1961.

"Both Sides of the Fence"

They called him "Saltpeter" Johnson, and he lived in a sod-roofed log cabin on the Chulitna River near Talkeetna. None of the locals really knew where he came from, but it was common rumor that he had once sailed around the Horn on a Norwegian windjammer. He lived alone, seldom came to town, and either caught or shot everything that he deemed necessary to assure his solitary happiness. Once in a while, he would slip into the B & K General Store to purchase some Rye Krisp and a few cans of sardines, but beyond these occasional forays to the "big city," solitude was his game, and he made all the rules. Saltpeter didn't like snoops. He demonstrated his dislike conclusively one day by shooting down a helicopter that hovered too low over the potato patch that grew in the sod of his cabin roof. The old-timer did have one redeeming grace—he could predict the long-term winter weather in any given year with uncanny accuracy.

If the north wall of his cabin was uncovered and exposed to the weather, the locals believed that a very mild winter could be expected. If a moose hide covered the wall, a moderate winter would ensue. Late November of 1962 had seen both a moose and a grizzly hide flapping gently in the cold wind on the north wall of Saltpeter Johnson's cabin on the Chulitna.

Though there were those who scoffed at the old man's reputation, Sheldon was not one of them. As he lifted the ski-equipped Cessna 180 from the Talkeetna strip on February 28, 1963, and passed over

Saltpeter's cabin on a northerly heading, he thought about the old man and the bitter cold that had persisted during the preceding weeks.

"I had some photographers aboard, and the trip was scheduled to last ten days. They had chartered me to fly them to the north coast to photograph polar bears and other wildlife."

The flight, with stops at Ruby, Kotzebue, and Point Hope, would terminate at Point Barrow, and all went well. On the last leg of the trip, along the shore ice between Point Hope and Barrow, they spotted a number of the white bears, and the men with the cameras had high hopes. But during the following week, because of the badly broken and rough ice Sheldon found it difficult and often impossible to land the crew on the ice pack. So he suggested that they return to Point Hope, where the crew could hire Eskimos with dog-sleds to take them out onto the ice.

"The 180 was too heavy for the kind of landings that these guys needed, and I knew that in addition to the natives with their sleds, there were several pilots with Super Cubs operating out of Point Hope who would be glad to charter the photographers. The Super Cubs would do the job, and since the ten days we'd agreed on were about up, we headed for Point Hope."

When the photographers were finally set up for at least an additional week on the ice, Sheldon decided to return to Talkeetna. As he lifted the Cessna off the packed snow of the Point Hope runway and set a southerly course along the coast, he looked ahead. The view at 2,000 feet confirmed the weather forecast that he had received just before takeoff. Dark clouds were piling up on the south horizon and racing inland over the snow-covered forelands.

"I landed at Kotzebue, gassed the plane, and immediately took off for Galena, about 200 miles to the south. The weather still looked ominous, and it seemed to be getting worse."

Sheldon figured that he was flying into a weather condition described by meteorologists as an overrunning warm front. The mass of moist less-dense warm air at higher altitudes, in this case moving at a rate of about 50 miles per hour, literally slides over the dense colder air layer below. The movement of such an overrunning front is almost invariably accompanied by high winds and extremely bad weather.

"The winds aloft were from the southwest while the wind at ground level was running from the west. I began to experience moderate to heavy turbulence, and it had started to snow. With the weather falling apart I decided to make a landing at either Nome or Moses Point."

After a quick position check, Sheldon decided on the tiny settlement of Moses Point, on the northwest coast of Norton Bay opposite Cape Denbigh. He landed in a heavy snowstorm. Prior to his arrival, he had encountered very heavy turbulence and icing conditions.

"The heavy storm had moved into the area at a tremendous rate, and there was no relief in sight, so I tied down the Cessna and decided to sit it out."

Sheldon holed up for two days in the FAA station at Moses Point. On the third morning, it began to clear over Cape Darby to the southwest. Because of the pattern that the moving storm had followed, he decided to set a course for the town of McGrath, on the Kuskokwim River.

"McGrath is south-southeast of Moses Point, and before I left, I checked the weather. Clearing skies along my route were predicted, and the storm seemed to be moving out."

The forecast was wrong. After an hour and a half, Sheldon again began to encounter turbulence, accompanied by more heavy, wet snow. He was forced to fly south to avoid the weather, which seemed to be still concentrated along the Kuskokwim Mountains.

"I was about 100 miles southwest of McGrath, and the weather, though localized, was extremely severe, so I decided to land at the old mining village of Flat. I topped off my tanks and spent about an hour shooting the breeze with some of the old-timers there. The snow had quit, and I looked at a fairly high overcast, about 5,000 or 6,000 feet. It didn't look too bad, so I started the engine and continued on my way to McGrath.

"Within ten minutes, I was again in another tremendous storm. I tried to return to Flat and found that the damned weather had closed in behind me. All I could do was play her by ear, so I flew for about 3½ hours looking for a landing possibility."

At this point, Sheldon was west of McGrath and skirting the Kuskokwim Mountains of south-central Alaska, rugged ranges of peaks that jut a moderate 5,000 to 6,000 feet above sea level.

"The aircraft was picking up ice on the wings, and the windshield had frosted over."

During the past hour, Sheldon's predicament had deteriorated from bad to highly dangerous. The powerful Cessna was heavy and slow to respond to control pressures. He could only see what lay ahead through a small spot on the lower portion of the windshield, where the defroster fought its own losing battle with the storm outside. The ghostly patches of spruce and rocky ridges that slipped by in the swirling snow were barely discernible. In a relatively short period of time, the high-performance aircraft had become a cocoon-like death trap.

"My objective was to put her down at the first opportunity. After looking over five or six possibilities, either the location would fade from view, or I'd make a cautious turn and try to get a second look—then I'd overfly the place and lose it."

Sheldon was now experiencing the often fatal "series of difficulties" that are grim companions to airplane disasters—subtle changes in flight conditions which magnify themselves at a breathtaking rate that often precludes any possibility of escape. There have been only a few times during his flying career that he has been caught in the vicious circle of events like those that engulfed him over the Kuskokwim Mountains.

He glanced at the dancing fuel gauges in the dimly lit instrument panel and saw that the white needles were nudging the empty mark on both tanks. With each fleeting minute, the airplane was growing more sluggish and difficult to control. In addition, what little light remained in the gray sky was quickly disappearing, and the swirling snow made forward visibility through the tiny hole melted in the ice on the windshield almost nonexistent.

"By now, the ice on the wings was so heavy that I dared not turn the plane or I'd stall. Most of the time, the mountains below me were lost in the snow, and what I could see of them looked mighty poor for a landing."

It was becoming increasingly difficult to hold the plane in level flight, and finding a place to land was imperative. As the gloomy, snow-blurred ridges flashed beneath him, Sheldon's right hand automatically reached for the radio mike on the panel.

"Ah, McGrath radio—Cessna 39er Tango."

"39er Tango, McGrath—Go ahead."

"Roger, Sam. I'm unable to continue and will put her down as soon as I get the chance. I'll radio position at that time."

"Ah, Roger 39er Tango—good luck, Don."

Sam Huff's voice was detached, and with its professional modulation, seemed almost insincere, but Sheldon knew that Sam would stay with him whatever happened.

"About this time, I got a quick glimpse of a fairly gradual slope running up the mountain ahead of me, and I knew it was now or never."

Sheldon tipped the nose of the heavy Cessna slightly and eased back on the throttle cautiously. He knew that with the heavy load of ice he carried, to slow the trundling plane too much would be inviting instant disaster. He also knew, however, that if he did not slow the plane enough he was risking a possibly fatal overshoot of his newfound "runway."

The Cessna settled heavily through the blowing snow and landed as though physically tired, the skis plowing twin trails in the fluffy snow of the slope. The 180's inertia died quickly as it slid upslope in the soft snow, the spring-steel landing-gear struts flexing gently. Finally all motion stopped.

During the entire landing, Sheldon had seen only a fleeting glimpse of snow-covered ground as he flared the plane at what he felt to be the right distance from the surface of the snow. If he had been too high, the plane would have stalled and possibly plunged nose first into the mountain. Had he been too low, he would not, in all probability, have had even that brief glimpse of white snow just before the skis touched down.

After shutdown, the silence was broken only by the drumming wind and the slight metallic clicking of the cooling engine. As the gyros wound down, the falling snow began to cover the silver plane.

"After I got stopped, I cranked up the HF radio again, and talked with my friend Huff at Northern Consolidated. I told him that the closest I could come on my position was that I was somewhere in the Kuskokwims, possibly near Von Frank Mountain, at about 5,000-foot elevation according to my altimeter. I signed off immediately because I didn't want to waste my battery."

Sheldon's situation had improved from potentially fatal to simply dangerous in the flicker of a few fleeting moments. That he was alive and unhurt was a minor miracle, and even more amazing, the Cessna had sustained no apparent structural damage in the blind landing. His final glimpse through the ice-free spot in the Plexiglas windshield before touching down had told him little about where

187

he was, and even what he had seen was now being covered by the heavily falling snow outside. In addition, the wind was now doing its best to drive the airplane over onto its back.

"I knew that my first job, besides keeping the engine warm, was to secure the plane. It was getting dark fast, and I wanted to get the job done while I could still see. I carried a French-made Thermex portable heater, which I filled with Blazo [white gas] to set under the cowling."

Sheldon grabbed a pair of snowshoes from the rear compartment and pushed the Cessna's door open. He was immediately struck by a driving wall of heavy, blowing snow. Staggering against the strong wind, he quickly located a clump of small gnarled spruce trees, which clung to the slope. After cutting several bundles of branches, he carried them back to the plane. With the nose of a snowshoe, he excavated a large hole in the snow beneath each wing strut and buried the spruce bundles after carefully attaching nylon lines to them. The lines were then tied to the wings of the lurching Cessna.

It was dark and cold, but Sheldon was perspiring heavily when he crawled back into the airplane to appraise his situation. In the dark, the only sounds were the humming wind and the dry hiss of the snow being driven against the aluminum skin of the plane. The snow continued unabated throughout the long night and the following day. Then, instead of stopping, it grew worse.

"I spent each day trying to stay ahead of the snow. I had to dig the plane out of the drifts on three different occasions, and in between diggings, I packed down about a 2,000-foot runway down the slope with the snowshoes, against the great event of flying out of the place."

Sheldon also cut and dragged more of the stubby, cold-brittled spruce to the edge of his crude runway and piled them in three separate heaps.

"The three piles of spruce were to be burned as signal flares, when and if they were needed. In my survival gear, I carried a brand-new five-gallon can of Blazo fuel, which I could dump in the spruce to make it light in a hurry. I made three piles of spruce because this is the International Distress Code signal in a situation of this kind."

There were a number of good reasons why Sheldon could not

risk an attempt to fly out during the infrequent and barely notice-able lulls in the storm, but the snow, which never stopped, and his almost empty wing tanks were at the head of the list. Although he did not know his location, he was not in any immediate danger, for the plane was well stocked with emergency rations and gear. His big Woods down sleeping bag would keep him warm while he slept, and for the moment, he was in good shape.

Sheldon figured that if he were to spend any considerable amount of time on the bleak slope waiting for the help that he expected, he would make his preparations "by the numbers."

"My radio still was functional, but my battery was becoming run down, so the procedure was to run the engine for short periods of time on the little gas I had left while I operated the radio. When the aircraft had come to a stop, it was pointed uphill at a steep angle, and while talking with Huff at McGrath on the third day, I noticed that the engine was faltering as though it wanted to quit."

Sheldon quickly identified the problem. The steep angle at which the plane rested had been retarding the flow of the remaining gaso-line to the carburetors. His solution was to crib the Cessna's tail up to a level attitude, after quickly checking to determine if the tanks had finally given up their final drop of fuel.

"On the fourth day, the storm was becoming intermittent, and I made another call to McGrath. Huff's voice was understandable but snarled in static."

"The Air Force is up and flying a grid pattern with some F-4Us over the area. When you hear the sonic boom, note the exact time and direction and call me," Huff said.

Sheldon heard the jets at 7 minutes past 10 o'clock that night and notified Huff at McGrath, "I think they're about 40 miles to my southwest. The time—22:07 hours."

Sheldon finished his transmission by asking Huff for "30 gallons of 80/87 fuel." From the information given by Sheldon on this trans-mission, the Air Force was able to plot his position.

Before clearing with Sheldon, Huff verified that he had read the pilot's last transmission and promised the gas as soon as somebody spotted him. Sheldon shut down the radio and began to listen for the telltale roar of jet engines and watch the clearing skies for a possible closer pass by the fighters.

"On the morning of the next day, I heard a transport aircraft approaching. It sounded like a C-54, and in the cold air, and at 20 miles, I thought he was right on the side of the mountain with me. I jumped into the plane and cranked up the radio. I told him over the 3411 frequency that I was socked in among mountain peaks and advised him to return the next day. The transmission took the last spark out of my batteries."

For the first time since his skidding stop on the snow-blasted mountainside, Sheldon could afford to relax. He was quite certain that the military had his approximate position located, and with a little help from the weather, he would soon be on his way. During the night, the weather began to break, and the wind died. The still air brought bitter cold, and when Sheldon crawled out of his sleeping bag the next morning, his outside air thermometer read exactly 40 degrees below zero.

While eating his breakfast of bologna, cheese, and an orange, he thought about those other pilots who had not been as fortunate as he, the ones who left their airplanes after only a few days to wander aimlessly through the snow-choked spruce and downed timber trying to get out. Many of them left their planes never to be seen again, or at best, their bones might later be found by some moose hunter or trapper.

Later that morning, with the coming of the 11:00 A.M. sunrise, the military C-54 returned. When he heard the first distant throbbing of the plane's engines, Sheldon wrenched open the Cessna's door and hit the snow running. As he ducked under the wing, he grabbed up the can of Blazo fuel and headed directly for the first of the three piles of spruce that he had gathered earlier. After dousing the piles with the Blazo, he threw a match on the first. It flared briefly without smoke and promptly went out. He tried the second and third piles, but the results were the same. When he threw the last match, the C-54 was only five miles from his perch on the mountainside.

"The Blazo was just burning right off the spruce without igniting it. It was bitterly cold, and I figured I'd had it for this time around, but I soon discovered that they didn't really need the flares. They knew right where I was. They overheaded me three times, and after the third pass, I was certain that they had me spotted because they pulled up and flew a wide circle."

Minutes later, the big airplane slowed down and slanted toward his position on the mountain. He watched with vast relief as three parachutes blossomed below and to the rear of the C-54, which pulled up and disappeared in the direction from which it had first come.

"The chutes landed quite near, and would you believe, the cans were filled with 30 gallons of dirty water."

The big plane returned from a different direction.

"This time they dropped six cans which contained 30 gallons of the most beautiful, bright-red 80/87 gasoline that I had ever seen."

The explanation of the fuel "mix-up" would come later, and Sheldon chuckles dryly as he remembers the military grins that accompanied it.

"We had worked very closely for years, and some of my friends in the C-54 thought it would be a real joke if they dropped the phony gas, which actually turned out to be dishwater. *It was hilarious.*"

The fuel drop had been made during the late afternoon, and Sheldon elected to hold fast in view of the failing light and go for an early-morning takeoff.

The next day dawned bright and clear. Sheldon busily roped the rimey frost of the previous night from the wings. He had, as always, chamoised every drop of the gasoline while pouring it into the thirsty wing tanks.

"The tanks were a long way from full, but it was all that I needed for 2½ hours in the air."

With the flight surfaces cleaned of frost, he began the arduous task of turning the heavy Cessna to a downhill position for the takeoff.

"This is a big job, especially when you're alone with a ton of airplane on skis. About that time, I heard a small aircraft approaching, and a few minutes after it landed, I was talking with my old friend Sam Parent from the Red Devil Mine near Flat, which, it turned out, was not far away. He'd been searching for me right from the time the storm began to break up and was a welcome sight."

The two pilots quickly turned the nose of the Cessna downslope, and with Parent off first, Sheldon firewalled the throttle. Lurching heavily, the silver plane crawled from its hole in the snow and picked up ground speed as it accelerated down the steep slope.

As the wings glinted in the early-morning sunlight, he gave his thanks for close friends who fly airplanes and the tiny portable heater that had ensured the start of the engine that now pulled 9339 Tango smoothly through the 40-below-zero air. Later, as he overflew the tiny settlement of McGrath, with its slowly rising spires of smoke from wood-fed barrel stoves, he pondered the thought that he had now "been on both sides of the fence." For the first time in his long flying career, he had been the object of an organized search by military aircraft.

Emergency on 3411

In 1962, the jeep was already old, with gouged paint and missing windshield. In some perverse way, the vehicle's decrepit appearance pleased the mechanically scrupulous Sheldon. The jeep constituted the entire Talkeetna Air Service ground fleet. It had been used on countless missions within a stone's throw of town, its range limited, among other things, by the degree of physical torture its driver and passengers were willing to endure. It had, however, served faithfully in the hauling of uncounted tons of mountain gear, drummed gasoline for Sheldon's airplanes, game meat, trophy horns, and most of the other freight that is part of the air-charter business. The odometer had been turned back several times, and it had finally quit working about the time the muffler fell off. To ride with Sheldon in this steed of dubious vintage was an experience not to be taken lightly, for even today, the man who daily becomes one with a sophisticated airplane costing $45,000 and capable of cruising at 145 miles per hour has, generously speaking, seemingly never learned the intricacies of traveling one-tenth that speed on the ground.

In fairness to Sheldon, there is an obvious reason for the erratic course he follows as he travels the fortunately unpopulated roads in the vicinity of Talkeetna. He is driving as he would fly, and while an airplane will hold a given course when properly trimmed, a jeep will not. This simple fact does not apparently concern Sheldon, who casually releases the wheel to search for the bag of toasted soybeans or other munchies that he always seems to have on hand. While his passenger is silently attempting to push his right foot through the floor, Sheldon casually glances up to adjust the slow flight of the vehicle in the direction taken by the road. He then refocuses his attention on whatever he is doing at the time, usually opening the goodies preparatory to offering some to his rider. At the present moment in early May 1962, however, the old jeep was safely parked in the forenoon shade of the railroad station a half block from Sheldon's office. The pilot, his eyes closed and his knit cap tipped back on his head, relaxed behind the wheel as he waited for the northbound train. He was tired.

Sheldon had arrived early, and the place was almost devoid of the regulars who daily wandered over to "meet the train." In one of his rare chances to idle away a few minutes, he silently toted up the climbers that were now on the mountain and under his care.

"The previous two days had been another hassle, and I'd just finished an uninterrupted 36-hour stretch, flying climbers in to McKinley and elsewhere. I had 60 climbers on the mountains and had wanted to put the burn on her while the good weather held."

One of the first parties that Sheldon had moved out was led by a "mountain climber extraordinaire." He was a German named Helmut Raithel, who, with a crew of six handpicked German and American experts, would attempt to scale Mount Russell, to the southwest of Mount Foraker and the McKinley Group. Raithel was one of many "old-school, old-world climbers," who, like others of their breed, have amassed brilliant careers in mountaineering the world over. He was a stern, hawk-eyed veteran, and his crew bore the unmistakable aura of having already measured up to his high expectations.

Mount Russell, a deceptively unimpressive 11,670 feet in height, had until 1962 been tried but remained unclimbed, principally because of the nature of the steep grade that must be overcome on all quadrants. The almost vertical sides of the entire mountain formed an unbroken, inverted cone of jagged, snow-encrusted granite. Raithel had chosen a worthy adversary on this his first climb in the Alaska Range.

After their arrival at Talkeetna in a murky overcast, Raithel and his crew had been grounded by continuing foul weather for several days, and when it finally broke, Sheldon and Raithel made a quick hop to the mountain. After studying the peak from the air, they mutually agreed upon a possible landing site on the Northwest Approach. Mount Russell is located near the settlement of Farewell on the Kuskokwim River's rocky South Fork, a place that Sheldon soberly describes as "the home of the winds."

"The jet-stream winds often dip toward the peaks of the Alaska Range. Monumental forces of moving warm frontal systems from the Gulf of Alaska crash headlong into semistationary continental polar cold fronts from the north side of the range. I had delivered the last of Raithel's gear to their base camp on the Northwest Approach and before I headed back, I noticed a distant roar from the direction of Mount Russell's summit. This indicated the approach of high-velocity winds. I could see great blocks of ice, some rock, and plumes of snow being swept from the summit and decided to get out quick.

"I immediately took off down-glacier just as the wind overtook my brand-new Cessna. I jumped crevasses and boulder piles for about a mile before clearing the glacier surface. Once airborne, I made a 180-degree turn into the wind and skyrocketed to 14,000 feet. I now planned to cross the range at Kahiltna Pass, and when I arrived there, I was shocked to find that I was flying backward, with the airspeed redlined at 192 miles per hour. All I would have needed at that point was some turbulence, and structural failure would surely have followed. I banked gently, got with the wind, and roared over to Minchumina, where I sat out the blow."

A slight creaking and expansion of the rails and the distant muted blast of air horns announced the arrival of the northbound train from Anchorage. It jogged Sheldon from his musings and reminded him that he was about to meet the ninth and last member of another expedition.

Sheldon had never met the man, a famous surgeon, but he had no trouble spotting him. Tall, distinguished, and sporting a monocle and saber scars, the man, called Dr. Von Wetzel by the rest of his crew, alighted from the train amid the hissing of locked air brakes and the thrumming idle of the diesel engine. Sheldon jumped out of the jeep to shake his hand, and the two were soon stowing both of Von Wetzel's well-worn medical bags in the jeep. With the usual amenities properly put to rest, the surgeon, who had covertly been studying the pilot, looked into Sheldon's bloodshot eyes, sighed deeply, and in a loud voice, expressed his professional opinion as to the treatment he deemed necessary for Sheldon's obvious state of exhaustion.

"Young man, vot you need, is a good night's sleep—alone."

Sheldon will always be amused by this completely erroneous diagnosis as to the cause of his fatigue by a world-famous surgeon of Von Wetzel's stature.

"We departed Talkeetna within 30 minutes of Von Wetzel's arrival. Despite his height of 6½ feet, I got the mustachioed surgeon, his two medical bags, and the rest of his gear wedged into the airplane, and as I climbed toward 6,000 feet, I tuned 3411 on the radio."

Sheldon and many other bush pilots of the north stand watch on the HF band whenever they can while aloft. This band is a prime source of random traffic, including distress calls originating from other airplanes and ground-base radios.

Sheldon leveled the Cessna as the altimeter wound to 6,000 feet, trimmed the plane, and automatically matched the directional gyro with the magnetic compass. Then, over the sounds of the smoothly drumming engine and the slight buzz of static, he heard the faint but unmistakable voice of someone in trouble.

"The call was originating at a construction camp about 50 miles north of Talkeetna, and we were headed to the northwest."

The frenzied voice on the radio continued in unabated panic, and Von Wetzel scowled slightly as he leaned forward and listened intently.

"Please, please, get some help," pleaded the anonymous voice. "A Caterpillar tractor has just run over one of our men, and he's in awful shape. Please hurry."

Von Wetzel winced at the abruptness in the almost irrational voice and glanced at Sheldon, who was already making the course change that would take them to Troublesome Creek, the scene of the accident. Sheldon asked Von Wetzel if he thought that he could help the man, and the surgeon replied, "Ja. You take me there—but quickly."

In minutes, the camp was under the nose of the Cessna, and Sheldon banked steeply, tipping the silver airplane on its right wing as he rapidly searched for a possible place to land. Luckily the air was smooth and flat, but during those first few moments of searching, this looked like the only blessing that the day was to

196

Ray Genet eating a baked potato after five days of lemon drops high on Mount McKinley.

Lloyd Sumpter, courtesy Terry Cartee

Don Sheldon poses with the John Day Expedition upon their arrival at Anchorage International Airport. Left to right: John Day, Pete Schoening, Sheldon, and the Whittaker twins.

Anchorage Daily Times

Photos by Anchorage *Daily Times*

Opposite page: Rescue camp
at 10,200 feet on the Kahiltna
Glacier. Activities centered
here in the rescues of Helga
Bading and the John Day team.

Sheldon at his 10,000-foot
landing strip. On the skyline,
the "pyramid of granite"
described by Washburn to
guide the pilot to the landing
site at 14,300 feet where
Helga Bading's rescue could
be effected.

A tiny bird in a hostile world.
Sheldon making his epic
flight to rescue Helga Bading.

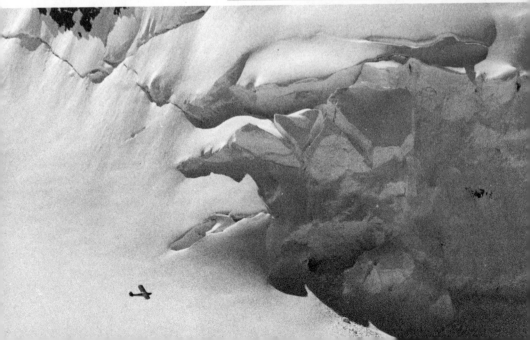

Bradford Washburn

Sheldon's 14,300-foot-high landing site, the highest
on McKinley. Note the crevasse field at the lower end of the
site and the nearly vertical wall at its upper end.

Opposite page (top): Link Luckett
prepares to risk his life to rescue members of
the John Day party, high above.

Opposite page (bottom): Sheldon
flying cover for Luckett in the heroic effort
to reach the Day crew.

Bradford Washburn

McKinley's West Buttress. The route of both the John Day
Expedition and the Anchorage party is at the left. (1) Sheldon's landing
strip at 10,000 feet; (2) Windy Corner; (3) Helga Bading's high camp
at 16,400 feet; (4) the point from which John Day was rescued by Link
Luckett (dotted line shows path of the Day party's fall); (5) South Summit;
(6) Sheldon's landing site at 14,300 feet. (A) The route via the Southwest
Buttress taken by the ill-fated Micheko Sekita team; (B) the point at
15,500 feet where the bodies of Sekita's three team members
were found (dotted line shows path of their fall).

Left to right: Sachiko Watanabe, Micheko Sekita, Alex Bertulis,
Mitsuko Toyama. The Sekita team's five girls occupied this two-man tent.

Tom Stewart, courtesy Alex Bertulis

James Wickwire

Above: Three members of the Sekita team ascending the Kahiltna
Glacier's Northeast Fork. Note the huge packs carried by the tiny
girls and the fact that they are not roped together on this
dangerous crevasse field. Below: The tragic end of a three-week
search. Micheko Sekita kneels beside the body of one of
three companions killed in a fall of nearly 4,000 feet.
In the background, the twisted climbing ropes.

Lloyd Sumpter, courtesy Terry Cartee

Bradford Washburn/Indication of locations by Steve Hackett

McKinley's East Face and the route taken by the doomed Wilcox team in 1967. (1) Harper Ice Fall; (2) Karstens Ridge; (3) upper Harper Glacier; (4) Denali Pass; (5) Archdeacon's Tower; (6) South Summit; (7) North Summit; (8) the area where seven members of Wilcox's team remain to this day.

Bill Babcock (left) and his brother Jeff on McKinley's South Summit after locating some of the lost members of the Wilcox party. Earlier they had found another frozen body in a wind-shredded tent (below) at the party's 17,900-foot camp.

Photos by Gayle Nienheuser

hold. Suddenly, he noticed a stretch of relatively smooth sand along a narrow, brush-studded bar in the creek that meandered near the construction camp, and without his usual cautious second look, simultaneously pulled on full flaps, chopped the throttle, and tipped the nose earthward.

It is said by most airmen that the best landings are the logical result of careful planning. The time allowed for deliberation on this one was severely curtailed by circumstance, but the landing was perfect. The plane rolled to a stop just as the wheels beneath the retractable skis touched the first half inch of creek water at the far end of the river bar.

"We came to a stop just opposite the site of the accident and about 300 yards away."

Von Wetzel, his medical bags clutched one in each hand and his monocle flashing in the sun, unhesitatingly waded the icy, waist-deep creek. He was closely followed by Sheldon, and in minutes, they were crouched at the side of the accident victim, Orville Englehorn, who had indeed been run over by a Caterpillar tractor, a huge D-9 model.

"By the time we got there, there were possibly a dozen members of the construction camp crowding around their injured compatriot. I noticed a cook, complete with a white cap and apron, rushing around and trying to make the victim, who was in excruciating pain, as comfortable as possible. The guy was crushed from his toes to his waist but was still conscious. Von Wetzel went to work immediately and soon had him splinted fore and aft. As I marveled at the job he had done in so short a time, it suddenly dawned on me that I'd never get the guy into the 180, because you couldn't bend him with all those splints."

Sheldon hurried back to the Cessna, reached in to tune the panel radio, and grabbed the mike. He hit the jackpot in one try—by extreme good fortune, a helicopter was cruising in the immediate area. The chopper was soon stirring the dry sand on the river bar as it landed, and in minutes, Sheldon and the others had the moaning construction worker lashed to the side rack of the machine. With a chuffing roar, the copter headed for Talkeetna, where the injured man was transferred to a Civil Air Patrol aircraft for a hurried trip to Anchorage's Providence Hospital.

Sheldon has often been called upon to rush to the scene of countless non-mountain-climbing accidents. Many are the foggy nights that he has been contacted on his base radio by the State Police and asked to rush to a cordoned segment of wet road and land with only the aid of flares and the headlights of patrol cars. He has been no stranger to the mutilation that follows a head-on collision and has, by necessity, become a proficient and knowledgeable medic in his own right. He has learned the symptoms of injuries that make transport even in his airplanes inadvisable, though his airborne ambulance service has accounted for many quick trips to Anchorage and not a few saved lives. Talkeetna is located many miles from the nearest clinic, and there are no doctors in town.

At one time, the pilot even kept a car parked at Merrill Field, Anchorage's oldest major airstrip, which happens to be closer to the hospital than the main airport. The car's purpose was singular— to occasionally provide the fastest available service to the hospital. The system worked well until someone stole the car, stripped the engine from beneath the hood, and deposited what was left of it in the Anchorage dump. Sheldon opted not to replace it.

Seven months after the construction worker was injured by the Caterpillar tractor at Troublesome Creek, Sheldon, on another hospital run to Anchorage, had just delivered his passenger and was walking down the main corridor of the hospital.

"I was surprised to see someone who looked very familiar. It was Englehorn, the man who'd been run over by the D-9. He was walking down the hall with the aid of crutches. After we had talked awhile, I said, 'Orville, tell me. What was the worst part of that whole episode?' "

Englehorn rested on his crutches and looked past Sheldon as he remembered. "I guess you probably think it was the pain," he grinned, "and sure as hell, I'll never forget it, what with my bones crushed clean to my hips. But the worst part was what that damned cook did to me. They no more'n got the Cat off when he comes a-runnin' with a fifth of cheap Scotch, which he forced me to drink, and there ain't *nothing* that I hate worse'n Scotch."

After the side trip to aid Englehorn, the aviator and surgeon had continued to the rendezvous with the latter's crew. Then Sheldon flew to Mount Russell to check on Raithel's progress.

On May 28, 1962, Klaus Ekkerlein, Robert Goodwin, and Peter Hennig, all members of Helmut Raithel's expedition, rested at the summit of 11,670-foot Mount Russell. Like ghosts in the summit haze, with McKinley vague in the background, they stood where

no man had ever stood before, and another neighbor of the towering Denali had been conquered.

Sheldon, more than any other man alive, has had intimate contact with the climbing of the peaks in the majestic McKinley Group.
He has taken part in all of the major first climbs since 1951 and has
shared the heartbreak of those that did not succeed. He is seldom surprised to hear of new innovations that climbers make in
their efforts to reach the high peaks, but Hans Metz, a Swiss mountaineer, had come up with one. It related to the trip down McKinley rather than its ascent—he would ski.

Sheldon liked the irrepressible Metz and was taken with the fact
that he planned to journey cross-country to the mountain from
Talkeetna, climb it with the aid of skis, and then return via the
same route. He agreed to deposit all 1,000 pounds of Metz's expedition gear on the Kahiltna Glacier, at the 7,000-foot level. One of
the expedition members, due to other commitments, had not yet
arrived and had to be flown into the drop area, where he would
join up with the rest of the party for the ski-climb to the South
Summit. Metz and his crew were successful and scaled the summit
with the aid of skis. Due to climbing conditions, it was impossible
for Metz to launch his ski descent from the summit, though he and
his companions did ski much of the long way down. They passed
the 7,000-foot landing site on the way out and eventually returned
to the bank of the Susitna River opposite the village of Talkeetna,
where they were met by a riverboat. On the way out, they had encountered the same difficulties that plagued the Heinrich Harrer
Expedition on the outbound course from Mount Hunter—bad
weather and bears.

On May 17, 1962, just eleven days before three members of the
Raithel Expedition reached the summit of Mount Russell, Metz
was credited with the 24th successful ascent of McKinley's South
Summit, but the first recognized ski descent from the top of the
continent's highest mountain did not occur until early in the month
of July 1970, when two Japanese, Kazuo Hoshikawa and Tsuyoshi
Ueki, accomplished the feat. However, Sheldon disputed their
claim. The pilot asserted that due to 3,000 feet of near-vertical rock
and ice beneath the summit, Hoshikawa and Ueki never actually
skied the *entire* route.

"Only Sylvan Saudan, a Frenchman, came close, skiing the entire
route from 19,300 feet down, and we photographed his descent

down the near-vertical avalanche chute to the 14,300-foot level on the West Approach."

By late 1962, McKinley's now well-known South Summit had been scaled an almost monotonous 30 times. The first lateral via the mountain's South Spur had been made by a 19-man party led by Boyd Everett, who was later killed in an avalanche on the treacherous Dhaulagiri in the Himalayas.

With the passage of time, McKinley, especially its South Summit, was becoming better explored, as were many of the lesser peaks in the McKinley Group. As a direct result, experienced climbers were turning to more and more difficult routes. One of the oldest of all adages began to be proven true—familiarity with the well-known and often-climbed routes was gradually breeding contempt for easy victories. Sheldon, always in tune with the trends in activity on the peak that was becoming known as "his mountain," recognized a change in the character of climbing on and near McKinley and couldn't help but wonder when he would be called upon to once again return to his 14,300-foot emergency runway.

Death on the Mountain

During the winter of 1962, Sheldon took time from his regular schedule to fly to Anchorage for a meeting of a very select aviators' club called the "Quiet Birdmen." Aspiring members of the organization had to meet very rigid and somewhat unusual qualifications, such as a stipulated number of hours aloft during wartime, and though no longer prerequisite, parachuting from an airplane in an emergency or other adverse conditions. Sheldon had met these qualifications as had his close friend Bob Reeve.

Before their departure for the QB meeting that evening, Sheldon met and chatted with Reeve's oldest daughter, the attractive and dark-haired Roberta. To say that she was interested in the famous pilot from Talkeetna would be to understate the truth.

On July 23, 1963, Roberta, with her mother, Tillie, and a friend, traveled north to Sheldon's base of operations for the purpose of "watching the solar eclipse." What factors made the view of this phenomenon more spectacular from Talkeetna are vague, but the day ended with Sheldon flying the three gals back to Anchorage, after a "whirlwind flying tour of the Talkeetna area," which included a stop for dinner at the Chelatna Lake Roadhouse. The pilot, with tongue in cheek, describes the occasion simply as one of "getting better acquainted."

Spring of 1964 began in Talkeetna when the warming weather once again released the Susitna from its hiding place beneath four feet of snow-covered ice. Sheldon was deluged with charter requests.

On March 28, Sheldon flew to Anchorage for Bob Reeve's birthday celebration. The party ended in an all-night discussion of the Good Friday earthquake that had blasted the city at 5:36 local time the evening before and what it had done to the still-shocked city. It was during a lull in the conversation that Roberta asked Don if he might need a secretary to handle the bookkeeping and correspondence for his hectic business in Talkeetna, and Sheldon replied that if he could get the right kind of secretary, "she'd be worth 18 grand a year and board." Reeve chuckled and allowed that opportunity was "rapping with brass knuckles."

Ten years later, having collected only the board, Roberta says she is still looking for the $18,000. Her chiding draws only a chuckle from her pilot husband. Brad Washburn says, "She's worth at least $24,000 a year to Don."

"Women are pretty smart," muses Sheldon. "In a dice game, the smart guys take the resource from the dumb ones; then the women relieve the smart ones of their winnings. Actually, if I paid Roberta twice $18,000 a year, it'd be the best deal in the Far North, 'cause in addition to running the radio, my dear wife bakes great cookies, raises smart beautiful children, grows flowers, answers telephone calls, and cajoles irate fishermen who think I should forget the guys on the mountain and haul them."

On April 11, Sheldon was invited to speak to his friends of the Search and Rescue Section at Elmendorf Air Force Base in Anchorage, and he asked Roberta to accompany him, which she did gladly. Then, after plying his future father-in-law with spicy moose sausage, Sheldon got the courage to propose to Roberta, and they were married on May 16, 1964. The pilot gained a permanent secretary in addition to a mighty fine wife.

Thinking about the sausage that he would no longer be forced to eat, Reeve cracks, "I might have lost a daughter, but I saved my liver."

Predictably, Sheldon planned a flying honeymoon and found upon checking his busy schedule that it would occur coincidentally with the arrival in Talkeetna of Lionel Terray, a French mountaineer of world fame who would later lose his life on a little-known peak in the Swiss Alps. Earlier in the spring, Sheldon had been impressed by a "16-cylinder" letter from Terray requesting that Sheldon transport men and supplies for the assault Terray planned on 12,240-foot Mount Huntington, which, because of its extreme difficulty, had never before been climbed.

But Terray's arrival would not disturb his honeymoon plans, for at this time he had on his payroll three fliers who worked on an as-needed basis. They were handpicked by Sheldon and were competent pilots.

Mike Fisher had flown for Talkeetna Air Service off and on since the late fifties. He was a flight and ground-school instructor in Fairbanks prior to moving to Talkeetna and had worked for the well-known Don Jonz, owner of PanAlaska Airways and a close friend of Sheldon's. In 1972, on a flight between Anchorage and Juneau, Jonz lost his life in the crash of a twin-engined Cessna 310. Also lost were his passengers, U.S. Representative Hale Boggs; Nick Begich, Alaska's lone U.S. representative; and Begich's assistant.

The second pilot, Lynn ("Pedro") Twigg, materialized one day at Sheldon's backyard strip and happened to mention that he "used to fly planes similar to Sheldon's back in Michigan." Sheldon gleefully remembers more of the details of the meeting.

"I really didn't take the guy seriously enough, I guess, and jokingly pointed to a huge stack of freight that weighed about 2,000 pounds and asked him if he knew where Cache Creek was. He says, 'Nope.' I say, 'Here's a chart,' and then I left to make a flight that I had scheduled. When I returned, there sat the Cub with a hot engine and out of gas. The freight was gone and so was Twigg. I was dumbfounded and went looking for him. When I caught up with him, I say, 'Where do you work?' "

"The Alaska Railroad."

" 'How much they paying you over there?' He named the figure, and I say, 'Lookee, I'll double that. Now all you got to do is forget that railroad jazz and come fly for me.' "

So it was that Sheldon hired the crafty and likable Twigg, who now works as a lubrication specialist in a large construction firm for a wage that even Sheldon can't afford.

Sheldon's third pilot, Fred Richards, now a senior captain with Fairbanks-based Wien Air Alaska, was an even older acquaintance of the pilot's than Twigg. On many occasions since the late forties, Richards had assisted with the Talkeetna "flying rat race."

Twigg and the highly capable Richards were the two men that Sheldon designated to fly support for the Terray climb of Mount Huntington. That Sheldon trusted these men explicitly was a high recommendation, and his decision to "take a few days off for a honeymoon" was ironclad proof that he wasn't taking his marriage lightly.

Sheldon remembers the hectic preparations that he made for Terray's arrival, but more than that, he remembers Terray, known as "La Piston" to his fellow climbers and countrymen.

"The Piston of France. He'd climbed about every 'impossible' mountain in Europe and also had spent considerable time climbing in the high peaks of the Himalayas. When not roped to the face of a mountain, he was an undercover agent for the Prefect of Police in Paris. Terray was a tremendous athlete with a brilliant mind, but what made him something special was his liking for tackling the most difficult of climbs imaginable—alone."

Terray had written Brad Washburn and asked for a really challenging goal in the McKinley area for a topflight group of French climbers. The scientist promptly sent him a picture of the Northwest Approach to the forbidding Huntington, with its knifelike summit ridge soaring at an impossible angle upward into the hazy Alaskan sky. When asked about Terray's credentials, Brad Washburn says, "At the time, he was unquestionably France's number-one alpinist."

Terray had decided against tackling the mountain solo and asked Sheldon if he could take him and his crew of eight to the base of Mount Huntington.

"The answer was yes. I had taken six crews to try the mountain, but all of them, though extremely talented, had failed to reach the summit. This means that 60 or 70 very capable mountaineers had tried the route that Terray planned and had not made it. The Northwest Approach has to be seen to be fully appreciated. It's a scimitarlike hogback, almost vertical, that carries a class-six rating in climbing circles."

The original system of grading the difficulties of climbing routes was based upon a sliding scale of one to seven. A class-six climb was rated as virtually impossible, even with the use of special assist hardware. The system has since been refined and the categories subdivided.

While the climb of Huntington was taking place, Sheldon and his bride went on their honeymoon. They flew to the village of Chitina, where the Copper River breakup was in full swing. Sheldon has always equated this place with the most beautiful of Alaskan scenery. After a detailed tour of McKinley and the mountains that stand at its feet, they ended the trip at Swan Lake, about 15 miles north of Talkeetna. The plane that Sheldon flew was his faithful Cessna 180 equipped with Fluidyne wheel-skis, since the snow and ice on the lakes had not yet melted. The landing near the tiny cabin on Swan Lake went without a hitch, and they taxied to a point relatively close to shore.

"During the night, a warm chinook wind deteriorated the lake ice, and as we taxied for takeoff, the ice failed, and my skis broke through. All I could do was put in a fast radio call to my base in Talkeetna for help."

Twigg and Richards flew full-bore to the lake, and though Sheldon had carefully staked out a landing place along the shore, they buzzed him and dropped a big box of Wheaties with a note pinned to its side. The note read, "Ice too thin. Can't land."

About 20 minutes later, the pair returned, landed easily along the lakeshore, and helped Sheldon erect a tripod of logs over the Cessna. Then they winched the plane high enough to place green poles beneath the ice-glazed skis. Sheldon taxied to thicker ice and took off. His friends have never let him live this down.

But one of the first things Sheldon did after returning to Talkeetna was to check on the progress that Terray and his crew were making on Huntington. As the Super Cub scaled upward along the ugly knifelike spine of the Northwest Approach, he spotted the climbers. They were near the summit and moving upward. He knew as he looked that the Frenchmen would be victorious, but it was not until several days later that he learned the full extent of the price they had paid for the privilege of standing atop the corniced summit of Huntington.

"When I went in for the pickup five days later, Terray and his crew were just coming down the sheer wall above their base camp. Their faces were badly lacerated beneath a Sahara-type sunburn, their ears and noses had been frostbitten and were peeling, and they told me they'd taken a terrible beating from the high wind on the top of the mountain. Worst of all, Terray had fallen only a couple of hundred yards from the summit. Soubis and a guy named Jacques ["Farine"] Batkin had saved his life with a belay, but the fall against the rope had damaged Terray's shoulder and almost broken his back. He had then, after a night's rest, continued the tough climb to the top but had terrible problems coming down.

"On the day of the pickup, I flew the 180 and had Roberta, Dorothy Jones, owner of a store in Talkeetna, three other local gals, and an old portable Victrola on board. Roberta and Dorothy were

213

dolled up in wolfskins, and one of the other three was wearing a genuine Hawaiian hula skirt with longjohns underneath. When we landed, the Terray crew was so whipped that someone had to put a recording of the French national anthem on the Victrola before they took heart and began to join in the fun. Terray produced a goatskin of vino, and I ended up having a hell of a time pouring those guys off the base of Mount Huntington."

The balance of the 1964 season saw Sheldon service several more climbing crews, many of them on McKinley. His name was becoming more than just synonymous with Alaskan mountain climbing, for it was being said that he considered McKinley to be his mountain, a claim that he refutes. He had, in his chosen specialty of bush flight, "gotten in on the ground floor of the mountain," but he will admit to no more than this.

Time passed quickly, and 1965 saw relatively little activity on McKinley and the other major peaks of the Alaska Range. A Japanese expedition made the 40th ascent of the popular South Summit on July 3 of that year, and the 41st was recorded a couple of weeks later by an American team. The most prominent feat of mountaineering of the 1965 season was accomplished by a four-man team representing the Harvard Mountaineering Club and led by Dave Roberts, a major in English literature. On July 30, they attained the summit of Mount Huntington, the same peak that Terray and his crew scaled just one year earlier. The Roberts Expedition ascended the spinelike Huntington up the West Face, a different route than that taken by Terray's team. Sadly, the successful climb was permanently marred by the tragic death of Edward Bernd, who fell while roping down the vertiginous rock wall after the victory. Sheldon had flown Roberts and his three companions to the mountain. After retrieving them, he flew for several days looking for Bernd's body, which he never found. The details of this epic climb are described in *The Mountain of My Fear*, written in an excellent style by Roberts. With each passing year, the proportion of Sheldon's time spent flying McKinley and other mountains was multiplying at a phenomenal rate. His increased activities have been due primarily to two factors—the increasing popularity of the McKinley Group as a climb area and his own flawless reputation. Though he has become known as the climber's patron saint in times of high-altitude emergency, the lion's share of his repute stems from the steady and reliable service that he has always rendered to the climbers that he transports. Most mountain-climbing expeditions do not make headlines, which is fortunate, for it is the efforts that end in injury and death that are most newsworthy.

It was late in the 1966 climbing season when Sheldon first heard from Art Davidson, a mountaineer who, along with seven other men, proposed to climb McKinley during the winter. Never before had this feat been attempted. Because he had often wondered about the possibility of success on such a venture, Sheldon was intrigued. He contracted to do the flying for the team of eight and learned that the climb would be made with the cooperation of the Institute of Arctic Biology of the University of Alaska in Fairbanks. Davidson and his crew would meet Sheldon in Talkeetna.

"It was about this time that I met Genet. Ray had come to Talkeetna to join the rest of the Davidson Expedition, and he sure was a character. Multilingual in European languages, he looked to me like he'd be an asset on any climb. I found out after several years that he's not only sharp but a hell of a high-powered guy. I never know when he's pulling my leg, and on a mountain, he's a wolverine in tiger's clothing. On a summit climb, he'll jab a guy in the pants with his ice ax to get him another hundred yards up the mountain. Then if he sees life in the guy's eyes, he'll feed him some kidney pills, and if that doesn't work, he'll drag him bodily the rest of the way."

During the winter ascent, Ray Genet would be dubbed the "Pirate" by the rest of Davidson's crew, yet when he first joined the expedition, his climbing ability was seriously doubted by Art Davidson. Even the firm recommendation of his friend and team member Jacques ("Farine") Batkin could not dispel all the doubts that Davidson and the others harbored. But in the final analysis, it was the Pirate who graciously shared his boundless tenacity for survival on the South Summit of McKinley. The dramatic description of this celebrated climb in January 1967 appears between the covers of Art Davidson's book *Minus 148°*.

Sheldon took Davidson and the rest to the mountain and left them at 7,000 feet on the wind-ripped surface of the Kahiltna Glacier. Eight men went to the "winter" of McKinley but only seven returned. Genet's close friend and countryman, the happy Farine, was killed when, climbing unroped, he fell into a crevasse shortly after the ascent began. As often happens, Sheldon was asked to go to the Kahiltna and bring the tarp-wrapped form back to the little red hangar in his backyard.

From their first meeting to the present, a very special relationship—almost like an informal partnership—has existed between Don Sheldon and the Swiss Genet. Sheldon has relied upon Genet's talents in a number of critical situations since they first met just before the McKinley winter climb in January 1967.

From the time he rendezvoused with the winter-climb team, Genet has called Talkeetna his home, and he has brought a small bit of old Europe to the little town by the Susitna. He is an expert cabin builder, and his tiny house sits close by the Big Sue and is dwarfed by the magnificent view of McKinley to the north. His headquarters is the Talkeetna Road House when he's in town, which he often is not, for much of his time is spent on the big mountain, and on occasion, he returns to Europe for a climbing visit. Like Sheldon, Genet is a guide, registered with the Alaska Department of Fish and Game, and during the autumn months, he works for the aviator in that capacity.

Genet, a bachelor, is a free spirit and as a friend once put it, "a funny guy. Before you meet him for the first time, you expect a giant of a man, bedecked in a black beard. After you've met him and know his abilities, you walk away still thinking that he's well over seven feet tall, but in reality he's five foot ten."

Ray Genet is as much a part of the Sheldon story as the pilot's knit cap and chamois gas strainer. Sheldon never tires of expressing his amazement at Genet's physical accomplishments, which have become legendary.

"Ray is a tireless climber, and at 42 years of age, he is more than ready when some uninitiated guy on a crew, not knowing the strength of the man, boasts that he will beat him up the mountain. With this, Ray shoulders a pack that is twice as heavy as the one on the kid, and then promptly walks him into the snow."

The summer of 1967, besides being a hot one, had been another of Sheldon's "Chinese fire drills."

"The hangar was full of climbing gear, you could cook eggs on the airplane engines almost 24 hours a day, and the charter traffic was so heavy it was like getting caught in a revolving door. But we were clobbering 'em. At that time, I hadn't yet heard of a guy named Joe Wilcox, who was in the Park to lead a party of 12 relatively inexperienced climbers on a try for the South Summit via Karstens Ridge."

Sheldon would later learn that the crew, which came to Alaska via the Alcan Highway, consisted of Wilcox and his original eight climbers and three others from Colorado. Howard Snyder, Jerry Lewis, and Paul Schlichter were trained climbers who were completely equipped to climb McKinley on their own, but they had to join up with Wilcox because Park Service rules would not allow such a small party to climb the mountain. Sheldon also discovered, at a later time, that Wilcox was a rather unusual climber, not because of his ability or lack thereof but because of his inordinate hunger for publicity on the climb. Wilcox had written to Brad Washburn asking numerous questions about what unusual climbing records relating to McKinley were still unbroken. He also immodestly informed Washburn that he would undoubtedly be followed north by various members of the news media, who were eager to record his climb for posterity. Washburn responded by stating that, to date, no nine-man crew had ever fallen into the same crevasse, nor had anyone ever climbed the mountain backward or blindfolded. Wilcox later expressed his displeasure by writing "BRAD IS BAD" in the Alcan Highway dust on the rear of his camper.

And so, Wilcox, the leader of the combined group, brought what now consisted of an 11-man team with him to McKinley National Park. From Wonder Lake, they transported their complete supply of gear to Cache Creek, with the aid of rented horses, and finally onto the lower surface of the vast Muldrow Glacier. The 12 men continued up the Muldrow to Karstens Ridge, over the top of the spectacular Harper Ice Fall, and up to 17,900 feet. From here, they would eventually attempt to reach the South Summit. The climb degenerated into an ordeal. Due to inept leadership and various errors in providing food for the expedition, the ascent was fraught with bickering and ill feelings. In addition, Wilcox refused to listen to the advice that Brad Washburn had given to other members of the expedition. Lack of experience in the use of portable stoves led to a vital tent being burned to the snow line. That the entire crew of 12 men reached the 17,900-foot level for the summit try was a minor miracle in itself.

Wilcox and the three men from Colorado—Lewis, Schlichter, and Snyder—were the first members of the Wilcox Expedition to attain the summit. Then they returned to the camp at 17,900 feet where the other members of the party were waiting. Anshel Schiff, who was having difficulty breathing at this elevation, decided to go down to a lower altitude with Wilcox and the three Coloradans.

After Wilcox and his group departed, one of the remaining seven men, Steve Taylor, decided to remain in camp because he began to feel ill. Thus only six men comprised the second team of the Wilcox Expedition. They did reach the summit, but they underestimated the time that would be required for the round trip and were trapped by one of McKinley's terrible summit storms. Forced to bivouac overnight without the tents that most teams take with them, they nearly perished in the gale-force winds and resultant whiteout conditions that enveloped the summit. Desperate after the vitality-robbing bivouac of the night before, suffering in the bitter cold and anemic air at 19,000 feet, and already in the process of slowly freezing to death as they walked, they made their last terrible mistake. Looking for a shortcut, they started down over the edge of the gentle shelf beneath the Archdeacon's Tower. They were still conscious of the need to mark their route with cane wands, but they were now walking unknowingly toward their deaths in the breath-sucking wind and choking snow of the storm. The probable fate of the crew is described in Howard Snyder's book *The Hall of the Mountain King*.

"I've spent most of my life watching the mountain do the same thing to any number of expeditions," says Sheldon. "She'll storm and blow, clear up and give you a glimpse of what you want to see, then go 180 degrees. It was snowing, sure, but this isn't what makes high-altitude storms fatal—it's the wind."

When described on the printed page, the wind at McKinley's crown assumes a tempered dimension that it does not deserve. Only those who have faced the screaming tumult that passes for wind at 20,320 feet and lower can understand its horrible magnitude. Art Davidson, in his book *Minus 148°*, compares the sound of this force to the overwhelming crescendo of Niagara Falls, while Sheldon likens it to the sound of two passing freight trains. Others claim that this force is so completely dominant that a climber ceases to consciously experience mere sound. Probably no man alive can describe what a McKinley windstorm is really like better than Howard Snyder, who was at 15,000 feet, descending with Wilcox and the others, when the second team became lost. He tells of a force that sucks breath from human lungs, making inhalation impossible while facing downwind. When facing the other direction, the opposite becomes true, and exhalation becomes impossible, no matter how hard one tries. In tents during the descent, Wilcox and his four companions experienced winds of such magnitude that static electric charges leaped three to four inches from the drum-tight nylon inner tent walls to ground out on the parka-clad climbers.

Sheldon was flying resupply missions to other teams on the mountain when he learned through McKinley Park authorities that Wilcox's crew was in trouble. He said he would take a look.

"I was in the vicinity of the Wilcox crew's lower camps and climbed up above Karstens Ridge with the Cub to take a quick look."

A quick look, for Sheldon, consisted of a detailed exploration of every nook and cranny on the mountain. As the wind-blown Cub bucked and howled beneath the rim of McGonagall Pass, he began his search. Because a heavy wind still swept the mountain, Sheldon was beginning to think that the blowing snow of the past two days had probably removed all traces of the missing party. He had flown for better than three hours and was beginning to think about gasoline for the Lycoming engine. Just as he made the decision to leave the area and refuel, Sheldon saw something through the shallow veil of blowing surface snow.

"I wasn't sure that I'd seen anything at first. It was sort of a hunch, and I banked to the left for a better look."

On the second pass, Sheldon dropped almost to the surface of the sidehill below the Archdeacon's Tower, his upslope wing missing the snow by scant feet. As the Cub ate up the short distance to what Sheldon now saw was a dark-orange, fluttering object protruding above the windswept surface of the slope, his eyes watered and burned with the strain of trying to focus before he hurtled by. At the last possible moment, he tipped the stick, kicked rudder, and slipped the tiny plane sideways. As he angled away from the slope, he got the look he needed.

"It was the rippling orange nylon of a jacket sleeve that had first caught my eye. I now saw a gnarled, twisted hand clutching an ice ax. The hair stood up on my neck, and I started sweating."

Sheldon knew that recovery of the body was far beyond his capabilities. After making several more close passes, he was positive that he could see no more of the hapless party than the parka-clad arm clutching the ice ax. He knew also that at this altitude, a helicopter would be useless. Sheldon quickly reasoned that with the wind direction having been what it was when the party disappeared beneath Archdeacon's Tower, the rest must be nearby.

Now his attention focused on a climbing team he had been watching as they steadily ascended. The crew was being led by Bill Babcock of Anchorage. Sheldon felt sure that the Babcock party, though they had passed above the site of the fall, were now in a position to verify his discovery.

"I was, of course, flying the Cub alone and on oxygen, so I set the plane up and gripped the stick between my knees, reached behind me, and found a brown paper bag with 12 big Hershey bars in it. I quickly sketched a map, which I hoped would show Babcock where the body was, attached a 50-foot chunk of blue surveyor's ribbon to the bag, rolled around, and dropped it among his crew."

Babcock read the map, waved to Sheldon, who was now circling at 19,500 feet, and then carefully led his crew toward the spot marked on the map.

"I watched them head directly to the hand with the ice ax, and they dug the body from the snow. They found a second body, which was buried completely, and that was it. Babcock's crew searched but never did find the remainder of the second summit team."

Sheldon later learned that on their ascent, the Babcock party had found Taylor's frozen body still in the tent at the 17,900-foot camp. Due to the weather, extreme elevation, and lack of available personnel, the bodies found by Sheldon and examined by Babcock were left to the mountain. The drifting snow quickly buried them along with the balance of the seven doomed climbers. To this day, they remain interred under the windswept surface of that slope beneath the Archdeacon's Tower.

The death of these seven tripled the number of fatalities on McKinley. Though it is small comfort, Sheldon firmly believes that this is the peace that would be preferred by these climbers.

The Mountains Strike Back

In spite of the tragedy of the Wilcox Expedition during the summer of 1967, seven more successful scalings of McKinley's popular South Summit were written into the annals of Alaskan mountaineering by the end of 1968. The tallest of McKinley's summits had now been attained on 64 separate occasions. The treacherous 20,320-foot giant holds a seemingly endless fascination for the mountaineering fraternity, both professional and amateur alike.

Brad Washburn probably best describes McKinley's appeal: "There is not yet a full and balanced understanding by the general public of the real difficulties and problems encountered during an ascent of Mount McKinley. Perhaps the most important factor to point out is that only a handful of the more than 500 persons who have now climbed the South Peak would be rated as first-class alpinists by world-accepted modern technical standards.

"The ascent of McKinley is a curious paradox. Under certain conditions, it can be disarmingly easy, while under others, it can be fiendishly difficult. It is just near enough to the highway so that a strong experienced party will someday make the round trip to the top in two weeks or less, given good breaks with the weather. Yet it is far enough and its weather so fickle and violent that even the most powerful group of climbers may be forced to take a month or more to make the ascent by the easiest route—or indeed, to fail if weather and snow conditions do not cooperate properly."

Much of what Washburn describes also applies to the climbing of other major mountains in the world. Sheldon, who has lived his entire life under the combined dictates of the forces collectively called weather, knows only too well the subtle side effects that are produced by warming trends, changing snow conditions, and a misplaced ice ax or Vibram-soled boot. He also believes fervently in the climber's axiom that a mountain is never really climbed until you're down.

"Most of the bad falls on McKinley have occurred on the descent," says Sheldon. "Avalanching is one of the most deadly and sudden fates that can befall the climber, and it has killed a bunch of 'em, like the one on Dhaulagiri in the Himalayas that killed Boyd Everett, Vin Hoeman, and their party. An avalanche also wiped out Hoeman's wife, Grace, at a later date here in Alaska."

The name Grace Hoeman evokes sad memories, and Sheldon relates her story with mixed emotions, for she was one of the few climbers that Sheldon found to be always quietly distant and somehow difficult to understand.

"Grace, a very capable student of the outdoors, was a Czech by birth. She was an anesthesiologist, as I recall, and she went to the mountains to escape the humdrum city life. She had a history of difficulties in climbing, and the main one was her altitude limit, which was about 13,000 or 14,000 feet. She always experienced the cramps, nausea, and problems in breathing that come before an attack of pulmonary edema [altitude sickness]. To combat this, she went into training on the peaks of Chile. After she returned, she organized a McKinley climb. Her heart's desire was to get to the top of the South Summit, and her team consisted of five capable international mountaineers."

Sheldon received Grace Hoeman's request for air support early in the spring of 1970 and agreed to airlift the team to a glacier base camp.

"This was an unusual expedition, and what made it so was not that all of the team members were of international origin but that they were all women."

The expedition was dubbed the "Denali Damsels." During the ascent, Grace Hoeman experienced tremendous difficulties due to a moderate attack of pulmonary edema during the climb through Denali Pass. However, in spite of her illness, on July 6, 1970, Grace Hoeman led her party to the summit. The Denali Damsels became the first all-female party to successfully climb McKinley and return safely. It was the 83rd ascent of the South Summit.

After the victory on McKinley, Grace Hoeman teamed up with Hans VanderLaan and another friend. The trio went to ski on Alaska's Eklutna Glacier, where she and VanderLaan were killed in a massive avalanche.

Grace Hoeman was a very knowledgeable climber and an expert in appraising the safety of any route she encountered. It has been said that the untimely death of her husband created a death wish that she carried with her to the August-rotted surface of the Eklutna Glacier.

Ironically, Grace Hoeman returned in death to McKinley's summit early in January of 1971. With possible premonition, she had written her last will and testament prior to her trip to the Eklutna, and the document clearly requested that her cremated remains be scattered by Don Sheldon over the route taken by the Denali Damsels. The pilot granted this last request in his Super Cub, and the icy blast of January air tore at his mittened hand as he gentled his engine and committed the climber's last remains to the ageless snows of Denali.

In a rather startling revelation, Sheldon explains that the Hoeman request was not an unusual one, and he estimates that at present he has been asked to perform the rite on almost an annual basis. With grim mirth, he describes his first encounter with the job.

"The first time I was asked to scatter ashes, I gave my attorney a quick call, and after a serial number check on the ashes he assured me that it was all perfectly legal. I was flying the 180 and figured the quickest way to get the job done would be to open the window and dump 'em out. I would have been okay if I hadn't opened the box in the plane. The wind sucked the ashes up like a vacuum sweeper, and spit 'em out in the cabin. They were in my eyes, ears, and mouth, and I had a hell of a time getting them outside. From that day on, I used a different strategy."

It seemed to Sheldon that he had no more than returned home after Grace Hoeman's last flight when he learned through an old acquaintance in the Army Search and Rescue Section that the search for a recent crash of a turboprop military aircraft with a crew of five was being abandoned. The plane, en route to Anchorage from Whitehorse in the Yukon Territory, had wandered from its course for some unknown reason and had gone down on Mount Sanford, in the Wrangell Mountains. The crash was known to have killed all crew members.

"Colonel Blair is an old friend of mine. He has made three tours of duty in Alaska, in the old Tenth Rescue, and we had worked closely in the location and recovery of many downed military and civil aircraft."

Blair told the aviator that after repeated attempts to reach the crash site with large military helicopters had failed, the search had been called off because of the high risk involved. The officer also made it very clear that the Army felt the crash site was literally impossible to reach on foot.

"The long and the short of the military operation on Sanford to reach the downed plane had ended in not much more than a lot of frostbite for the guys who went there. The Army had been reluctant to hang it up because they wanted to get the bodies as well as pictures of the panel instruments for examination."

Sheldon could immediately visualize the terrible winds in the vicinity of the crash, because having airlifted climbers and cold-weather test crews into the area, he was no stranger to the 16,237-foot peak in the Wrangell Mountains. In his mind's eye, he could see the exact place at which the crash had occurred, and he shared the colonel's lack of optimism with regard to the chances of ever reaching the aircraft. Sheldon was about to say so when he thought of Ray Genet.

"I told the colonel that we had just the hand here in Talkeetna who might solve all his problems—Genet, the rope artist and a tremendous talent on rescue work. Right then he was the only McKinley guide in the area. To this Colonel Blair said that he'd heard of Ray, and asked me where he could be found. I told him that Genet was living in a tent out in the brush near town, and we went looking for him."

Ray Genet agreed without hesitation to give the climb a try and requested just enough time to get his hardware together. He wanted an anchorman, and his choice was Dave Johnston, one of the climbers who had survived with him in an ice cave on the South Summit of McKinley for five days during the winter climb in 1967.

Johnston agreed to accompany Genet, and they were soon hovering in a military helicopter at the 13,000-foot level of Mount Sanford, below the site of the crash. As the big helicopter bucked and yawed wildly in the turbulence they descended a rope ladder into a cloud of swirling snow.

Genet knew they were in trouble as soon as they took their bearings. They were in a howling gale, the driving sandlike snow stinging their faces like unseen wasps. Quickly, they dug a cave in the packed snow with their ice axes. It looked like 1967 all over again—only the mountain was different.

"They were at 13,000 feet, and the way it turned out, they got hung up there for 7 full days. They couldn't climb—hell, they couldn't even start a Primus stove in the blasting wind. They had a radio that the military had supplied, but it was useless to call for a pickup because the wind, which was steadily increasing, made it impossible for a chopper to even hover. After the seven days, the storm blew itself out as suddenly as it had started, and Genet cranked up the radio.

"During the stay in the snow cave, they had managed to get outside just long enough to set about 100 yards of fixed line, and by the time the chopper got there, their sleeping bags were solid ice from condensation and weighed about 100 pounds each."

The Air Force chopper took Genet and Johnston to nearby Glennallen for a two-day recovery period. While they were there, Johnston's wife, who was about to give birth, sent word that she wanted him back in Talkeetna for obvious reasons. His departure left Genet without an anchorman for the climb that he planned to resume as soon as possible.

In a phone conversation with a friend, Rex Post, Sheldon mentioned that Genet was looking for a new anchorman, and Post expressed his desire to fill the slot.

"Post, a senior Pan Am captain based in Seattle, was flying the overseas schedule. When I called, he said, 'Good, I'll switch off a shift to Japan, come to Anchorage, and be up there tomorrow.'"

Post was with Genet on a chopper en route for Sanford the next morning.

The helicopter off-loaded the two climbers beneath Mount Sanford's crown, at the 13,000-foot level where Genet and Johnston had based earlier. Their objective lay almost 900 vertical feet above them on a shelf just under the summit.

"Rex Post had been on McKinley with Genet on an earlier expedition and had done a lot of climbing in the Post River area, photographing Dall sheep with me."

With the monotony of a pounding gong, and as soon as the helicopter had departed, the area again was enveloped in a fierce snowstorm that lasted all night. When it subsided the following morning,

Post and Genet began to laboriously set steel pitons in the rock and ice of the steep slope. As they inched upward along the route of the fixed line that they were slowly establishing, Post seemed to be enjoying his work immensely, but Genet soon noticed that his companion's movements were beginning to slow and his breathing was becoming labored. They were above 13,000 feet, where the air can supply only about half of the oxygen that is available at sea level. On many other occasions, the Pirate had seen the effect of this shortage on climbers. Then Post started to cough, and Genet began to worry.

"Ray asked Post how he felt, and he allowed that he didn't feel too well, so Genet carefully helped him back down the fixed line to 13,000 feet and put him into two down sleeping bags—Post's and his own. Within two hours, the athletic Captain Rex Post was dead."

Genet was stunned at the suddenness with which the edema had struck Post down. He had not realized that the man was dying until it was too late. Genet spent the first half of the black overcast night keeping a macabre vigil with the corpse. Shortly after midnight, the cloud cover fragmented. Moments after Post died, Genet had radioed the Air Force for an immediate pickup, and the chopper arrived soon after the weather broke. After Genet and Post were loaded aboard, the chopper departed Mount Sanford just as another in the seemingly endless series of violent storms engulfed the crown of the mountain. This storm would last a week.

"Ten days later, Genet made up his mind," Sheldon states with a helpless grin. "But he now had to fight the general. There was no one around to help, as he had run out of anchormen, so he said, 'I'll do it alone.'"

The Air Force objected strenuously and told Genet that it was too dangerous—one man had already lost his life—and they would not take him in. There followed an argument with the black-bearded Genet that lasted two full days.

Genet, showing his special brand of tenacity, won the debate, and after signing a release, he was once again in a chopper roaring to the summit of Sanford. Genet, with his gear, off-loaded down the rope ladder. This time something was different—the weather was perfect.

In the unnatural tranquility of this place that had come to mean nothing but psychological pain and death to Genet, he continued placing the pitons, starting where ten days before Rex Post had begun to die. In a relatively short time, he reached the wreckage and verified that the crew had all been killed instantly. Genet removed personal items, photographed the instruments that had frozen in position on impact, and then returned to the 13,000-foot level where he called for a final helicopter pickup.

Because the mission was carried on under strict military classification, Genet cannot describe in detail his findings in the broken aircraft. For the effort he expended, a grateful U.S. Army Air Force offered Genet a position as a civilian cold-weather test expert. Since that time, he has guided more than a dozen military cold-weather expeditions to high altitudes on Mount McKinley. While he works, Ray Genet is retained at the pay rate of a full colonel, a situation that Sheldon says "takes quite a bit of the slack out of a mountaineer's winter pocketbook."

Genet's return to Talkeetna found Sheldon and his wife, Roberta, "negotiating 52 miles of correspondence" necessary to schedule the airlifts of climbing crews during the approaching spring and summer. They were also anxiously awaiting the arrival of the third addition to their family. They already had two girls. Holly was born on March 26, 1966, and Kate on September 25, 1968. Robert Donald arrived on April 6, 1971. The blond-haired apple of Sheldon's eye was named for Bob Reeve, his grandfather, and his father—a fitting summary of the old, the new, and the best in Alaskan bush aviation.

With the coming of the endless days of yet another summer, Sheldon tuned his airplanes to their accustomed fine edge in preparation for the 1971 season of 5:00 A.M. to 1:00 A.M. flying.

When asked how her husband's revolving-door operation affects her, Roberta replies, "In all honesty, I can't say I don't ever worry about him, and during the average business season, I experience controlled panic about four or five times. I'll never forget the time he was flying up on McKinley, and I heard him getting giddy over the radio from lack of oxygen. He figures that he's been loafing if he doesn't get at least 900 hours charter during a given season."

On June 16, Sheldon routinely polished the windshield of his most powerful airplane, a Cessna 185. The plane had been equipped with a Robertson Short Takeoff and Landing (STOL) kit, a modification that enables the plane to take off and land at less than the factory-designed speed. With the STOL kit and the 300-horsepower Continental engine, the Cessna promised much improved bush performance. Later that same morning, Sheldon took off over the

Susitna, bound for the crossroad settlement of Paxson, at the junction of the Richardson and Denali Highways, south of the Alaska Range.

At Paxson, he met five Japanese climbers whom he had agreed to fly to the Hayes Glacier on nearby Mount Hayes, a 13,832-foot-high peak—43 miles southwest of the village of Delta Junction—in the Alaska Range. He decided to make his first trip with a load of the party's gear and three of the climbers and was soon settling gently to a landing on the glacier at the slow airspeed that the STOL kit guaranteed to be safe. The broad retractable skis touched down on the granular snow of the glacier, and with the usual upslope run, the big Cessna began to slow. Suddenly, without warning, a heavy gust of wind caught the right wing and drove the left ski deeply into the snow. Sheldon responded instantly by applying full power, and slowly, with its 300-horsepower engine howling, the plane began to recover. At this precise moment, the left landing gear collapsed, and the plane flipped over onto its back.

The high-octane gasoline gushing from the broken wing roots made the danger of fire imminent. Sheldon and his three passengers bailed out of the plane from every available exit. The pilot had again escaped, this time with no more than a cut forehead, a black eye, and an abiding distrust for the slow-flight modifications that make an airplane fly slower than the factory-designed speed. His passengers emerged without a scratch.

Back at Paxson, the two remaining climbers telephoned Roberta in Talkeetna. In broken English, they expressed their concern, and she then called Jack Wilson, a well-known bush pilot and personal friend of Sheldon's, who was based at Gulkana, about 60 miles due south of Paxson. Wilson flew directly to the Hayes Glacier, but by the time he arrived, the weather had closed in. Returning to his home base, he phoned Search and Rescue at Elmendorf Air Force Base in Anchorage.

Later, a rescue helicopter plucked Sheldon from the glacier and returned him to Talkeetna, where he immediately began readying his Super Cub. He then returned to Paxson and completed the airlift, during which freak wind conditions necessitated several down-glacier landings before the job was done. These unorthodox landings were made over the crushed Cessna and constituted but one more part of the pilot's bad day on Mount Hayes.

Back home, Sheldon's tiny office was jammed with boot-clad

fishermen, all waiting their turn to be taken in Sheldon's float-equipped Cessna to places—such as Papa Bear Lake and the Talchulitna and Yentna Rivers—that held the promise of slab-sided rainbow trout. Though still sporting minor cuts and the black eye, Sheldon began relaying the fishermen to their various destinations while plying them with his usual running commentary on the passing scenery.

That Sheldon has never been seriously hurt in an airplane mishap is a mystery to his colleagues and friends. For years, the slight limp that affects his walk has been erroneously associated with some obscure crash but instead was caused by the repeated pressure of heavy packs during his earlier guiding days. His one serious injury took place miles from the nearest airplane.

"On a sheep hunt with two clients in the Wrangell Mountains, I was negotiating a knife-edged slate ridge. If the sheep could use the trail, so could I. Then the whole ridge avalanched, and I tumbled about 400 feet into a jumble of sharp rocks. When the dust cleared, I found that I had dislocated my right shoulder and was cut from head to toe. The clients wanted to cover me with their coats, but I insisted that they rope me back up to the top of the ridge. From there, I staggered 16 miles back up the mountain to the plane, stopping every three or four steps along the way to keep from blacking out. One of my clients, Dan Cuddy, a longtime Alaskan and old friend, flew the airplane back to civilization."

On June 28, the last day of a three-day series of freight hauls to the 10,100-foot level of the rugged Muldrow Glacier on McKinley, he suddenly found himself looking down at the scene of an accident.

"I had been making 40-pound precision airdrops to the Outdoor Leadership Program Expedition and had already moved almost 5,000 pounds of gear to the foot of the Harper Ice Fall. There were 31 climbers in the big team, and they were led by world-famous anatomist Dr. Robert W. Bullard, of Indiana University. He was a big man, as climbers go—about 6 feet 4 inches—and weighed about 235 pounds."

As soon as he saw the unmistakable confusion below, he knew that something had gone wrong. The knot of milling climbers was on a large pressure ridge in the breaks below the Harper Ice Fall, where the Muldrow Glacier begins. As Sheldon circled lower, he spotted the telltale hole in the snow surface which bore chilling testimony that a member of the expedition or, worse, several members had fallen into what looked like a deep crevasse. Sheldon knew the area well, and it was treacherous—a known concentration of deep, bottomless crevasses. From the group's position on the glacier, the pilot saw that the team had halted about 100 feet below and about a quarter of a mile laterally from the supply cache, which consisted of expedition gear and fuel. Seeing tents nearby, he reasoned that they had been in the process of setting up camp when the accident occurred. He was right.

"The team had stamped out a sign for me on the snow, with snowshoes, and it said LAND, but it would have been impossible for even a helicopter to put down there. Looking down, I could see the shadowy contours of the crevasses beneath the ice bridge, and the whole area was thinly veiled by only a six-inch cover of snow that had been drifted and then had crusted over. Had I landed, I would have been caught by the same trap that had caused the fall."

Sheldon circled once more and dropped a hastily scrawled note that instructed the crew to sled the victim, or victims, down to the 7,600-foot level of the glacier, a place where he felt he could effect a recovery. The note was written with a felt-tip pen on the cover of a cardboard box full of gear.

After the drop, Sheldon climbed the silver Cessna at full power and flew to the East Approach of McKinley to look for a man named Weiskopf, who had apparently crashed while dropping supplies to another group of climbers. In minutes, Sheldon's know-how on the mountain paid off again, and he spotted the tiny plane "rolled up in a ball on the Traleika Glacier. It turned out the pilot had broken only his arm and his reputation." Climbing at full power, for the necessary radio-range altitude, he called Talkeetna and reported the position of the downed aircraft. A helicopter flew in immediately to pick up Weiskopf.

Another of McKinley's storms enveloped the area, and for two days, gale winds and snow lashed the slopes, dropping visibility to less than nothing. On June 30, with the storm abating slightly, Sheldon returned in buffeting turbulence to the Muldrow Glacier's 7,600-foot plateau at 4:00 P.M. Unknown to Sheldon, the weakening storm had caused the air temperature at this altitude to rise dramatically. As he touched down under full power, he felt the heavy tug of slushy snow on the skis of the Cub. He taxied up the 15-

percent grade on a pressure ridge, and just a few feet short of the waiting climbers, the floor of his landing field suddenly fell from beneath his skis.

"The plane lurched to a stop in its tracks and then began to slide slowly backward, and as it did, the nose came up to about a 40-degree angle. All I could see was mountaintops and clouds."

Instantly, and instinctively, Sheldon advanced the Cub's throttle in a smooth but gentle motion with his left hand. Had he over-controlled, he would most certainly have lost his life to the bottomless chasm that now gaped beneath the yellow fabric of the plane's belly.

"It was like hanging on the edge of a huge knife. When I finally got the backward slide stopped, I was hanging onto the lip of the hole by the heels of my skis, with the tail assembly stuck down in the hole and out of sight."

The climbers jumped to help. In the still-blowing snow, which was perversely picking up new momentum, they hastily dug from in front of the skis with snowshoes, working quickly within scant inches of the whirling knifelike aluminum propeller. The path clear, Sheldon, with the help of the climbers, blasted the tiny Cub away from the lip of the crevasse, which proved to be big enough to engulf a train.

The gaping hole had only been part of the trap that had suddenly engulfed Sheldon. The snow was like flypaper, making it difficult for Sheldon and the climbers to pack a runway for the take-off. As he looked at the new snow that had begun to fall and felt the heavy gusting of the mounting wind, he wondered if he would get away before his plane was literally blown from the surface of the mountain.

"I had planned to get one of the victims, or the only victim, on this first trip, but the way the wind was building, I knew it would be impossible. As soon as the strip was completely packed down, I jumped in the Cub, firewalled her, and made it off alone by the skin of my teeth. The takeoff was downwind, and there was slush snow blowing 40 feet into the air as I finally lifted off."

During the brief time that he had been with the climbing crew, Sheldon learned the details of the tragedy. Dr. Bullard, the 42-year-old expedition leader, had been the only victim. As the group prepared to set up their camp higher on the mountain, he had lost a basic gamble that few experienced climbers are willing to take. Due to badly chafed hips, incurred during the long day's climb that had just ended, Bullard removed his harness and ropes, which attached him to the rest of the team. Surrounded by his 31-man crew, he took several short steps and then plunged through the thin surface of the snow into a completely hidden 200-foot crevasse. He fell headfirst, frantically groping for the rope he had just removed, and the impact killed him instantly. It had taken the crew ten full hours of concentrated effort to remove his body from the crevasse, after which seven of them had sledded it to the lower reaches of the Muldrow. Sheldon also was told that after the accident, George Hunker, the other adult leader of the all teen-age expedition, along with Randy Cerf, one of the students, had left the expedition for a rush to the far-off headquarters in McKinley Park. They had attempted to raise the Park personnel on their radio but failed, and they did not know that Sheldon was effecting a rescue coincidental with their long march.

But Sheldon had been forced to run before the weather, which he respects more than any other natural or man-made force. Back in Talkeetna, he kept a close eye on the weather for two more days, and on July 2, he started the Cub for a second try.

"I knew that the climbers who brought Bullard down would pull back and return to the main expedition after I had left the first time, and I needed help. I called Genet, who as far as I'm concerned, is worth any three men on a deal like that. He was behind me in the Cub when I left Talkeetna the second time."

Ray Genet has climbed to the summit of McKinley more often than any man alive, having made the ascent 15 times during a 7-year period. The Pirate was operating his own mountain-expedition business and was specializing in the scheduling and supervision of organized climbs. He was slated to join one of these expeditions the day he agreed to accompany Sheldon to the Muldrow, and his crew was part of a large group of climbers that Sheldon was booked to fly to the mountain that same day. Sheldon, in recalling the event, cannot resist a final description of the bearded Swiss.

"Genet is a man of small physical stature and weighs about 155 pounds. He has tremendously broad wrists and a powerful set of lungs, but his knuckles don't quite drag on the ground.

"On July 2, Ray had a 16-man expedition scheduled to start on the West Approach of McKinley. In addition, I was booked to haul three more crews up there for a total of 49 climbers. To move this crew and get Bullard, I had to have some strategy. Part of my strategy was to get started at three in the morning with Genet, who was scheduled for the first trip anyway."

With Genet, an interested but only slightly impressed observer, peering over his shoulder, Sheldon successfully landed on the Muldrow, where the frozen, canvas-swathed body of the scientist waited beneath an inch of fluffy new snow. The second part of Sheldon's "strategy" would cause ordinary bush pilots to shudder.

"Since Bullard was six foot four, I took the precaution of lashing a clear spruce two-by-eight plank to the wing struts and the tail section prior to leaving Talkeetna. I knew that, frozen solid, Bullard would be too big to get inside the Cub, so I had elected to tie him on the outside which, after no small struggle, we did."

With the body thus secured, Sheldon, flying alone, effected a successful takeoff from the still-roiled surface of the big glacier and flew directly to the nearby mining strip of Kantishna.

"At Kantishna, I met three very nervous people; two were members of the Outdoor Leadership Program who had walked out from the accident scene, and the other was a wild-eyed park ranger. They were really shocked that I'd brought Bullard out the way I did, tied to the outside of the Cub, but after I got them calmed down, the ranger volunteered to go for additional help, and I told him to hop to it."

Sheldon loaded the two climbers aboard the Cub, quickly returned to the 7,600-foot level on the Muldrow, off-loaded them, picked up Genet, and then returned to Talkeetna. Forty-two hours later, after another period of almost nonstop flying, he had distributed Genet's climbers and the crews for three other expeditions to their various destinations in the Alaska Range. The pilot then hit the sack for a well-earned and desperately needed rest. On November 21 of this year, he would celebrate his 50th birthday.

"Five Little Flowers"

In the clammy, frost-teased air of the tiny two-man parachute tent, Micheko Sekita clenched her small hands in frustration. The campsite at 9,500 feet was still in deep shadow, and the weak late-June sun illuminated only the high mountain walls around the tent, causing the red nylon to glow. Her fever, the result of a chest cold, seemed to have dissipated somewhat during the long night, and the discomfort she had experienced for several days was forgotten. Micheko Sekita was worried. Five days before, early on the bright morning of June 25, her crew of four had reluctantly bade her farewell and departed for the summit of McKinley. Now all that remained to remind her of them was the feeble hiss of the Sony walkie-talkie, its batteries too weak to function.

The five-girl team had come from Japan in high spirits for their planned ascent of the white mountain and had arrived in Talkeetna on June 5, 1972. As they detrained and piled their 800-pound load of expedition gear aboard Sheldon's venerable jeep, their quiet, laughing voices had a birdlike quality, and the entire world was theirs for the asking. The warm sunshine-flooded air was alive with the sounds of a new spring, and the five girls immediately established a permanent niche in Sheldon's heart.

"They were like tiny fragile dolls, and they reminded me of wild flowers as they chattered and laughed at the world around them, but make no mistake, they were athletes in the true sense of the word. I guess the one thing that struck me first was how completely happy they seemed to be. They couldn't have weighed more than

90 pounds apiece, and it didn't require a mathematical genius to figure that, even relaying, they would have to carry packs that would weigh almost as much as they did."

The girls were all from the vicinity of Tokyo, where 32-year-old Micheko Sekita was a teacher of handicapped children. Her close companion, Matsuko Inoue, nine years her junior, was also from Tokyo as was Mitsuko Toyama. Nobue Yajimi called the Prefecture of Saitama her home, while the final member, Sachiko Watanabe, came from Sapporo.

These Japanese girls would represent the first all-woman team from their country to attack the 20,320-foot mountain. In Japan, all-woman mountain-climbing teams are commonplace, but before 1972, McKinley's summit had seen only one all-woman team, the Denali Damsels.

Micheko Sekita had selected experienced climbers, and the Mc-Kinley ascent would be done under the banner of the Ryosetsu Climbing Club of Japan. That they were proud of their mission was unmistakable to Sheldon, though Micheko, the leader, was the only member who spoke fair English.

"They had good gear and a tremendous amount of rope. Their food supply seemed adequate and consisted of items that I had seen so many times before on Oriental climbs—powdered vinegar; dried bonito, which is a kind of fish; lots of rice and rice products; instant seaweed soup; and of course, chopsticks. Their gear seemed to be well chosen too, and they carried good snowshoes, which they called *wakans*. They also packed skis."

Ostensibly, the purpose of the Sekita Expedition was to scale McKinley's summit via the Southwest Buttress, a route that would offer the opportunity for rock and ice climbing as well as the necessary work on snow, for which the mountain is famous. But this climb to McKinley's summit had another purpose—to give them experience and to test their climbing abilities. In 1974, Micheko Sekita's team hoped to be the first all-girl team to scale the mighty and inaccessible Everest.

As he watched their preparations and learned of the route that they would attempt, Sheldon began to feel uneasy. He wondered about their ability on a long and sustained climb in the deep snow and with the associated chill factors on McKinley. It was the same feeling he'd had when the great Riccardo Cassin came to Alaska.

"The last 9,000 feet of the mountain on the route they planned to cover is exposed and along a stretch where many expeditions—like those of Wilcox, John Day, and others—had already come to grief. The chill factor on the mountain seemed to be the one condition that these gals, like so many other climbers I've flown to the mountain, had not really considered as much as they should have. In spite of the fact that these kids were rock artists in the true sense, McKinley is a different cat than they were used to.

"I took Sekita and her crew of four to the Kahiltna on June 7 and left them chattering amid their 800-pound load of gear. About a half hour later, I overflew them and was amazed that they'd already covered about four lateral miles on skis and couldn't believe my eyes when I saw the packs they carried. They must have weighed at least 60 pounds apiece."

By June 9, the girls had established a temporary cache at 7,900 feet on the Kahiltna, after relaying their gear on skis. On June 10, three of them climbed up-glacier to scout for a suitable place at which to locate their base camp. They selected a site at the 9,500-foot level, beneath the base of McKinley's Southwest Buttress. More than a week of constant effort was consumed relaying gear to this place from which the assault of the mountain would begin.

Sheldon, as was his habit, had checked on the progress that the girls were making. He again marveled at the stamina they showed, but he would have been even more amazed if he had been aware that the expedition leader, Micheko Sekita, had spent the last several days laboring under the effects of a chest cold and an accompanying fever, which climbed as each day slipped by. By the time the base camp was established at 9,500 feet, she was finding the simple act of breathing increasingly difficult. On the night of June 24, in the glow of the Primus stoves, Micheko decided to stay behind while the rest continued to the summit. This must have been the most difficult decision that she would make on the entire climb, for in Japan, the highest honor accrues when all team members are victorious.

Now, it was early morning on June 30, and she had spent the last five days trying to shake the suffocating effects of the chest cold and fever, which at lower altitudes would be merely uncomfortable. Here at 9,500 feet, in the damp cold of the tent, the thin air, with only about a third of its sea-level complement of the life-sustaining oxygen, aggravated her problem. Then, as if to squelch what little cheer that she had been able to cling to while her teammates ascended above her, the radio had apparently gone dead. The last words that she had heard from her companions had been received at eight o'clock in the evening of June 29. The failure of the radio was now confirmed, for she would certainly have heard more news of the summit team during the long night, through which she had tossed fitfully, half awake and listening to the tiny hiss of the radio beneath her parka, where she kept it to warm the failing batteries. In addition to all these concerns, she had been told that Matsuko Inoue had also become ill, and as a result, had stayed in a bivouac at 17,500 feet. The remaining three girls had then decided on a dash for the summit, a climb they assumed would take about six hours. In a radio transmission at noon on June 29, they had estimated that they would require "about three hours to reach the summit ridge [19,000 feet]," and at 4:00 P.M., they radioed after negotiating a steep and snow-choked gully that "they would like to get the summit and then go back to Camp V [17,500 feet] where Inoue wait." Mitsuko Toyama's voice had been clearly heard at four o'clock, and Micheko felt that she would soon learn of her party's victory on the summit. Then, at exactly eight o'clock, she had heard the Sony click with an incoming carrier signal and the words "calling you at eight o'clock"—and then complete silence. Had the radio died in Toyama's hand, or had her own set failed? Micheko could not be certain but quickly found that she could no longer contact her companions, for she triggered the transmit button immediately with no success. All she could do was wait.

Micheko Sekita, her thinking clouded by the nagging worry about the fate of her crew and the fever, which though beginning to subside still weakened her, had possibly created further problems with her radio by mistakenly leaving it on during the night. Now, on the morning of June 30, she could wait no longer. She sensed that she was needed above and climbed to a "white peak" at 12,900 feet, where she "waited all day" but saw and heard nothing. She then returned to the camp at 9,500 feet for another miserable night alone.

On July 2, she left the 9,500-foot camp carrying food for her companions and climbed to 14,500 feet. At the day's end, she erected the parachute tent she carried and spent the night.

Above Micheko's position, Matsuko Inoue was also beginning to worry about the summit team. Trying desperately to remain optimistic, she calculated that, due to some unknown emergency, her companions had been forced to descend the mountain via another route. However, this was a theory that she did not really trust, for due to her higher position on the mountain, she had seen and felt the storm that had shrouded the peak late in the afternoon of the day her companions struck out for the summit. The wind had moaned above her campsite, and the top of this mountain that now seemed to rebel at her mere presence became obscured in a white-out as the southwest wind pushed a great undulating plume of snow over the summit. She tried to summon the strength to go up and look for her teammates, but could not, for the pain in her abdomen was now so severe that she could scarcely stand upright. To climb up would be to invite collapse, and so she did the only other thing that seemed possible; she began to descend with hopes of rejoining her leader.

On July 4, at about 17,000 feet, she met Sekita, who was in the process of ascending. After a brief and depressing reunion, the two sick girls spent the night there, protected only by their special shelter-type clothing.

The following morning, July 5, Inoue waited while Micheko began to climb the route followed by her team earlier, and in a herculean effort, reached the desolate crest of the summit plateau, where she looked upward at the lonely windblown ridge that leads to the top of the world. She saw no sign of her companions and sank into the snow to spend the night, a huddled form exposed to whatever kind of weather the mountain might devise. Her exhausted mind cared little for such things as mere weather. Micheko was now but a short step away from the total despair that would consume her the following morning, July 6, when she topped the highest point on the summit plateau at 19,500 feet. Tears of frustration rolled down her cheeks as she gazed at the last gentle wind-swept slope between her position and the South Summit. Moaning in despair, she surrendered to the physical and mental exhaustion that had stopped powerful men far short of Denali Pass.

After what would later seem like interminable hours, Micheko arose from the snow and resolutely began to retrace her steps down to the 17,000-foot level where she had left her companion. All she remembers of the descent was that she found herself talking with Matsuko Inoue just before she could have continued no farther. After another night on the mountain without tents, the two girls continued downward, slowly "inching" their way where but a few days earlier the climbing had been done at a pace that spoke of a victory in the offing. Somehow, the two girls reached the site of the base camp at 9,500 feet and sank into an almost comatose sleep in the tiny two-man shelter that had housed all five of the Sekita Expedition team members simultaneously during the early days of the climb. It was the evening of July 7.

July 8 dawned with Inoue much worse. She now vomited blood and was in desperate need of help. Micheko Sekita knew that she must act swiftly, and she decided to call Sheldon. Before leaving the base camp, she stamped the word SICK in the snow and then prepared to leave, after carefully wrapping Inoue in sleeping bags. She skied down to Sheldon's 7,000-foot landing site, and using a powerful radio transceiver he keeps there, called Talkeetna. It was with this brief transmission that the world learned of the new tragedy that was well under way on Denali, and Sheldon immediately gassed the Cessna and departed for the Kahiltna Glacier.

"I decided to take a quick look. When I arrived over their base camp at 9,500 feet, the first thing that I spotted was the word SICK stamped out in the snow, but I was helpless. I couldn't land there."

Looking down, Sheldon immediately recognized that a change had occurred in the surface of the glacier. Where once there had been a relatively safe landing place, he now detected the swells and undulations on the snow surface that signaled new crevasse activity, which rendered a landing impossible. Without pause, he banked steeply to study the surface of the glacier one more time to be certain that he could not possibly get down and then reached for the mike on his radio.

As he talked with his base at Talkeetna requesting helicopter aid, he was already setting the Cessna up for a landing to pick up Micheko Sekita, who waited farther down the Kahiltna at 7,000 feet. The pilot offered the grieving climber a spare oxygen unit, which she put on as they climbed upward. The vast Kahiltna disappeared beneath the tail of the plane as Sheldon climbed over the route of the ascent, and he quartered the slope until they reached the 16,000-foot level.

"I couldn't get more than 16,000 because of a cloud deck, but we really gave the mountain a going over for about 2½ hours. Even with two sets of eyes looking at everything that might mean something, we drew a blank—no tracks, no nothing. Then the weather began to go sour."

As they circled, Sheldon once more marveled at the strength this tiny climber possessed. She had already been through an exhausting ordeal and now, after 2½ tiring hours flying on oxygen, she was reluctant to abandon the search. Sheldon knew that there was no other choice, for both fuel and oxygen were getting low. He placed the Cessna in a long, gradual glide to a final landing at 7,000 feet. Sekita got out, to climb back on skis to the 9,500-foot camp and her ailing companion.

Sheldon returned to Talkeetna, and as he did, the weather closed in behind him. He watched as the lower levels of the big mountain faded from sight beneath a rapidly moving storm front, and his frustration became almost tangible. It would be four days before McKinley allowed the rescue operation to continue. On July 12, an Air Force helicopter removed both girls from the 9,500-foot camp and transported them to Providence Hospital in Anchorage, where Inoue was judged to be critically ill with a badly perforated ulcer. Sekita returned to Talkeetna the following day by train to take up residence with the Sheldons during the search for the missing girls that would soon begin.

The following two-week period was one of massive confusion. The military directed Ray Genet, who was on the mountain when the search was mounted, to take his group of Special Forces survival trainees to the area where the three girls were last heard from. After an extensive search of the area beneath the summit, they returned to their base camp and reported that they had found nothing. The weather was stormy, and high winds pummeled the slopes of the mountain, making sustained search impossible. Genet then left the mountain.

Back in Talkeetna, the news of the apparent disaster on the mountain had Sheldon's office phone ringing constantly.

"A huge press was on. Micheko was on the phone more than she was off it. There were calls from everywhere, reporters from half-a-dozen papers, relatives and loved ones of the climbers, and the Japanese consulate. I couldn't help but notice the trend of the conversations, and both my heart and Roberta's went out to the poor girl."

The responsibility that Micheko had assumed as leader of the expedition to McKinley now became a stifling burden. The Japanese consulate demanded that she be personally responsible for all expenses incurred in both the expedition and the rescue or recovery of the climbers from the mountain. Micheko Sekita found that she was bound not only financially but morally, for unless she could comply with the demands of the consulate and the people of her country, she would not be allowed to return home. She would have to somehow return with her whole team or not return at all.

Time began to pass with almost confusing rapidity. Sheldon had taken his second prolonged look on July 12. He was at that time servicing several crews on the mountain, and when he failed to find any trace of the girls, he overflew four of his expeditions and dropped notes telling the climbers to be on the lookout for them. The weather on the mountain was reasonably mild and offered comparatively good flying conditions. When he could, Sheldon was aloft at these times and flew as long as either the weather or his fuel and oxygen tanks allowed.

"When Micheko and I flew that first day, [July 8], I concentrated on the East Approach, because I estimated that if the three gals had been blown off the mountain, the wind, which had been from the west, would have blown them over the East Approach. As a matter of fact, I half-expected that the area that had killed Joe Wilcox's crew would be where we'd find 'em."

An Air Force C-130 had circled the mountain several times, but no helicopters were pressed into service. Sheldon learned later that the three girls had been seen by another team at the 19,000-foot level in Denali Pass, just beneath the mountain's summit. A Dr. Gerstman and his teammates had tried without success to convince the girls that they were climbing into a dangerous weather condition. In a statement to Sheldon, Gerstman said that he was appalled that the girls did not carry sleeping bags, only small day packs, and were very obviously making a rather desperate dash for the summit. Sheldon's early appraisal of the "flaw" in the Micheko Sekita party's planning was proving to be a chilling reality. Due primarily to his conversation with Dr. Gerstman, he now determined that the girls had to be somewhere near the summit.

Following his search on July 8 with Micheko on board, Sheldon became obsessed with finding the girls, but years of experience looking not only for climbers but for any manner of things on the mountain had taught him patience. He knew that any day he flew could bring success, for the snows of McKinley, or any other mountain, are constantly shifting. With the changing landscape below, each day's search was a completely new one.

Sachiko Watanabe's husband suddenly arrived in Talkeetna from Sapporo. Each day, he paced aimlessly between Sheldon's hangar and office, watching the sky to the northwest and waiting for news of his lost wife.

On the afternoon of July 22, Sheldon discussed the search with Ray Genet, and though the Pirate was due to join a climb already in progress on the mountain, he agreed to help. His first assistance came in the form of sound advice, and with an almost casual shrug, Genet recalls what happened.

"Watanabe was wandering around there, and it was really sad, so I said, 'Well heck, the best way to look really good is with a helicopter.' I called the Japanese consulate and asked them if they would pay for a helicopter. At that time, nobody really figured that it was a rescue anymore. I figured we were simply looking for bodies. The Air Force wasn't much help, if any, because the limit with their helicopters was about 14,000 feet. The Army had machines that could fly to the summit, but since it was no longer a search for survivors, they wouldn't help us. I figured that a private helicopter would be our only chance."

Genet explained to the consulate in Anchorage why he felt the use of a helicopter would be best at this time and offered to ride the chopper and supply his expert knowledge of the terrain in the search. He was then informed that another team of Japanese climbers was being staged in Japan and would arrive at a later date.

"I said, 'Well, that doesn't make too much sense, because they would all be strangers to the mountain, and too much time would be used up waiting for them. The longer we waited, the better the chances would be that their bodies, wherever they were, would be snowed over and never found.'"

The Japanese consulate reluctantly agreed to Genet's plan but stated that the limit for a helicopter charter would be seven hours of flying time. Genet then contacted Gay Helicopter Service in Anchorage and arranged for use of an Allouette III, a turbo-supercharged machine capable of high-altitude operation.

Chuckling, Genet says, "The pilot, Quakenbush, who finally agreed to fly to McKinley had never been above 10,000 feet. He took the job after the first pilot scheduled 'turned up sick.' We started the search by taking a wide swing around the summit and then flew back and forth over the slopes, gradually losing altitude, until we got to just above 15,000 feet, below the crest of the Southwest Buttress. It was here that I spotted something that at the moment only looked like tiny dots."

Genet asked the pilot to turn around and make another approach, this time at a little lower altitude, which he did.

"As we hovered there, I could see that it was part of the bodies, sticking out of the snow."

Genet carefully marked the spot in his mind and told the chopper pilot to return him to Talkeetna. They had been in the air several hours, and on the way back, he calculated that if they had been required to continue the search for another 30 minutes, they would have reached the charter limit placed upon the flight by the Japanese consulate. Sheldon met Genet in Talkeetna and quickly learned about the apparent fate of the three girls.

"From what Ray told me, I could visualize the route that the fall had taken, and it was down at least a 70-percent grade of rock and hard ice. Hell, a guy could parachute down that slope, and it ends almost exactly 1,000 feet above my strip at 14,300 feet. We figured that the gals had made the summit and then got caught in a sudden storm accompanied by tremendous winds. They could probably see the tents of my other people down at the 14,000-foot level and maybe thought that they could take a shortcut down to them. Whatever happened to them, they either fell or were blown over the lip and tumbled at least 4,000 feet."

When asked if he considered the Japanese girls experienced enough for the mountain, Genet's laconic reply carried a world of wisdom, "What is experience? On the mountain you learn all the time."

The following day, Sheldon loaded Genet and his vivacious girl friend Marlene Titus, Micheko Sekita, and Sachiko Watanabe's husband into his supercharged Cessna 180 and flew them to 10,000 feet on Kahiltna Pass, within the park boundary. This was done at Genet's request so that his party could become acclimatized to the lower oxygen level in which they would work. Sheldon had asked for and received special permission to land here, since this was a mission to retrieve the bodies of the girls as opposed to the routine start of a climb. Prior to leaving Talkeetna, Genet, for very obvious reasons, had been less than enthusiastic about Watanabe accompanying his group.

After the arrival at 10,000 feet, Genet, Titus, Micheko Sekita, and Watanabe immediately started for the 14,300-foot level and Sheldon's Super Cub landing strip, where they joined one of Genet's expeditions already on the mountain. The climb to this point took the party two full days and consisted of two herculean 18-hour climbing sessions. Once at 14,300 feet, they were in a position to reach the bodies. Genet described the actual recovery with a clinical detachment.

"Titus stayed at 14,300 feet, and we started to climb with a crew of nine, including myself. Micheko Sekita and Watanabe were with us, and we reached the seracs at 15,500 feet, the exact level where the bodies were, in a relatively short time. It took us some time to get the bodies untangled and the drifted snow cleared away, and I then knew that they had fallen a great distance. They were rolled up in the climbing rope that they were tied together with, and several shoes had been lost. We used black plastic sheeting to slide the bodies down to the 14,300-foot level, and it took three guys for each of the bodies. It was so steep we had to belay."

With the bodies recovered and resting at 14,300 feet, Genet explained to Micheko Sekita and Watanabe how and where to tramp down a runway for Sheldon, who would be arriving on July 27. Genet and Titus, along with Genet's expedition, then continued up the mountain. As they climbed, they kept watch over the two Japanese and also watched Sheldon land in the Super Cub. Genet had been in radio contact with the pilot over a small shortwave set that he carries whenever he is on the mountain.

Marlene Titus remembers that Sheldon, for reasons of his own, had chosen to land next to the runway that had been tramped down by the Japanese. Grimacing at the wasted effort, she said, "I'd rather climb the mountain any day than tramp down a runway."

Sheldon explained that he landed "off runway" so that a turn onto the packed area could be made, thus eliminating the danger of bogging down in five feet of soft snow in the turn. If he failed here, it could have easily taken four or five hours to prepare for takeoff.

Whatever Sheldon's reasons for the off-runway landing, his arrival in the Super Cub was as precise as ever, and he immediately relayed the bodies, one at a time, down to the landing site at 10,000

244

feet, where he would later return with the Cessna and transport them to Talkeetna.

During the next few days, Sheldon returned to the Kahiltna with Micheko Sekita to recover the party's climbing gear at 8,700 feet. Soon all traces of Sheldon's "five little flowers" had been removed from a mountain that remained unchanged by their brief presence.

The bodies of Mitsuko Toyama, Nobue Yajimi, and Sachiko Watanabe were cremated in Anchorage and sent on their long trip home. Micheko Sekita also returned to her homeland to begin the interminable task of forgetting and reimbursing her government for the high cost of a mountain climb that most of her countrymen would consider a failure. Sheldon does not.

"I'm sure that the girls made the summit because of little things that happened, like their watches stopped at nine o'clock by the fall. This would have given them plenty of time to make it, and besides, Genet reported their tracks there at 19,000 feet. I can't say for sure, but I'd never bet against it."

Finally, since Sheldon, like his ex-partner Morrison, is a firm believer in backing a winner, he and his wife Roberta wrote off most of the considerable flying expenses, with the hope that it would help a small dark-eyed friend of theirs called Micheko Sekita rebuild her shattered dreams.

Postscript

Over the years, Talkeetna, Mount McKinley, and Don Sheldon have remained virtually unchanged. The town, with its graveled main street and weathered log buildings, still rests easy on the eye. "Beautiful Downtown Talkeetna," as the hand-lettered sign along the road into town proclaims, has succeeded in warding off most of the pressures of our modern world, and for the past 40 years, its population has averaged 125 souls and 200 dogs.

Olie Dahl, the aviator's next-door neighbor, rocks at his front window and nods to Sheldon as he passes. Evil Alice Powell still runs the best motel in town, and the yeasty aroma of fresh-baked bread still drifts through the doorway of the Talkeetna Road House when the Closes bake their 30-odd loaves for the weekly trade.

The big mountain to the northwest of town has changed even less than Talkeetna, and it will remain virtually unchanged with the passage of many hundreds of decades, for McKinley is still young as mountains go. The years since the turn of the century have been little more than drops of spray in some huge waterfall, and the sky-blue ice that moves at an invisible rate beneath countless tons of snow on the Muldrow Glacier is at least 5,000 years old.

Ironically, Sheldon's workday is reminiscent of his description of the job at the Step And A Half Dairy in Anchorage so long ago— "25 hours a day, 9 days a week." During the 1973 season, he single-handed his 10-year-old Super Cub and the expensive silver Cessnas for a total of 900 hours aloft. The almost complete absence of daylight during six months of the year makes this truly a staggering total. He eats on the run, and the monthly flight schedules his wife keeps look like the "want list" at a busy general store. Over the years, Sheldon has received many attractive offers from various flight agencies but has turned them all down. To explain why, he says, "Lookee, in a year's time, I fly for a thousand bosses and enjoy it more than I ever would flying for one."

The red frame hangar still stands in sag-roofed dignity at the main-street end of Sheldon's 900-foot dirt strip. It has been christened the "Sheldon Sheraton" or the "Hangar Hilton" by climbing teams from 12 nations who have unrolled their sleeping bags on its planked floor. Japanese-figured burlap bags, courtesy of the house, serve as ground cloths.

In 1973, Sheldon managed to find the time to supervise the construction of a new and bigger metal hangar adjacent to the old one. The red frame building will remain, however, and be used for storage.

A counterpart of his strip in Talkeetna is 60 air miles away at the 7,000-foot level of the Kahiltna Glacier and has been dubbed "Talkeetna International Airport" in deference to the continental nature of the clientele who use it. The aviator's mountain house on the Ruth Glacier is referred to as the "Sheldon International Hotel" for the same reason.

Charter flying is an expensive business, especially in Alaska, and Sheldon pays thousands of dollars each year to adequately insure his passengers. Like most other fixed-base operators, he does not buy the "gold-plated" hull insurance for his airplanes.

"That stuff is so expensive that I'd end up paying three times the value of each aircraft every four years."

As for his own personal insurance, even the record of high safety that Sheldon has amassed during more than 30 years of flying does not count. Bush pilots pay 35 to 75 percent extra for their insurance, while the men who fly commercial jets pay the same rate as does the plumber down the street.

Some of the years have been financially tough, with the company books ending up decorated in red ink, but most seasons allow Sheldon to show a fair profit.

"That $45,000 Cessna 185 that I stacked on the Hayes Glacier back in June 1971 lay there on its back for all the world to see, including me, for six months. I had to make several landings over it the day after she flipped and it's still up there, under an avalanche of talus ice blocks. I paid eight grand for the privilege of naming my own lake, and the pretty Cessna 180 floatplane that still decorates the tundra up at Yellowjacket Lake went for $35,000. Add the $9,000 worth of airplane that I hung in the cottonwoods north of Anchorage and then later sold for scrap for 50 bucks, and even an idiot can see that all the resource isn't going into the cash register."

The numbers game, as Sheldon plays it, has been a one-way street for many less tenacious Alaskan pilots, and many of those who managed to stay out of bankruptcy have become nervous wrecks. Even with his losses, Sheldon remains philosophically cheerful, and the years sit lightly on his shoulders. He seems to have the unbridled exuberance of a kid with a new toy whenever he buys another airplane, and his suntanned face splits in mirth as he recalls Roberta's reaction to a purchase he made shortly after their marriage.

"I guess she didn't know me quite well enough yet. I went out and signed up for 100 grand worth of new airplanes."

Sheldon brought a 40,000-gallon fuel bulk plant to Talkeetna, ran a riverboat business, and even a Tasti-Freez ice-cream stand, which made "$67 one morning while I tried to mow the front lawn." Though his airtight schedules often make punctuality difficult, he has managed to build a rock-solid reputation based upon old-fashioned good service. One of his strongest backers is Evil Alice Powell, who often sends prospective clients to Talkeetna Air Service.

"Don's not only a fine pilot," she says, "but if I have someone, I sure don't have to pull him off a bar stool somewhere. He never touches a drop of booze."

Not all of Sheldon's problems stem from his specialty of high-risk flying. Sometimes, on routine flights, the passengers themselves provide unexpected complications.

"I had a call to pick up a woman over at Cantwell, near Broad Pass, a number of years back and take her to the hospital in Anchorage. I got her strapped into the airplane, and just as we lifted off, she went nuts. She began to jerk and heave on the control wheel, and we ended up in a cloud of dust off the embankment at the end of the strip. I got the plane straightened around, it was fortunately undamaged, and taxied back to get her husband, who agreed to ride along and see that she behaved. I took off, got level at 2,000, and the gal goes ape again. This time, she decides that she wants to get out and walk and was halfway through the door before we could stop her. Her husband and I made a grab for her at the same time, but she was jammed in the door by the slipstream. After doing whifferdills all over the valley, we managed to get her back in the plane, and I radioed ahead to Talkeetna for a pair of hand-cuffs. We landed, cuffed her to the baggage compartment, and had an uneventful trip the rest of the way to Anchorage."

Other Sheldon flights have assumed unexpected dimensions. On one flight, he lost a race with the stork and helped an Indian woman give birth in the rear seat of his Cessna. He flew one-handed and followed directions from a doctor at the Anchorage CAA control tower. When Sheldon tells about this episode, he winks, blushes slightly, and says matter-of-factly, "The operation was a success, but I've been allergic to screaming women ever since."

Sheldon's passengers are not always on the receiving end of the service he offers. On a sight-seeing jaunt with three Baptist minis-ters, he landed amidst several thousand caribou for pictures. On the takeoff, the right ski rigging parted company, causing the front of the ski to point straight down. "I had a minister hanging out the door, standing on the heel of the ski so I could safely land the air-plane. It was about 20 below outside in the slipstream and 40 miles back to Talkeetna."

To relate all of the exciting incidents in Sheldon's life would re-quire a book double the size of this one. The episodes that have appeared here hopefully describe the real Don Sheldon. He is a man who is admired not only by the vast and highly competent fraternity of Alaskan bush pilots but by all who know him.

Harmon ("Bud") Helmericks, veteran Arctic pilot and competi-tor, probably best summed up the enigma who owns Talkeetna Air Service: "Don is a guy that just can't be stopped. He's a leader in the true sense, and I don't mean that he's just another fine pilot who sees a challenge and then tackles it. I don't think Don ever really identifies any job as a challenge, he just sizes it up and *does* it. If it weren't that way, he'd have been dead long ago."

About the only thing that Sheldon ever really gambled on was the outcome of one of his four-five-six games. He takes time in his stride, and though a firm believer in the practical and logical ap-proach to all flying situations, he admits that there is no such thing as aces straight in the flying business. At 53, Sheldon has many "Chinese fire drills" to supervise before he retires his knit cap and chamois gas strainer, but it's anyone's safe bet that when he does, he'll still be a long way ahead of the game.

Bibliography

Davidson, Art. *Minus 148°: The Winter Ascent of Mt. McKinley*. New York: W. W. Norton & Company, 1969.

Day, Beth. *Glacier Pilot: The Story of Bob Reeve and the Flyers Who Pushed Back Alaska's Air Frontiers*. New York: Henry Holt and Company, 1957.

Francis, Devon. *Mr. Piper and His Cubs*. Ames: The Iowa State University Press, 1973.

Helmericks, Harmon. *The Last of the Bush Pilots*. New York: Alfred A. Knopf, 1969.

Mills, Stephen E., and Phillips, James W. *Sourdough Sky: A Pictorial History of Flights and Flyers in the Bush Country*. Seattle: Superior Publishing Company, 1969.

Orth, Donald J. *Dictionary of Alaska Place Names*. Washington: United States Government Printing Office, 1967.

Pearson, Grant H., with Newill, Philip. *My Life of High Adventure*. Englewood Cliffs, N.J.: Prentice-Hall, Inc., 1962.

Potter, Jean Clark. *The Flying North*. New York: Macmillan Company, 1947.

Roberts, David. *The Mountain of My Fear*. New York: The Vanguard Press, Inc., 1968.

Snyder, Howard H. *The Hall of the Mountain King*. New York: Charles Scribner's Sons, 1973.

Washburn, Bradford. *A Tourist Guide to Mount McKinley*. Anchorage: Alaska Northwest Publishing Company, 1971.

_____. "Mount McKinley (Alaska)—History and Evaluation." *The Mountain World*, edited by Malcolm Barnes. New York: Harper & Brothers, 1956–7, pp. 55–81.

Index

Aeronca Sedan, 64
Alaska, Territory of, 15, 16, 17, 26
Alaska Airlines, 66
Alaska Railroad, 26, 29
Alaska Range, 66, 77, 95, 102, 103, 124, 128
Alaska Road Commission, 62
Alcan Highway, 15
Alpine Club of Italy, 178
Amarillo Air Force Base, Texas, 55
American Alpine Club, 178, 182
Anchorage, 26–7, 110, 111, 128, 210
Anchorage climbing expedition, 162–4
Anderson, Lawrence, 37, 38, 40
Anderson Glacier, 98: UCLA climbing expedition on, 98–102
Athabascan Indians, 38

Babcock, Bill, 220
Babcock expedition, 220
Bading, Mrs. Helga, 162, 163, 164, 167, 172
Barrille, Edward, 120
Barrow, 112, 117
Bates, Bob, 76
Batkin, Jacques, 213, 215, 216
Beckey, Fred, 102
Beckwith, Edward P., 75
Begich, Nick, 211
Bering Glacier, 93, 94
Bernd, Edward, 214
Blair, Colonel, 224
Boecher, Roy, 144, 153–4
Boggs, Hale, 211
Boston Museum of Science, 71, 77, 78, 83
Brauchli, Andrew, 162
Breitenbach, John, 142
Brooks Glacier, 76, 161
Browne, Belmore, 120–1
Bucket of Blood Bar, Talkeetna, 22, 35–6
Bullard, Dr. Robert W., 229, 231–2, 233
Burtel, Joey, 33, 34

Bush aviation, in Alaska, 15–16, 17. See also Pioneer bush pilots

Cache Creek, 30, 32, 33
Canali, Jack, 181, 182
Carpé, Allen, 75, 93
Carpé, Mount, 93
Carpé-Koven expedition, 75
Cassin, Riccardo, 178, 179, 182
Cassin Expedition, 179–82
Cerf, Randy, 232
Cessna-180, 94, 160
Chitina Glacier, 98
Christensen, Haakon, 77, 78, 123–4
Chugach Mountains, 93
Chulitna River, 29, 128
Civil Aeronautic Authority (CAA), 34, 40, 123, 125
Civilian Pilot Training Corps (CPTC), 51, 52
Clancy, E. I., 51
Close, Caroll, 122, 246
Close, Verna, 122, 246
Cook, Dr. Frederick A., 120, 121
Cook, Jim, 28, 30, 31, 32
Cook's fake peak, 120, 121
Cordova, 93
Cordova Airlines, 93, 94
Crews, Paul, 162, 164, 172
Crillon, Mount, 72
Crosson, Joe, 15, 16, 74–5, 83, 110
Crosson, Mount, 157
Cuddy, Dan, 229

Dahl, Olie, 246
Darling, Oscar, 74
Davidson, Art, 215, 218
Davidson Expedition, 215–16, 224
Day, John, 159, 160, 161, 164, 173, 174
Day Expedition, 162, 163, 164
Dease, Ira, 33, 34, 35, 36, 37
Deborah, Mount, 102: Harrer Expedition on, 102–3

Denali. See McKinley, Mount
Denali Damsels (Hoeman expedition), 222, 235
Denali Highway, 62
Denali Pass, 241
Devil's Canyon, 66, 128–9, 130, 131: rescue at, 130–5; Sheldon's citation for, 133–4
DEW-line site, 112–13
Dickey, William, 123
Dickey, Mount, 122, 123
Dodson, Jim, 49
Driggs, Howard, 144

East Kahiltna Peak, 157
Eielson, Carl Ben, 15, 16, 58, 110, 155
Ekkerlein, Klaus, 206
Eklutna Glacier, 223
Elliott, Sergeant Robert, 165
Elmendorf Air Force Base, 19, 210, 228
Englehorn, Orville, 205, 206
Everett, Boyd, 208, 222

Fairbanks, 15, 37, 58
Fairview Inn, Talkeetna, 29, 60, 127, 142
Fairweather, Mount, 72
Fisher, David, 123
Fisher, Mike, 211
Flat, 185
Foraker, Mount, 82, 93
Fort Richardson, 129

Gay, Ward, 50
Genet, Ray, 215, 216, 224–7, 232, 233, 240, 242–3, 244, 245
Gerstman, Dr., 241
Gibson, Jim, 168–9
Gillam, Harold, 15, 16
Glacier landings, 74, 76, 77, 78, 94, 95, 98–101, 121, 161–2, 228, 230–1, 233: at 14,300 feet, 167, 169, 170–5; Sheldon on, 83–4, 85, 93, 169
Goodwin, Robert, 178, 179, 182, 206

Graham, Roy, 26
Grand Canyon, Arizona, 122–3, 124
Grubb, Wally, 137, 138, 139

Hackett, Major William, 94
Hackett Expedition, 94, 95
Haggland, Pete, 93
Haley, Herb, 93, 94
Hall of the Mountain King, The, 218
Harper Ice Fall, 229
Harrer, Heinrich, 102
Harrer Expedition, 102–4
Harvard Mountaineering Club, 214
Hayes, Mount, 228
Hayes Glacier, 228
Helicopter search and rescue missions, 139, 165, 166, 173–4, 205, 242–3
Helmericks, Harmon, 249
Hennig, Peter, 206
Hiebert, Augie, 122, 123–4
Higgins, Cecil, 74
Hoeman, Grace, 222–3
Hoeman, Vin, 222
Hoshikawa, Kazuo, 207
Huff, Sam, 186–7, 189
Hunker, George, 232
Hunter, Mount, 93, 103: Harrer Expedition on, 103–4
Huntington, Mount, 210, 212, 214: Roberts Expedition on, 214; Terray Expedition on, 211, 212, 213–14

Iliamna, Mount, 20, 22
Inoue, Matsuko, 235, 237, 237–8, 238–9, 240
Inside Passage, 26
International Distress Code, 188

Jenkins Mine, 32–3, 35, 36: murders at, 34–5
Johnson, Lars, 51
Johnson, "Saltpeter," 183–4
Johnston, Dave, 224–5
Jones, Dorothy, 213–14
Jones, Jerry, 75
Jonz, Don, 211

K-2, Kashmir, 160
Kahiltna Glacier, 77, 78, 96, 207, 236, 245: Sheldon's airstrip on, 161, 247
Kahiltna Pass, 73, 161, 170, 195, 243
Katalla, 93
Kitchen, George, 168, 169, 170, 172
Kokrines, 40
Kotzebue, 117–18
Koven, Theodore, 75, 93
Koven, Mount, 93
Kroto Creek, 33, 35, 37, 38

Ladd Air Force Base, 76
Lander, Wyo., 23, 25
Lars Larson flight school, 49, 50, 52
Lenin Peak, Soviet Union, 159–60
Lewis, Jerry, 217
Life magazine: on Sheldon, 135, 175
Lilley, Barbara, 102
Lindley-Liek Expedition, 75, 122
Logan, Mount, 94, 95, 97, 98: Hackett Expedition on, 94, 95
Lucania, Mount, 76, 98–102
Luckett, Link, 173–4
Luz, John, 182

McDonald, Belle, 31, 32
McGonagall Pass, 74
McGrath, 49, 51, 52, 185, 192
McKinley, Mount, 17, 19, 72, 73, 74, 75, 77, 78, 82, 84, 93, 96, 120, 121, 123, 140, 142, 143, 157, 163, 167, 168, 172, 174, 177, 179, 180, 182, 207, 208, 214, 218, 220, 221, 235, 246. *See also* Kahiltna Glacier; Kahiltna Pass; Muldrow Glacier; Ruth Amphitheater; Ruth Glacier expeditions on: Anchorage team, 162–4; Babcock, 220; Carpé-Koven, 75; Cassin, 179–82; Davidson (winter

McKinley (*continued*)
climb), 215–16, 224; Day, 162, 163, 164; Denali Damsels, 222, 235; Lindley-Liek, 75, 122; Metz, 207; Outdoor Leadership Program team, 229–30, 231–2, 233; Sekita, 234, 235–9, 240, 242; U.S. Army research team, 75; Washburn, 77, 78; Wilcox, 217–20
mapping project, 71, 72, 73, 77, 82, 93, 121, 124, 177
Sheldon's house on, 123, 247
McKinley Group, of Alaska Range, 103, 124, 157, 177, 207, 208, 214
McKinley Park Station, 102
Marcus Baker, Mount, 76
Martin, James, 15
May Creek, 94, 98, 99, 101–2
Mayfield, Commissioner Benjamin, 30, 31, 34
Merrill, Russell, 49
Merrill Field, 49, 206
Metz, Hans, 207
Metz expedition, 207
Metzger, Charles, 162, 172
Meybohm, Fred, 102
Miller, Dick, 49, 50
Miller, Jake, 54, 55–6
Miller, Dr. Maynard, 93, 94
Minto, 38
Minto Flats, 34, 38
Minus 148°, 215, 218
Moennikes, Frank, 64, 65
Moller, Fred, 15
Moore, Terris, 77, 78, 82
Moose's Tooth, 73, 121, 122
Morrison, Lena, 60, 81
Morrison, Professor, 84
Morrison, Robert ("Stub"), 59–60, 61, 70, 81
Moses Point, 185
Mountain climbing, 157, 158–9, 177, 178, 179, 180, 208, 212, 221–2, 225–6: expeditions. *See* Anderson Glacier; Deborah, Mount; Hun-

Mountain climbing (*cont.*) ter, Mount; Hunting- ton, Mount; Logan, Mount; McKinley, Mount; Russell, Mount; Silverthrone, Mount

Mountaineering Club of Alaska, 162

Mountain of My Fear, The, 214

Mountain World, The, 177: quotation from, 177

Mount McKinley National Park, 93, 160–1, 174, 181, 217, 232, 243

Mt. Morrison, Colo., 23

Muldrow Glacier, 74, 75, 76, 77, 161, 229, 230, 233, 246

National Geographic, 73

Nieminen, Matt, 74, 83

Norman, LaVerne, 25

Norman, Pat, 25

North Pole, 120, 143

Olten, Percy, 75

Otter Lake, 130

Outdoor Leadership Pro- gram Expedition, 229– 30, 231–2, 233

Parent, Sam, 191

Parker, Herschel, 120–1

Paxson, 227–8

Pearl Harbor, 50

Pearson, Grant, 122

Peary, Admiral Robert, 120

Pioneer bush pilots, 15, 16–17, 49, 74–5, 76– 7, 83, 110

Piper Aircraft Corporation, 54, 56

Point Hope, 143, 144, 153

Point Lay, 112, 113

Post, Rex, 225–6

Powell, Evil Alice, 246, 248

Quiet Birdmen (QB), 209

Ragle, Captain Richard, 76

Raithel, Helmut, 194

Raithel Expedition, 194–5, 206

Reeve, Bob, 15, 16, 49, 76– 7, 78, 83, 209, 210, 227: on Sheldon, 79

Reeve, Roberta, 209, 210. *See also* Sheldon, Ro- berta

Reeve, Tillie, 209

Reeve Aleutian Airways, 16

Richards, Fred, 211, 213

Riverton, Wyo., 25, 26, 56

Roberts, Dave, 214

Roberts Expedition, 214

Ruby, 40, 49, 110, 112

Rumohr, John, 75

Russell, Mount, 194, 195, 206, 207: Raithel Ex- pedition on, 194–5, 206–7

Ruth Amphitheater, 73, 121, 123

Ruth Glacier, 71, 72, 73, 82, 83, 120–1, 122–3

Ryosetsu Climbing Club, 235

St. Elias Mountains, 72, 93, 94, 97

Sanford, Mount, 223, 224

Saudan, Sylvan, 207–8

Schiff, Anshel, 217–18

Schlicter, Paul, 217

Schoening, Peter K., 159– 60, 173, 174

Schultz, Skunahog, 52

Seattle, Wash., 26, 52

Second World War, 20, 50, 51, 52: Sheldon in, 52–3

Sekita, Micheko, 234, 235, 236–7, 238–40, 240– 1, 243, 244, 245

Sekita Expedition, 234, 235–9, 240, 242

Seltenrick, Fred, 58

Shatto, Charlie ("Yarlie"), 26, 37, 38, 40

Sheldon, Berniece, 24, 25, 56

Sheldon, Donald Edward begins air-charter ser- vice, 59. *See also* Talkeetna Air Ser- vice

as big-game guide, 143– 4, 153–6, 229

birth, 23

as bush pilot, 59, 62, 64–8, 109–19, 135, 136, 176–7, 184,

Sheldon (*continued*) 195–6, 205–6, 228– 9, 248–9

character and personal- ity, 50–1, 176

children of, 227

citations awarded, 22, 108, 133–4: quoted, 134

crash landings, 64–5, 68–70, 138–9, 228

early life, 16, 23–6

education, 36, 37, 52, 56

emergency landings, 56, 57, 67–8, 114–15, 185–7

flight training, 49–50, 52, 69

flying skills, 62–3, 70, 131–2, 138, 140

and Ray Genet, 215, 216, 232, 233, 243– 4

glacier landings, 83, 94, 95, 98–101, 121, 161–2, 228, 230–1, 233: at 14,300 feet, 167, 169, 170–5; on glacier landings, 83, 84, 85, 93, 169

honeymoon trip, 210–11, 212–13

house on Mount McKin- ley, 123, 247

and mapping of Mount McKinley, 82, 83

marriage, 210. *See also* Sheldon, Roberta

and Lena Morrison, 81

and Stub Morrison, 59– 60, 61, 70, 81

on mountain climbing, 179, 180, 221–2

and mountain-climbing expeditions, 157–8, 176–7, 178, 194, 207, 214, 228, 232, 233: Anchorage team, 162; Cassin team, 178, 179; Davidson (winter- climb) team, 215, 216; Day team, 160, 161–2; Harrer team, 102–4; Metz team, 207; Outdoor Lead- ership Program team, 229, 233; Raithel team, 194–

Sheldon (*continued*)
  5, 206; Roberts team, 214–15; Sekita team, 234, 235–6, 243, 244, 245; Terray team, 212, 213–14; UCLA team, 98–102
  purchases first plane, 55
  rescues of, 139, 189–91, 228
  search and rescue missions by, 125–7, 130–5, 164–5, 166, 167–74, 196, 205–6, 219–20, 229–33, 239–40, 241, 242, 243, 244–5: for the military, 19, 20–2, 104–8, 223–4
  in Second World War, 52–3: medals won, 53
  and "specialty flying." *See* Sheldon: glacier landings
  at Step And A Half Dairy, 27–8
  and Tanana River trip, 37, 38–40
  in television and movies, 175
  with timber-cutting crew, 25–6
  and Bradford Washburn, 71–2, 78, 82, 83, 84, 120, 121, 122
Sheldon, Roberta, 210, 227, 228, 245: quoted, 227
Shemya Air Force Base, 19–20, 22
Silverthrone, Mount, 76, 93: U.S. Air Force research expeditions on, 75, 76, 77; and Bradford Washburn, 76, 77
Smith, Jerrold R., 182
Smith, Merle, 94
Snetterton Heath Air Base, England, 53
Snyder, Howard, 217, 218, 219
Solum, Adolf, 25–6
Spadavecchia, Nicholas, 75
Sports Illustrated: and Sheldon, 135
Step And A Half Dairy, Anchorage, 27, 29

Stevenson, William, 165
Super Cub, 71, 72, 77, 94–5, 98, 100, 140, 167–8
Susitna ("Big Sue") River, 29, 128–9
Swan Lake, 212–13
Swisher, Lee, 75

Talkeetna, 28, 29–30, 34, 35–6, 38, 40, 59, 60, 142, 157, 158, 206, 246
Talkeetna Air Service, 17, 60, 61, 70, 81, 142, 154–5, 177, 193, 211, 216, 247, 248: "hangar hotel," 158, 247
Talkeetna Mountains, 63, 66, 137
Talkeetna River, 29, 124
Talkeetna Road House, 122, 216, 246
Taylor, Steve, 218, 220
Terray, Lionel, 210–11, 212
Terray Expedition, 211, 212, 213–14
Titus, Marlene, 243, 244
Toyama, Mitsuko, 235, 237, 245
Traleika Glacier, 161, 230
Twigg, Lynn ("Pedro"), 126, 211, 213

UCLA climbing expedition, 98, 102
Ueki, Tsuyoshi, 207
Underdahl, Berniece. *See* Sheldon, Berniece
U.S. Air Force, 22, 52, 75, 76, 77, 104, 106, 107, 189, 225, 226, 227, 242: Mount Silverthrone research expedition, 75, 76, 77
U.S. Army, 94, 129, 165–6, 166–7, 172, 223–4, 242: Mount McKinley research expedition, 75; Sheldon's citation from, 133–4; quoted, 134
U.S. Geological Mineral Mapping Survey, 93, 94
U.S. Geological Survey (USGS), 66, 93

University of Alaska, 36, 37, 84, 215
University of Denver, 78

Valdez, 76
VanderLaan, Hans, 223
Von Wetzel, Dr., 195, 196, 205

Wainwright, 113, 117
Walsh Glacier, 76
Washburn, Barbara, 169–70: McKinley climb, 77
Washburn, Bradford, 71, 72, 73, 79, 82–3, 120, 121–2, 169–70, 177, 180, 212, 217
  McKinley Group mapping project, 71, 72, 77, 78, 93, 121, 122, 123, 124
  Mount McKinley photographic project, 72–3
  quoted, 120, 121, 122, 123, 170, 181, 210, 212, 221: *Mountain World,* 177
  research climbing expeditions, 75–6, 77, 78, 94, 123
Watanabe, Sachiko, 235, 245
Waugh, Hal, 159
Weeks Field, 58, 59
Wells, Ward, 122, 123–4
Wheeler, Floyd, 144, 153
Whittaker, Jim, 159, 160, 174
Whittaker, Lou, 159, 160, 174
Wickersham, James, 102
Wien, Noel, 15, 16
Wien Air Alaska, Inc., 16, 211
Wilcox, Joe, 216, 217
Wilcox Expedition, 217–20
Williamsport Technical Institute, Pa., 56
Wilson, Jack, 168–9, 228
Wilson, Dr. Rodman, 162, 172, 173
Winchell, Oscar, 49
Wrangell Mountains, 93, 95, 97, 223, 224

Yajimi, Nobue, 235, 245
Yellowjacket Lake, 137

Inset map (upper left):

MT. RUSSELL 11670
MT. DALL 8756
ALASKA RANGE
Curry
Talkeetna
TALKEETNA
MTS.
L. Louise
Gakona
Gulkana
Glennallen
MT. SANFORD 16237
WRANGELL
MT. WRANGELL 14163
Matanuska
Copper Center
MT. BLACKBURN 16523
MTS.
Susitna
MT. GERDINE 11258
MT. TORBERT 11600
MT. SPURR 11068
VALLEY Eklutna
Chitina
MT. MARCUS BAKER 13176
MT. WITHERSPOON
CHUGACH 12003
MT. GOODE 10810
Anchorage
Tyonek Spenard
Elmendorf AFB
Fort Richardson
MTS.
Valdez
CORDOVA PK. 7730
Cordova
LEUTIAN RANGE
MT. REDOUBT VOLCANO 10197
Kenai
KALGIN I.
Prince William Sound
KNIGHT I.
HINCHINBROOK I.
MONTAGUE PEAK 2160
ILIAMNA VOLCANO 10016
Cook Inlet
Tustumena L.
KENAI PENINSULA
Seward
KENAI MTS.
Blying Sd.
MONTAGUE I.
Chakachamna Lake
BARREN IS.
CHUGACH IS.
Gulf of Alaska

1 Inch = 94.5 Statute Miles

Main map:

Arctic

OSTROV VRANGELYA (WRANGEL I.)

Point La

Chukchi Sea

C. LISBURNE
Point Hope
PT. HOPE

ANADYR RANGE
Vankarem
Neshkan
Kivalina
Noatak

CHUKCHI PENINSULA
Arctic Circle
Kotzebue
CAPE DEZHNEV (EAST CAPE)
Shishmaref
Kotzebu Sd.
PIONEER I.
BIG LITTLE DIOMEDE IS.
C. PR. OF WALES
Wales
Kiwal

KORYAK MOUNTAINS
Gulf of Anadyr
Anadyr
Providenija
C. CHUKOTSKY
Providenija
SEWARD PENINSU

Tilichiki
Karacha
C. OLYUTORSKIY
Vilyuneyskaya
C. NAVARIN

U.S.S.R.
U.S.
Bering Strait
Nome
White Mtn
Norton Sound
Shaktoo

ST. LAWRENCE ISLAND

Alakanuk
C. ROMANZOF
St. Mich

Fortuna Ledg

Bering

HALL I.
ST. MATTHEW I.

Hazen Bay
Baird Inlet
Begheli

ROBERT MTN. 1675
NUNIVAK ISLAND

Eek

Sea

Kwigillingok
Kuskokwim Bay

C. NEWENHAM
HAGEMEISTER

ST. PAUL I.
PRIBILOF ISLANDS
ST. GEORGE I.

Bristo Bay

Port Moller

ATTU I.
NEAR ISLANDS
AGATTU I.

A L E U T I A N   I S L A N

PAVLOF VOL. 8261
Ungo
UNIMAK I. 9372
SHISHALDIN VOL.
Unimak Pass
SANAK I.

BULDIR I. SEMISOPOCHNOI
KISKA I.
RAT ISLANDS
AMCHITKA I.
Amchitka Pass

MAKUSHIN VOL. 6680
Dutch Harbor
UNALASKA I.

TANAGA I. KANAGA
KOROVIN VOL. 4852
Atka
ADAK I.
ANDREANOF ISLANDS
Kanaga Pass
Seguam Pass
ATKA I.
SEGUAM I.
ANLIA I.
Amukta Pass
ISLANDS OF THE FOUR MTS.
MT. VSEVIDOF 6920
MT. UMNAK 6680
FOX IS.

ULAK I.
AMATIGNAK I.

Longitude West of Greenwich